CLIFFSCOMPLETE™

Shakespeare's

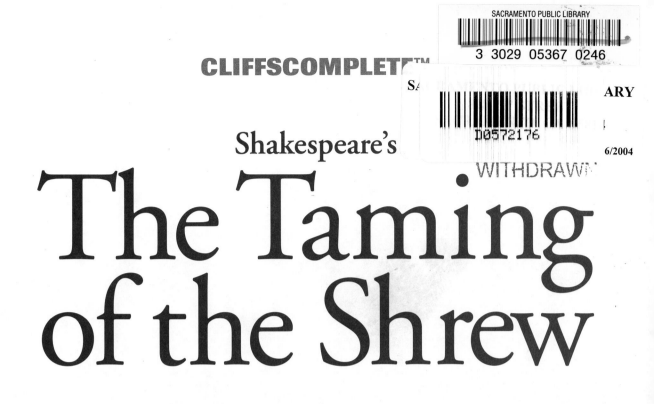

The Taming of the Shrew

Edited and commentary by Diana Sweeney

Master of Arts from the Shakespeare Institute

Complete Text + Commentary + Glossary

Hungry Minds™

Hungry Minds, Inc.

An International Data Group Company

Indianapolis, IN • New York, NY

CLIFFSCOMPLETE™

Shakespeare's

The Taming of the Shrew

About the Author

Diana Sweeney has been teaching English in Los Angeles, California, for over fifteen years. She is also the author of the CliffsComplete *Julius Caesar*.

Publisher's Acknowledgments

Editorial

Project Editor: Sherri Fugit

Acquisitions Editor: Gregory W. Tubach

Copy Editor: Robert Annis

Editorial Manager: Jennifer Ehrlich

Special Help: Jennifer Young, Melissa Bennett

Production

Indexer: Sharon Hilgenberg

Proofreader: Laura L. Bowman

Hungry Minds Indianapolis Production Services

CliffsComplete™ Shakespeare's *The Taming of the Shrew*

Published by

Hungry Minds, Inc.

An International Data Group Company

909 third Avenue

New York, NY 10022

www.hungryminds.com (Hungry Minds Web site)

www.cliffsnotes.com (CliffsNotes Web site)

Library of Congress Control No.: 2001087533

ISBN: 0-7645-8729-3

Printed in the United States of America

10 9 8 7 6 5 4 3 2 1

1O/QX/QT/QR/IN

Distributed in the United States by Hungry Minds, Inc.

Distributed by CDG Books Canada Inc. for Canada; by Transworld Publishers Limited in the United Kingdom; by IDG Norge Books for Norway; by IDG Sweden Books for Sweden; by IDG Books Australia Publishing Corporation Pty. Ltd. for Australia and New Zealand; by TransQuest Publishers Pte Ltd. for Singapore, Malaysia, Thailand, Indonesia, and Hong Kong; by Gotop Information Inc. for Taiwan; by ICG Muse, Inc. for Japan; by Norma Comunicaciones S.A. for Columbia; by Intersoft for South Africa; by Eyrolles for France; by International Thomson Publishing for Germany, Austria and Switzerland; by Distribuidora Cuspide for Argentina; by LR International for Brazil; by Galileo Libros for Chile; by Ediciones ZETA S.C.R. Ltda. for Peru; by WS Computer Publishing Corporation, Inc., for the Philippines; by Contemporanea de Ediciones for Venezuela; by Express Computer Distributors for the Caribbean and West Indies; by Micronesia Media Distributor, Inc. for Micronesia; by Grupo Editorial Norma S.A. for Guatemala; by Chips Computadoras S.A. de C.V. for Mexico; by Editorial Norma de Panama S.A. for Panama; by American Bookshops for Finland. Authorized Sales Agent: Anthony Rudkin Associates for the Middle East and North Africa.

For general information on Hungry Minds' products and services please contact our Customer Care department; within the U.S. at 800-762-2974, outside the U.S. at 317-572-3993 or fax 317-572-4002.

For sales inquiries and resellers information, including discounts, premium and bulk quantity sales and foreign language translations please contact our Customer Care department at 800-434-3422, fax 317-572-4002 or write to Hungry Minds, Inc., Attn: Customer Care department, 10475 Crosspoint Boulevard, Indianapolis, IN 46256.

For information on licensing foreign or domestic rights, please contact our Sub-Rights Customer Care department at 650-653-7098.

For information on using Hungry Minds' products and services in the classroom or for ordering examination copies, please contact our Educational Sales department at 800-434-2086 or fax 317-572-4005.

Please contact our Public Relations department at 212-884-5163 for press review copies or 212-884-5000 for author interviews and other publicity information or fax 212-884-5400.

For authorization to photocopy items for corporate, personal, or educational use, please contact Copyright Clearance Center, 222 Rosewood Drive, Danvers, MA 01923, or fax 978-750-4470.

CLIFFSCOMPLETE

Shakespeare's

The Taming of the Shrew
CONTENTS AT A GLANCE

CLIFFSCOMPLETE

Shakespeare's

The Taming of the Shrew
TABLE OF CONTENTS

Shakespeare's

THE TAMING OF THE SHREW

INTRODUCTION TO WILLIAM SHAKESPEARE

William Shakespeare, or the "Bard" as people fondly call him, permeates almost all aspects of our society. He can be found in our classrooms, on our televisions, in our theatres, and in our cinemas. Speaking to us through his plays, Shakespeare comments on his life and culture, as well as our own. Actors still regularly perform his plays on the modern stage and screen. The 1990s, for example, saw the release of cinematic versions of *Romeo and Juliet*, *Hamlet*, *Othello*, *A Midsummer Night's Dream*, and many more of his works.

In addition to the popularity of Shakespeare's plays as he wrote them, other writers have modernized his works to attract new audiences. For example, *West Side Story* places *Romeo and Juliet* in New York City, and *A Thousand Acres* sets *King Lear* in Iowa corn country. Beyond adaptations and productions, his life and works have captured our cultural imagination. The twentieth century witnessed the production of a play about two minor characters from Shakespeare's *Hamlet* in *Rosencrantz and Guildenstern are Dead* and a fictional movie about Shakespeare's early life and poetic inspiration in *Shakespeare in Love*.

Despite his monumental presence in our culture, Shakespeare remains enigmatic. He does not tell us which plays he wrote alone, on which plays he collaborated with other playwrights, or which versions of his plays to read and perform. Furthermore, with only a handful of documents available about his life, he does not tell us much about Shakespeare the person, forcing critics and scholars to look to historical references to uncover the true-life great dramatist.

Anti-Stratfordians—modern scholars who question the authorship of Shakespeare's plays—have used this lack of information to argue that William Shakespeare either never existed, or if he did exist, did not write any of the plays attributed to him. They believe that another historical figure, such as Francis Bacon or Queen Elizabeth I, used the name as a cover. Whether or not a man named William Shakespeare ever actually existed is ultimately secondary to the recognition that the group of plays bound together by that name does exist and continues to educate, enlighten, and entertain us.

An engraved portrait of Shakespeare by an unknown artist, ca. 1607. Culver Pictures, Inc./SuperStock

Family life

Though scholars are unsure of the exact date of Shakespeare's birth, records indicate that his parents, Mary and John Shakespeare, baptized him on April 26, 1564, in the small provincial town of Stratford-upon-Avon, so named because it sat on the banks of the Avon river. Because common practice was to baptize infants a few days after they were born, scholars generally recognize April 23, 1564, as Shakespeare's birthday. Coincidentally, April 23 is the day of St. George, the patron saint of England, as well as the day upon which Shakespeare would die 52 years later. William was the third of Mary and John's eight children and the first of four sons. The house where scholars believe Shakespeare was born stands on Henley Street, and despite many modifications over the years, you can still visit it today.

Shakespeare's father

Prior to Shakespeare's birth, John Shakespeare lived in Snitterfield, where he married Mary Arden, the daughter of his landlord. After moving to Stratford in 1552, he worked as a glover, a moneylender, and a dealer in agricultural products such as wool and grain. He also pursued public office and achieved a variety of posts including bailiff, Stratford's highest elected position, equivalent to a small town's mayor. At the height of his career, sometime near 1576, he petitioned the Herald's Office for a coat of arms and thus the right to be a gentleman. But the rise from the middle class to the gentry did not come right away, and the costly petition expired without being granted.

About this time, John Shakespeare mysteriously fell into financial difficulty. He became involved in serious litigation, was assessed heavy fines, and even lost his seat on the town council. Some scholars suggest that this decline could have resulted from religious discrimination because the Shakespeare family may have supported Catholicism, the practice of which was illegal in England. However, other scholars point out that not all religious dissenters (both

Shakespeare's birthplace.
SuperStock

Catholics and radical Puritans) lost their posts due to their religion. Whatever the cause of his decline, John did regain some prosperity toward the end of his life. In 1596, the Herald's Office granted the Shakespeare family a coat of arms at the petition of William, by now a successful playwright in London. And John, prior to his death in 1601, regained his seat on Stratford's town council.

Childhood and education

Our understanding of William Shakespeare's childhood in Stratford is primarily speculative because children do not often appear in the legal records from which many scholars attempt to reconstruct Shakespeare's life. Based on his father's local prominence, scholars speculate that Shakespeare most likely attended King's New School, a school that usually employed Oxford graduates and was generally well respected. Shakespeare would have started *petty school*—the rough equivalent to modern preschool—at the age of four or five. He would have learned to read on a *hornbook*, which was a sheet of parchment or paper on which the alphabet and the Lord's Prayer were written. This sheet was framed in wood and covered with a transparent piece of horn for durability. After two years in petty school, he would have transferred to grammar school, where his school day would have probably lasted from 6 or 7 o'clock in the morning (depending on the time of year) until 5 o'clock in the evening, with only a handful of holidays.

While in grammar school, Shakespeare would primarily have studied Latin, reciting and reading the works of classical Roman authors such as Plautus, Ovid, Seneca, and Horace. Traces of these authors' works can be seen in his dramatic texts. Toward his last years in grammar school, Shakespeare would have acquired some basic skills in Greek as well. Thus the remark made by Ben Jonson, Shakespeare's well-educated friend and contemporary playwright, that Shakespeare knew "small Latin and less Greek" is accurate. Jonson is not saying that when Shakespeare left grammar school he was only semi-literate; he merely indicates that Shakespeare did not attend any university, where he would have gained more Latin and Greek instruction.

Wife and children

When Shakespeare became an adult, the historical records documenting his existence began to increase. In November 1582, at the age of 18, he married 26-year-old Anne Hathaway from the nearby village of Shottery. The disparity in their ages, coupled with the fact that they baptized their first daughter, Susanna, only six months later in May 1583, has caused a great deal of modern speculation about the nature of their relationship. However, sixteenth-century conceptions of marriage differed slightly from modern notions. Though all marriages needed to be performed before a member of the clergy, many of Shakespeare's contemporaries believed that a couple could establish a relationship through a premarital contract by exchanging vows in front of witnesses. This contract removed the social stigma of pregnancy before marriage. (Shakespeare's plays contain instances of marriage prompted by pregnancy, and *Measure for Measure* includes this kind of premarital contract.) Two years later, in February 1585, Shakespeare baptized his twins Hamnet and Judith. Hamnet would die at the age of 11 when Shakespeare was primarily living away from his family in London.

For seven years after the twins' baptism, the records remain silent on Shakespeare. At some point, he traveled to London and became involved with the theatre, but he could have been anywhere between 21 and 28 years old when he did. Though some have suggested that he may have served as an assistant to a schoolmaster at a provincial school, it seems likely that he went to London to become an actor, gradually becoming a playwright and gaining attention.

The plays: On stage and in print

The next mention of Shakespeare comes in 1592 by a university wit named Robert Greene when Shakespeare apparently was already a rising actor and playwright for the London stage. Greene, no longer a successful playwright, tried to warn other university wits about Shakespeare. He wrote:

> For there is an upstart crow, beautified with our feathers, that with his "Tiger's heart wrapped in a player's hide" supposes he is as well able to bombast out a blank verse as the best of you, and, being an absolute Johannes Factotum, is in his own conceit the only Shake-scene in a country.

This statement comes at a point in time when men without a university education, such as Shakespeare, were starting to compete as dramatists with the university wits. As many critics have pointed out, Greene's statement recalls a line from *Henry VI, Part 3*, which reads, "O tiger's heart wrapped in a woman's hide!" (I.4.137). Greene's remark does not indicate that Shakespeare was generally disliked. On the contrary, another university wit, Thomas Nashe, wrote of the great theatrical success of *Henry VI*, and Henry Chettle, Greene's publisher, later printed a flattering apology to Shakespeare. What Greene's statement does show us is that Shakespeare's reputation for poetry had reached enough of a prominence to provoke the envy of a failing competitor.

In the following year, 1593, the government closed London's theatres due to an outbreak of the bubonic plague. Publication history suggests that during this closure, Shakespeare may have written his two narrative poems, *Venus and Adonis*, published in 1593, and *The Rape of Lucrece*, published in 1594. These are the only two works that Shakespeare seems to have helped into print; each carries a dedication by Shakespeare to Henry Wriothesley, Earl of Southampton.

Stage success

When the theatres reopened in 1594, Shakespeare joined the Lord Chamberlain's Men, an acting company. Though uncertain about the history of his early dramatic works, scholars believe that by this point he had written *The Two Gentlemen of Verona*, *The Taming of the Shrew*, the *Henry VI* trilogy, and *Titus Andronicus*. During his early years in the theatre, he primarily wrote history plays, with his romantic comedies emerging in the 1590s. Even at this early stage in his career, Shakespeare was a success. In 1597, he was able to purchase New Place, one of the two largest houses in Stratford, and secure a coat of arms for his family.

In 1597, the lease expired on the Lord Chamberlain's playhouse, called The Theatre. Because the owner of The Theatre refused to renew the lease, the acting company was forced to perform at various playhouses until the 1599 opening of the now famous Globe Theatre, which was literally built with lumber from The Theatre. (The Globe, later destroyed by fire, has recently been reconstructed in London and can be visited today.)

Recent scholars suggest that Shakespeare's great tragedy, *Julius Caesar*, may have been the first of Shakespeare's plays performed in the original playhouse. When this open-air theatre on the Thames River opened, financial papers listed Shakespeare's name as one of the principal investors. Already an actor and a playwright, Shakespeare was now becoming a "Company Man." This new status allowed him to share in the profits of the theatre rather than merely getting paid for his plays, some of which publishers were beginning to release in quarto format.

Publications

A *quarto* was a small, inexpensive book typically used for leisure books such as plays; the term itself indicates that the printer folded the paper four times. The modern day equivalent of a quarto would be a paperback. In contrast, the first collected works of Shakespeare were in *folio format*, which means that the printer folded each sheet only once. Scholars call the collected edition of Shakespeare's works the *First Folio*. A folio was a larger and more prestigious book than

A ground plan of London after the fire of 1666, drawn by Marcus Willemsz Doornik.
Guildhall Library, London/AKG, Berlin/SuperStock

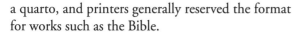

a quarto, and printers generally reserved the format for works such as the Bible.

No evidence exists that Shakespeare participated in the publication of any of his plays. Members of Shakespeare's acting company printed the First Folio seven years after Shakespeare's death. Generally, playwrights wrote their works to be performed on stage, and publishing them was a novel innovation at the time. Shakespeare probably would not have thought of them as books in the way we do. In fact, as a principal investor in the acting company (which purchased the play as well as the exclusive right to perform it), he may not have even thought of them as his own. He would probably have thought of his plays as belonging to the company.

For this reason, scholars have generally characterized most quartos printed before the Folio as "bad" by arguing that printers pirated the plays and published them illegally. How would a printer have received a pirated copy of a play? The theories range from someone stealing a copy to an actor (or actors) selling the play by relating it from memory to a printer. Many times, major differences exist between a quarto version of the play and a folio version, causing uncertainty about which is Shakespeare's true creation. *Hamlet*, for example, is almost twice as long in the Folio as in quarto versions. Recently, scholars have come to realize the value of the different versions. The *Norton Shakespeare*, for example, includes all three versions of *King Lear*—the quarto, the folio, and the *conflated* version (the combination of the quarto and folio).

Prolific productions

The first decade of the 1600s witnessed the publication of additional quartos as well as the production of most of Shakespeare's great tragedies, with *Julius Caesar* appearing in 1599 and *Hamlet* in 1600–1601. After the death of Queen Elizabeth in 1603, the Lord Chamberlain's Men became the King's Men under James I, Elizabeth's successor. Around the time of this transition in the English monarchy, the

famous tragedy *Othello* (1603–1604) was most likely written and performed, followed closely by *King Lear* (1605–1606), *Antony and Cleopatra* (1606), and *Macbeth* (1606) in the next two years.

Shakespeare's name also appears as a major investor in the 1609 acquisition of an indoor theatre known as the Blackfriars. This last period of Shakespeare's career, which includes plays that considered the acting conditions both at the Blackfriars and the open-air Globe Theatre, consists primarily of romances or tragicomedies such as *The Winter's Tale* and *The Tempest*. On June 29, 1613, during a performance of *All is True*, or *Henry VIII*, the thatching on top of the Globe caught fire and the playhouse burned to the ground. After this incident, the King's Men moved solely into the indoor Blackfriars Theatre.

Final days

During the last years of his career, Shakespeare collaborated on a couple of plays with contemporary dramatist John Fletcher, even possibly coming out of retirement, which scholars believe began sometime in 1613, to work on *The Two Noble Kinsmen* (1613–1614). Three years later, Shakespeare died on April 23, 1616. Though the exact cause of death remains unknown, a vicar from Stratford in the mid-seventeenth-century wrote in his diary that Shakespeare, perhaps celebrating the marriage of his daughter, Judith, contracted a fever during a night of revelry with fellow literary figures Ben Jonson and Michael Drayton. Regardless, Shakespeare may have felt his death was imminent in March of that year because he altered his will. Interestingly, his will mentions no book or theatrical manuscripts, perhaps indicating the lack of value that he put on printed versions of his dramatic works and their status as company property.

Seven years after Shakespeare's death, John Heminges and Henry Condell, fellow members of the King's Men, published his collected works. In their preface, they claim that they are publishing the true versions of Shakespeare's plays partially as a response to the previous quarto printings of 18 of his plays, most of these with multiple printings. This Folio contains 36 plays to which scholars generally add *Pericles* and *The Two Noble Kinsmen*. This volume of Shakespeare's plays began the process of constructing Shakespeare not only as England's national poet but also as a monumental figure whose plays would continue to captivate imaginations at the end of the millennium with no signs of stopping. Ben Jonson's prophetic line about Shakespeare in the First Folio—"He was not of an age, but for all time!"—certainly holds true.

Chronology of Shakespeare's plays

1590–1591	*The Two Gentlemen of Verona*
	The Taming of the Shrew
1591	*Henry VI, Part 2*
	Henry VI, Part 3
1592	*Henry VI, Part 1*
	Titus Andronicus
1592–1593	*Richard III*
	Venus and Adonis
1593–1594	*The Rape of Lucrece*
1594	*The Comedy of Errors*
1594–1595	*Love's Labour's Lost*
1595	*Richard II*
	Romeo and Juliet
	A Midsummer Night's Dream
1595–1596	*Love's Labour's Won*
	(This manuscript was lost.)
1596	*King John*
1596–1597	*The Merchant of Venice*
	Henry IV, Part 1
1597–1598	*The Merry Wives of Windsor*
	Henry IV, Part 2
1598	*Much Ado About Nothing*
1598–1599	*Henry V*
1599	*Julius Caesar*
1599–1600	*As You Like It*

1600–1601	*Hamlet*
1601	*Twelfth Night,* or *What You Will*
1602	*Troilus and Cressida*
1593–1603	*Sonnets*
1603	*Measure for Measure*
1603–1604	*A Lover's Complaint*
	Othello
1604–1605	*All's Well That Ends Well*
1605	*Timon of Athens*
1605–1606	*King Lear*
1606	*Macbeth*
	Antony and Cleopatra
1607	*Pericles*
1608	*Coriolanus*
1609	*The Winter's Tale*
1610	*Cymbeline*
1611	*The Tempest*
1612–1613	*Cardenio* (with John Fletcher; this manuscript was lost.)
1613	*All is True (Henry VIII)*
1613–1614	*The Two Noble Kinsmen* (with John Fletcher)

This chronology is derived from Stanley Wells's and Gary Taylor's *William Shakespeare: A Textual Companion*, which is listed in the "Works consulted" section that follows.

A note on Shakespeare's language

Readers encountering Shakespeare for the first time usually find Early Modern English difficult to understand. Yet, rather than serving as a barrier to Shakespeare, the richness of this language should form part of one's appreciation of the Bard.

One of the first things readers usually notice about the language is the use of pronouns. Like the King James Version of the Bible, Shakespeare's pronouns are slightly different from our own and can cause confusion. Words like "thou" (you), "thee" and "ye" (objective cases of you), and "thy" and "thine" (your/yours) appear throughout Shakespeare's plays. You may need a little time to get used to these changes. You can find the definitions for other words that commonly cause confusion in the notes column on the right side of each page in this edition.

Iambic pentameter

Though Shakespeare sometimes wrote in prose, he wrote most of his plays in poetry, specifically blank verse. Blank verse consists of lines in unrhymed *iambic pentameter. Iambic* refers to the stress patterns of the line. An *iamb* is an element of sound that consists of two beats—the first unstressed (da) and the second stressed (DA). A good example of an iambic line is Hamlet's famous line "To be or not to be," in which you do not stress "to," "or," and "to," but you do stress "be," "not," and "be." *Pentameter* refers to the meter or number of stressed syllables in a line. *Penta*-meter has five stressed syllables. Thus, Juliet's line "But soft, what light through yonder window breaks?" (II.2.2) is a good example of an iambic pentameter line.

Wordplay

Shakespeare's language is also verbally rich as he, along with many dramatists of his period, had a fondness for wordplay. This wordplay often takes the form of double meanings, called *puns*, where a word can mean more than one thing in a given context. Shakespeare often employs these puns as a way of illustrating the distance between what is on the surface—*apparent* meanings—and what meanings lie underneath. Though recognizing these puns may be difficult at first, the notes in the far right column point many of them out to you.

If you are encountering Shakespeare's plays for the first time, the following reading tips may help ease you into the plays. Shakespeare's lines were meant to be spoken; therefore, reading them aloud or speaking them should help with comprehension. Also, though most of the lines are poetic, do not forget to read complete sentences—move from period to period as well as from line to line. Although

Shakespeare's language can be difficult at first, the rewards of immersing yourself in the richness and fluidity of the lines are immeasurable.

Works consulted

For more information on Shakespeare's life and works, see the following:

Bevington, David, ed. *The Complete Works of Shakespeare*. New York: Longman, 1997.

Evans, G.Blakemore, ed. *The Riverside Shakespeare*. Boston: Houghton Mifflin Co., 1997.

Greenblatt, Stephen, ed. *The Norton Shakespeare*. New York: W.W. Norton and Co., 1997.

Kastan, David Scott, ed. *A Companion to Shakespeare*. Oxford: Blackwell, 1999.

McDonald, Russ. *The Bedford Companion to Shakespeare: An Introduction with Documents*. Boston: Bedford-St. Martin's Press, 1996.

Wells, Stanley and Gary Taylor. *William Shakespeare: A Textual Companion*. New York: W.W. Norton and Co., 1997.

Introduction to Early Modern England

William Shakespeare (1564–1616) lived during a period in England's history that people have generally referred to as the English Renaissance. The term *renaissance*, meaning rebirth, was applied to this period of English history as a way of celebrating what was perceived as the rapid development of art, literature, science, and politics; in many ways, the rebirth of classical Rome.

Recently, scholars have challenged the name "English Renaissance" on two grounds. First, some scholars argue that the term should not be used because women did not share in the advancements of English culture during this time period; their legal status was still below that of men. Second, other scholars have challenged the basic notion that this period saw a sudden explosion of culture. A rebirth of civilization suggests that the previous period of time was not civilized. This second group of scholars sees a much more gradual transition between the Middle Ages and Shakespeare's time.

Some people use the terms *Elizabethan* and *Jacobean* when referring to periods of the sixteenth and seventeenth centuries. These terms correspond to the reigns of Elizabeth I (1558–1603) and James I (1603–1625). The problem with these terms is that they do not cover large spans of time; for example, Shakespeare's life and career spans both monarchies.

Scholars are now beginning to replace Renaissance with the term *Early Modern* when referring to this time period, but people still use both terms interchangeably. Early Modern recognizes that this period established many of the foundations of our modern culture. Though critics still disagree about the exact dates of the period, generally, the dates range from 1450 to 1750. Thus, Shakespeare's life clearly falls within the Early Modern period.

Shakespeare's plays live on in our culture, but it must be recognized that Shakespeare's culture differed greatly from our own. Though his understanding of human nature and relationships seems to apply to our modern lives, historical context must be taken into consideration; one must understand the world he lived in so that his plays can be understood in the historical context that they were written. This introduction helps you do just that. It examines the intellectual, religious, political, and social contexts of Shakespeare's work before turning to the importance of the theatre and the printing press.

Intellectual context

Generally, people in Early Modern England looked at the universe, the human body, and science very differently from the way people do today. While we do not share their same beliefs, people during Shakespeare's time did not lack in intelligence or education. Discoveries made during the Early Modern period concerning the universe and the human body provide the basis of modern science.

Cosmology

One subject we view very differently than Early Modern thinkers is cosmology. Shakespeare's contemporaries believed in the astronomy of Ptolemy, an intellectual from Alexandria in the second century A.D. Ptolemy thought that the earth stood at the center of the universe, surrounded by nine concentric rings. The celestial bodies circled the earth in the following order: the moon, Mercury, Venus, the sun, Mars, Jupiter, Saturn, and the stars. The entire system was controlled by the *primum mobile*, or Prime Mover, which initiated and maintained the movement of the celestial bodies. No one had yet discovered the last three planets in the solar system: Uranus, Neptune, and Pluto.

In 1543, Nicolaus Copernicus published his theory of a sun-based solar system, in which the sun stood at the center and the planets revolved around it. Though this theory appeared prior to Shakespeare's birth, people didn't really start to change their minds until 1610, when Galileo used his telescope to confirm Copernicus's theory. David Bevington asserts in the general introduction to his edition of Shakespeare's works that during most of Shakespeare's writing career, the cosmology of the universe was in question, and this sense of uncertainty influences some of his plays.

Universal hierarchy

Closely related to Ptolemy's hierarchical view of the universe is a hierarchical conception of the Earth (sometimes referred to as the Chain of Being). During the Early Modern period, many people believed that all of creation was organized hierarchically. God existed at the top, followed by the angels, men, women, animals, plants, and rocks. (Because all women were thought to exist below all men on the chain, you can easily imagine the confusion that Elizabeth I caused when she became Queen of England. She was literally "out of order," an expression that still exists in our society.) Though the concept of this hierarchy is a useful one when beginning to study Shakespeare, keep in mind that distinctions in this hierarchical view were not always clear and that one should not reduce all Early Modern thinking to a simple chain.

Elements and humors

The belief in a hierarchical scheme of existence created a comforting sense of order and balance that carried over into science as well. Shakespeare's contemporaries generally accepted that four different elements composed everything in the universe: earth, air, water, and fire. People associated these four elements with four qualities of being. These qualities—hot, cold, moist, and dry—appeared in different combinations in the elements. For example, air was hot and moist; water was cold and moist; earth was cold and dry; and fire was hot and dry.

Additionally, people believed that the human body contained all four elements in the form of *humors*—blood, phlegm, yellow bile, and black bile—each of which corresponded to an element. Blood corresponded to air (hot and moist), phlegm to water (cold and moist), yellow bile to fire (hot and dry), and black bile to earth (cold and dry). When someone was sick, physicians generally believed that the patient's humors were not in the proper balance. For example, if someone were diagnosed with an abundance of blood, the physician would bleed the patient (using leeches or cutting the skin) to restore the balance.

Shakespeare's contemporaries also believed that the humors determined personality and temperament. If a person's dominant humor was blood, he was considered light-hearted. If dominated by yellow bile (or choler), that person was irritable. The dominance of phlegm led a person to be dull and kind. And if black bile prevailed, he was melancholy or sad. Women were thought to have an abundance of moist humors which made them more apt to being naturally lascivious and more loquacious than men. In *The Taming of the Shrew,* all of the women characters display distinctive traits brought about by their excessively moist humors. Thus, people of Early Modern England often used the humors to explain behavior and emotional outbursts. Throughout Shakespeare's plays, he uses the concept of the humors to define and explain various characters.

The Reformation

Prior to the early sixteenth century in Europe, the only Christian church was the Catholic or "universal," church. Beginning in the early sixteenth century, religious thinkers such as Martin Luther and John Calvin, who claimed that the Roman Catholic Church had become corrupt and was no longer following the word of God, began what has become known as the *Protestant Reformation.* The Protestants ("protestors") believed in salvation by faith rather than works. They also believed in the primacy of the Bible and advocated giving all people access to reading the Bible.

Many of the English initially resisted Protestant ideas. However, the Reformation in England began in 1527 during the reign of Henry VIII, prior to Shakespeare's birth. In that year, Henry VIII decided to divorce his wife, Catherine of Aragon, for her failure to produce a male heir. (Only one of their children, Mary, survived past infancy.) Rome denied Henry's petitions for a divorce, forcing him to divorce Catherine without the Church's approval, which he did in 1533.

The Act of Supremacy

The following year, the Pope excommunicated Henry VIII while Parliament confirmed his divorce and the legitimacy of his new marriage through the *Act of Succession.* Later in 1534, Parliament passed

A portrait of King Henry VIII, artist unknown, ca. 1542.
National Portrait Gallery, London/SuperStock

the *Act of Supremacy*, naming Henry the "Supreme Head of the Church in England." Henry continued to persecute both radical Protestant reformers and Catholics who remained loyal to Rome.

Henry VIII's death in 1547 brought Edward VI, his 10-year-old son by Jane Seymour (the king's third wife), to the throne. This succession gave Protestant reformers the chance to solidify their break with the Catholic Church. During Edward's reign, Archbishop Thomas Cranmer established the foundation for the Anglican Church (Church of England) through his 42 articles of religion. He also wrote the first *Book of Common Prayer*, adopted in 1549, which was the official text for worship services in England.

Bloody Mary

Catholics continued to be persecuted until 1553, when the sickly Edward VI died and was succeeded by Mary, his half-sister and the Catholic daughter of Catherine of Aragon. The reign of Mary witnessed the reversal of religion in England through the restoration of Catholic authority and obedience to Rome. Protestants were executed in large numbers, which earned the monarch the nickname *Bloody Mary*. Many Protestants fled to Europe to escape persecution.

Elizabeth I, the daughter of Henry VIII and Anne Boleyn, outwardly complied with the mandated Catholicism during her half-sister Mary's reign, but she restored Protestantism when she took the throne in 1558 after Mary's death. Thus, in the space of a single decade, England's throne passed from Protestant to Catholic to Protestant, with each change carrying serious and deadly consequences.

Though Elizabeth reigned in relative peace from 1558 to her death in 1603, religion was still a serious concern for her subjects. During Shakespeare's life, a great deal of religious dissent existed in England. Many Catholics, who remained loyal to Rome and their church, were persecuted for their beliefs. At the other end of the spectrum, the Puritans were persecuted for their belief that the Reformation was not complete. (The English pejoratively applied the term *Puritan* to religious groups that wanted to continue purifying the English church by such measures as removing the *episcopacy*, or the structure of bishops.)

The Great Bible

One thing agreed upon by both the Anglicans and Puritans was the importance of a Bible written in English. Translated by William Tyndale in 1525, the first authorized Bible in English, published in 1539, was known as the Great Bible. An English version of the Bible made it easier for everyone to read and interpret the scriptures in their own way. This became an especially dangerous thing as women began to realize that a man's supremacy was not an act of God but an act of men. So, in 1543, an "Act for the Advancement of True Religion" was established. This Act forbade women to read the

Bible in English. This Bible was later revised during Elizabeth's reign into what was known as the Bishop's Bible. As Stephen Greenblatt points out in his introduction to the *Norton Shakespeare*, Shakespeare would probably have been familiar with both the Bishop's Bible, heard aloud in Mass, and the Geneva Bible, which was written by English exiles in Geneva. The last authorized Bible produced during Shakespeare's lifetime came within the last decade of his life when James I's commissioned edition, known as the King James Bible, appeared in 1611.

Political context

Politics and religion were closely related in Shakespeare's England. Both of the monarchs under whom Shakespeare lived had to deal with religious and political dissenters.

Elizabeth I

Despite being a Protestant, Elizabeth I tried to take a middle road on the question of religion. She allowed Catholics to practice their religion in private as long as they outwardly appeared Anglican and remained loyal to the throne.

Elizabeth's monarchy was one of absolute supremacy. Believing in the divine right of kings, she styled herself as being appointed by God to rule England. To oppose the Queen's will was the equivalent of opposing God's will. Known as *passive obedience*, this doctrine did not allow any opposition even to a tyrannical monarch because God had appointed the king or queen for reasons unknown to His subjects on earth. However, as Bevington notes, Elizabeth's power was not as absolute as her rhetoric suggested. Parliament, already well established in England, reserved some power, such as the authority to levy taxes, for itself.

Elizabeth I lived in a society that restricted women from possessing any political or personal autonomy and power. As queen, Elizabeth violated and called

into question many of the prejudices and practices against women. In a way, her society forced her to "overcome" her sex to rule effectively. Although her position did nothing to increase the status of women in England, her strength and boldness perhaps served as a prototype for some of Shakespeare's more powerful women such as Kate in *The Taming of the Shrew*.

One of the rhetorical strategies that Elizabeth adopted to rule effectively was to separate her position as monarch of England from her natural body—to separate her *body politic* from her *body natural*. Additionally, throughout her reign, Elizabeth brilliantly negotiated between domestic and foreign factions—some of whom were anxious about a female monarch and wanted her to marry—appeasing both sides without ever committing to one.

She remained unmarried throughout her 45-year reign, partially by styling herself as the Virgin Queen

A portrait of Elizabeth I by George Gower, ca. 1588. National Portrait Gallery, London/SuperStock

whose purity represented England herself. Her refusal to marry and her habit of hinting and promising marriage with suitors both foreign and domestic helped Elizabeth maintain internal and external peace. Not marrying allowed her to retain her independence, but it left the succession of the English throne in question. In 1603, on her deathbed, she named James VI, King of Scotland and son of her cousin Mary, as her successor.

James I

When he assumed the English crown, James VI of Scotland became James I of England. (Some historians refer to him as James VI and I.) Like Elizabeth, James was a strong believer in the divine right of kings and their absolute authority.

Upon his arrival in London to claim the English throne, James made his plans to unite Scotland and England clear. However, a long-standing history of enmity existed between the two countries. Partially as a result of this history and the influx of Scottish courtiers into English society, anti-Scottish prejudice abounded in England. When James asked Parliament for the title of "King of Great Britain," he was denied.

As scholars such as Bevington have pointed out, James was less successful than Elizabeth was in negotiating between the different religious and political factions in England. Although he was a Protestant, he began to have problems with the Puritan sect of the House of Commons, which ultimately led to a rift between the court (which also started to have Catholic sympathies) and the Parliament. This rift between the monarchy and Parliament eventually escalated into the Civil War that would erupt during the reign of James's son, Charles I.

In spite of its difficulties with Parliament, James's court was a site of wealth, luxury, and extravagance. James I commissioned elaborate feasts, masques, and pageants, and in doing so he more than doubled the royal debt. Stephen Greenblatt suggests that Shakespeare's *The Tempest* may reflect this extravagance through Prospero's magnificent banquet and accompanying masque. Reigning from 1603 to 1625, James I remained the King of England throughout the last years of Shakespeare's life.

Social context

Shakespeare's England divided itself roughly into two social classes: the aristocrats (or nobility) and everyone else. The primary distinctions between these two classes were ancestry, wealth, and power. Simply put, the aristocrats were the only ones who possessed all three.

Aristocrats were born with their wealth, but the growth of trade and the development of skilled professions began to provide wealth for those not born with it. Although the notion of a middle class did not begin to develop until after Shakespeare's death, the possibility of some social mobility did exist in Early Modern England. Shakespeare himself used the wealth gained from the theatre to move into the lower ranks of the aristocracy by securing a coat of arms for his family.

Shakespeare was not unique in this movement, but not all people received the opportunity to increase their social status. Members of the aristocracy feared this social movement, and as a result, promoted harsh laws of apprenticeship and fashion, restricting certain styles of dress and material. These laws dictated that only the aristocracy could wear certain articles of clothing, colors, and materials. Though enforcement was a difficult task, the Early Modern aristocracy considered dressing above one's station a moral and ethical violation.

The status of women

The legal status of women did not allow them much public or private autonomy. English society functioned on a system of patriarchy and hierarchy, which means that men controlled society beginning with the individual family. In fact, the family metaphorically corresponded to the state. For example, the husband was the king of his family. His authority to control his family was absolute and based on divine right, similar to that of the country's king. People also saw the family itself differently than today, considering apprentices and servants part of the whole family.

The practice of *primogeniture*—a system of inheritance that passed all of a family's wealth through the first male child—accompanied this system of patriarchy. Thus women did not generally inherit their family's wealth and titles. In the absence of a male heir, some women, such as Queen Elizabeth, did. But after women married, they lost almost all of their already limited legal rights, such as the right to inherit and own property, and to sign contracts. In all likelihood, Elizabeth I would have lost much of her power and authority if she married.

Furthermore, women did not generally receive an education outside of the home, and could not enter certain professions, including acting. Just as Bianca is taught literature and music in *The Taming of the Shrew,* many daughters of wealthy fathers received private instruction in their homes and became quite capable of reading and writing. Still, society continued to relegate women to the domestic sphere of the home.

Daily life

Daily life in Early Modern England began before sun-up—exactly how early depended on one's station in life. A servant's responsibilities usually included preparing the house for the day. Families usually possessed limited living space, and even among wealthy families multiple family members tended to share a small number of rooms, suggesting that privacy may not have been important or practical.

Working through the morning, Elizabethans usually had lunch about noon. This midday meal was the primary meal of the day, much like dinner is for modern families. The workday usually ended around sundown or 5 p.m., depending on the season. Before an early bedtime, Elizabethans usually ate a light repast and then settled in for a couple of hours of reading (if the family members were literate and could bear the high cost of books) or socializing.

Mortality rates

Mortality rates in Early Modern England were high compared to our standards, especially among infants. Infection and disease ran rampant because physicians did not realize the need for antiseptics and sterile equipment. As a result, communicable diseases often spread very rapidly in cities, particularly London.

In addition, the bubonic plague frequently ravaged England, with two major outbreaks—from 1592–1594 and in 1603—occurring during Shakespeare's lifetime. People did not understand the plague and generally perceived it as God's punishment. (We now know that the plague was spread by fleas and could not be spread directly from human to human.) Without a cure or an understanding of what transmitted the disease, physicians could do nothing to stop the thousands of deaths that resulted from each outbreak. These outbreaks had a direct effect on Shakespeare's career, because the government often closed the theatres in an effort to impede the spread of the disease.

London life

In the sixteenth century, London, though small compared to modern cities, was the largest city of Europe, with a population of about 200,000 inhabitants in the city and surrounding suburbs. London was a crowded city without a sewer system, which facilitated epidemics such as the plague. In addition, crime rates were high in the city due to inefficient law enforcement and the lack of street lighting.

Despite these drawbacks, London was the cultural, political, and social heart of England. As the home of the monarch and most of England's trade,

London was a bustling metropolis. Not surprisingly, a young Shakespeare moved to London to begin his professional career. Because of the many references to people and places that actually existed in Shakespeare's hometown of Stratford-upon-Avon, many scholars speculate that *The Taming of the Shrew* was written shortly after Shakespeare moved to London.

The theatre

Most theatres were not actually located within the city of London. Rather, theatre owners built them on the South bank of the Thames River (in Southwark) across from the city to avoid the strict regulations that applied within the city's walls. These restrictions stemmed from a mistrust of public performances as locations of plague and riotous behavior. Furthermore, because theatre performances took place during the day, they took laborers away from their jobs. Opposition to the theatres also came from Puritans who believed that they fostered immorality. Therefore, theatres moved out of the city to areas near other sites of restricted activities, such as dog fighting, bear- and bull-baiting, and prostitution.

Despite the move, the theatre was not free from censorship or regulation. In fact, a branch of the government known as the Office of the Revels attempted to ensure that plays did not present politically or socially sensitive material. Prior to each performance, the Master of the Revels would read a complete text of each play, cutting out offending sections or, in some cases, not approving the play for public performance.

Performance spaces

Theatres in Early Modern England were quite different from our modern facilities. They were usually open-air, relying heavily on natural light and good weather. The rectangular stage extended out into an area that people called the *pit*—a circular, uncovered area about 70 feet in diameter. Audience members had two choices when purchasing admission to a

The recently reconstructed Globe Theatre.
Chris Parker/PAL

theatre. Admission to the pit, where the lower classes (or *groundlings*) stood for the performances, was the cheaper option. People of wealth could purchase a seat in one of the three covered tiers of seats that ringed the pit. At full capacity, a public theatre in Early Modern England could hold between 2,000 and 3,000 people.

The stage, which projected into the pit and was raised about five feet above it, had a covered portion called the *heavens*. The heavens enclosed theatrical equipment for lowering and raising actors to and from the stage. A trapdoor in the middle of the stage provided theatrical graves for characters such as Ophelia and also allowed ghosts, such as Banquo in *Macbeth*, to rise from the earth. A wall separated the back of the stage from the actors' dressing room, known as the *tiring house*. At each end of the wall stood a door for major entrances and exits. Above the wall and doors stood a gallery directly above the stage, reserved for the wealthiest spectators. Actors occasionally used this area when a performance called for a difference in height—for example, to represent Juliet's balcony or the walls of a besieged city. A good example of this type of theatre was the original Globe Theatre in London in which Shakespeare's company, The Lord Chamberlain's Men (later the King's Men), staged its plays. However, indoor theatres, such as the Blackfriars, differed slightly because the pit was filled with chairs that faced a rectangular stage. Because only the wealthy could afford the cost of admission, the public generally considered these theatres private.

Actors and staging

Performances in Shakespeare's England do not appear to have employed scenery. However, theatre companies developed their costumes with great care and expense. In fact, a playing company's costumes were its most valuable items. These extravagant costumes were the object of much controversy because some aristocrats feared that the actors could use them to disguise their social status on the streets of London.

Costumes also disguised a player's gender. All actors on the stage during Shakespeare's lifetime were men. Young boys whose voices had not reached maturity played female parts. This practice no doubt influenced Shakespeare's and his contemporary playwrights' thematic explorations of crossdressing.

Shakespeare was a man of the theatre and his relationship to the theatre pervades many of his plays including *The Taming of the Shrew*. In the Induction scene, a group of traveling players are hired to entertain Christopher Sly by performing the play within the play that tells the story of Kate and Petruchio.

Though historians have managed to reconstruct the appearance of the early modern theatre, such as the recent construction of the Globe in London, much of the information regarding how plays were performed during this era has been lost. Scholars of Early Modern theatre have turned to the scant external and internal stage directions in manuscripts in an effort to find these answers. While a hindrance for modern critics and scholars, the lack of detail about Early Modern performances has allowed modern directors and actors a great deal of flexibility and room to be creative.

The printing press

If not for the printing press, many Early Modern plays may not have survived until today. In Shakespeare's time, printers produced all books by *sheet*—a single large piece of paper that the printer would fold to produce the desired book size. For example, a folio required folding the sheet once, a quarto four times, an octavo eight, and so on. Sheets would be printed one side at a time; thus, printers had to print simultaneously multiple nonconsecutive pages.

To estimate what section of the text would be on each page, the printer would *cast off* copy. After the printer made these estimates, *compositors* would set the type upside down, letter by letter. This process of setting type produced textual errors, some of which a proofreader would catch.

Shakespeare in Love *shows how the interior of the Globe would have appeared.*
The Everett Collection

When a proofreader found an error, the compositors would fix the piece or pieces of type. Printers called corrections made after printing began *stop-press* corrections because they literally had to stop the press to fix the error. Because of the high cost of paper, printers would still sell the sheets printed before they made the correction.

Printers placed frames of text in the bed of the printing press and used them to imprint the paper. They then folded and grouped the sheets of paper into gatherings, after which the pages were ready for sale. The buyer had the option of getting the new play bound.

The printing process was crucial to the preservation of Shakespeare's works, but the printing of drama in Early Modern England was not a standardized practice. Many of the first editions of Shakespeare's plays appear in quarto format, and until recently, scholars regarded them as "corrupt." In fact, scholars still debate how close a relationship exists between what appeared on the stage in the sixteenth and seventeenth centuries and what appears on the printed page. The inconsistent and scant appearance of stage directions, for example, makes it difficult to determine how close this relationship was.

It is known that the practice of the theatre allowed the alteration of plays by a variety of hands other than the author's, further complicating any efforts to extract what a playwright wrote and what was changed by either the players, the printers, or the government censors. Theatre was a collaborative environment. In fact, many scholars feel that *The Taming of the Shrew* was a collaboration, citing the inferior Bianca/Lucentio plot as evidence of a second hand. Rather than lament our inability to determine authorship and what exactly Shakespeare wrote, we should work to understand this collaborative nature and learn from it.

Shakespeare wrote his plays for the stage, and the existing published texts reflect the collaborative nature of the theatre as well as the unavoidable changes made during the printing process. A play's first written version would have been the author's *foul papers*, which invariably consisted of blotted lines and revised text. From there, a scribe would recopy the play and produce a *fair copy*. The theatre manager would then copy out and annotate this copy into a playbook (what people today call a *promptbook*).

At this point, scrolls of individual parts were copied out for actors to memorize. (Due to the high cost of paper, theatre companies could not afford to provide their actors with a complete copy of the play.) The government required the company to send the playbook to the Master of the Revels, the government official who would make any necessary changes or mark any passages considered unacceptable for performance.

Printers could have used any one of these copies to print a play. It cannot be determined whether a printer used the author's version, the modified theatrical version, the censored version, or a combination when printing a given play. Refer back to the "Publications" section of the Introduction to William Shakespeare for further discussion of the impact that printing practices has on the understanding of Shakespeare's works.

Works cited

For more information regarding Early Modern England, consult the following works:

Bevington, David. "General Introduction." *The Complete Works of William Shakespeare.* Updated Fourth edition. New York: Longman, 1997.

Greenblatt, Stephen. "Shakespeare's World." *Norton Shakespeare.* New York: W.W. Norton and Co., 1997.

Kastan, David Scott, ed. *A Companion to Shakespeare.* Oxford: Blackwell, 1999.

McDonald, Russ. *The Bedford Companion to Shakespeare: An Introduction with Documents.* Boston: Bedford-St. Martin's Press, 1996.

INTRODUCTION TO *THE TAMING OF THE SHREW*

William Shakespeare was always interested in the concept that life imitated art and this theme showed up in many of his plays. Shakespeare often explored this concept by creating the play-within-the-play episodes that are seen in such plays as *Hamlet, A Midsummer Night's Dream*, and *The Taming of the Shrew*. The Induction scenes in *The Taming of the Shrew* introduce the reader to Christopher Sly, a drunken tinker who is booted out of a tavern just before he passes out. While he is in his alcohol induced sleep, a Lord returns from hunting to find Sly and then devises the plan of dressing Sly in the clothes of the aristocracy and tricking him into believing that he is a wealthy Lord. Sly awakens to find himself surrounded by splendor, and even though he doesn't really believe he is a wealthy Lord, he plays along hoping that maybe it is true. A troupe of players is brought in to entertain the new Lord Sly and the play they perform is the story of the taming of a shrew. The themes of illusion versus reality, class struggles, male-female relationships, and transformation are reflected in both the Induction framework and the play within the play.

In writing his comedies, Shakespeare was greatly influenced by classical Roman and Italian farce and comedy. *The Taming of the Shrew* follows closely a form of Italian comedy known as *Commedia dell'arte*. This style of theatre, a product of the Italian Renaissance, was an almost spontaneous sort of theatre where the actor was given an outlined scenario and, using stock characters, improvised the dialogue and developed the situations the scenario called for. The stock characters included sets of lovers, the Pantalone, a foolish old man who was often a suitor of one of the young lovers, and servants who were frequently much smarter than their masters and aided them in solving their love problems. These stock characters closely resemble Bianca and Lucentio, Gremio and Tranio in Shakespeare's play.

The majority of Shakespeare's plays are written in blank verse and *The Taming of the Shrew* is no exception. *Blank verse* is a form of poetry in iambic pentameter. Each line has ten syllables—five unstressed syllables alternating with five stressed syllables. Occasionally, a word that is usually pronounced as one syllable is accompanied by a grave accent. The accent is an indication that the word should be spoken with two syllables. For example, the word "moved," usually a one-syllable word, with a grave accent would be pronounced as "move-ed." This allows the line to fall correctly into the rhythm of the iambic pentameter. While Shakespeare put poetry into the mouths of kings, he also regularly used prose, relying on the use of colloquial diction, to indicate a character of lower social standing. This is seen with several characters in *The Taming of the Shrew*.

Text

The Taming of the Shrew first appeared in print in the 1623 Folio collection of William Shakespeare's Histories, Comedies and Tragedies. Textually, this play is one of the most difficult in the canon, complicated by the existence of a play printed in quarto form and entered on the Stationer's Register on May 2, 1594 titled, *A Pleasant Conceited Historie called The Taming of A Shrew*. The existence of this anonymous play, printed twenty-nine years before *The Taming of the Shrew* appeared in the 1623 Folio, has raised many questions about Shakespeare's text.

There are many similarities between the two plays but the discrepancies in language, structure, and characters are enough to encourage a closer examination of the sources of the two plays. The character of Christopher Sly appears in both plays, although the framework ends in Act I of *The Taming of the Shrew*, while it is completed in *The Taming of A Shrew*. The shrew is tamed by the same method in both plays and is brought to submission while each play ends with a feast where the husbands bet on their wives' obedience. The dialogue is close

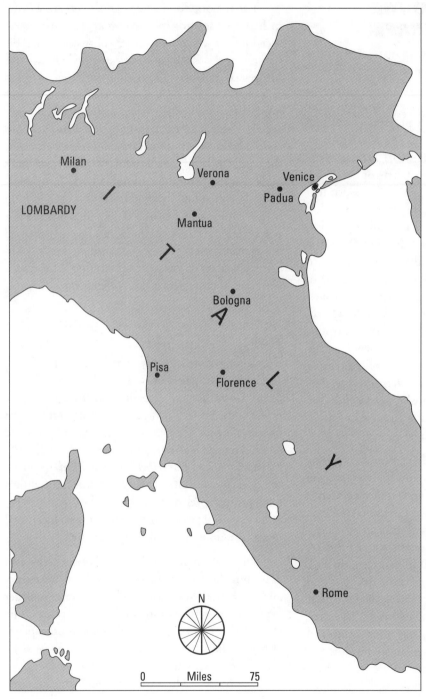

A map of Italy.

Padua and includes three sisters instead of the two in *The Taming of the Shrew.* Except for Kate, the names of the characters in *A Shrew* differ considerably from *The Shrew.*

In the almost 400 years of Shakespearean study, three theories have emerged concerning the relationship of *The Taming of A Shrew* to *The Taming of the Shrew.* For many years, scholars believed that *The Taming of A Shrew* had been written by someone other than Shakespeare (perhaps even Christopher Marlowe) but that Shakespeare had used the play as his principal source for *The Taming of the Shrew.* Other scholars conjectured that both *A Shrew* and *The Shrew* were two different plays that had been derived from a lost play that dealt with the shrew issue. The more recent and most currently accepted theory is that *The Taming of A Shrew* was a memorial reconstruction of Shakespeare's play, *The Taming of the Shrew.*

Because of the time and expense of having plays printed during the time that Shakespeare was writing, very few plays were actually printed for publication. Also, the attitude prevailed that plays were to be performed and observed, not read in many cases and occasionally runs word for word. *The Taming of A Shrew* is set in Athens rather than or studied. A writer would create the original copy of the play called the *foul papers*. Occasionally these foul papers were given to a scrivener to make a clean copy of the script. This script would then be given to the playhouse where the play was being performed and with the addition of exits, entrances, sound cues, and prop lists, the script became what was termed the *prompt book*. The actors in the production were not even given a complete copy of a play but only pieces of the script that contained their lines and perhaps a word or two of the cue lines. Thus it was possible that only one or two copies of any given play were ever in existence. On occasion, it would be necessary to recall a play without benefit of access to the original script. This recalling of the script has been termed *memorial reconstruction*. The usual process of memorial reconstruction consisted of an actor or group of actors who had played minor roles in an authorized production of the play coming together to reconstruct the script. This was done from memory and it is often easy to determine which actor or actors were responsible for the reconstruction by looking at the accuracy of the lines when compared to the authoritative script. In the case of *The Taming of the Shrew*, it has been hypothesized that the actor who played Grumio was primarily responsible for the memorial reconstruction, which when printed, was mistakenly titled, *The Taming of A Shrew*.

If *The Taming of A Shrew* is a memorial reconstruction of Shakespeare's play, the question remains as to why there are no concluding Sly scenes in *The Taming of the Shrew* as it was printed in the 1623 Folio even though they exist in *The Taming of A Shrew*. Writing in Studies in English Literature in 1978, Karl P. Wentersdorf addressed the problem in his article, "The Original Ending of *The Taming of the Shrew*: A Reconsideration." Wentersdorff postulates that the framework of the Induction, interludes, and an epilogue was complete in Shakespeare's original version of the play. Continuing, he explains that during the plague years of 1592-1594 there is evidence that plays were often cut due to the lack of

actors to play the parts. If the play actually included two or three final Sly scenes, Wentersdorff suggests that it would have taken sixteen adult actors and 5 boys to stage the play, but if the Sly scenes were cut from Acts IV and V then Sly and the Lord could double as the Pedant and Vincentio while the boy who played the page could double as the Widow. This would cut the company enough to allow for more efficient casting during a time when actors may have been scarce. The abridged copy of the script was most likely the one to end up as the printer's copy when compiling the 1623 Folio.

Until recently, the most accepted date for the writing of *The Taming of the Shrew* was set in 1597, but with the current recognition of *The Taming of A Shrew* as a memorial reconstruction of Shakespeare's play, the date must be altered. Published in May of 1594, *The Taming of A Shrew* was possibly reconstructed for a tour of the play in September of 1592, meaning Shakespeare's play had to have been written before that time. Although no date can be certain, scholars, including Marco Mincoff in his article, "The Dating of *The Taming of the Shrew*" in the 1973 issue of English Studies, now estimate that *The Taming of the Shrew* was written in the autumn of 1589 when Shakespeare was approximately 25 years old.

Despite the quandary around the exact date that Shakespeare wrote *The Taming of the Shrew*, there is little question, evidenced by the maturity of the style in which the play was written, that this was one of Shakespeare's earliest plays and possibly his first comedy. Based on the play's many references to Stratford, Shakespeare's hometown, some even speculate that it was his first play, written while he was either still in Stratford or having recently left, although there is no concrete proof for that hypothesis.

SOURCES

Folktales and ballads abounded throughout Europe detailing accounts of shrewish wives being tamed by their aggressive husbands. The theme was a popular one, showing up in Chaucer's "Wife of Bath" and some of the Miracle Plays. One of these tales by an anonymous author and printed around 1550 was "Here Begynneth a Merry Jest of a Shrewde and Curste Wyfe, Lapped in Morels Skin, for Her Good Behavyour." The tale, often sited as one of Shakespeare's principal sources for *The Taming of the Shrew,* relates the story of a willful woman whose sister was favored by their father. Upon her marriage, the husband beat the shrew until she was bloody and broken. He then wrapped her in the salted skin of his old plow horse, Morel, until she agreed to be submissive and obedient.

That Shakespeare refused to tell the stereotypically violent story of the taming of a shrew is a credit to his genius as a writer as well as his enlightened sense of humanity. Perhaps Shakespeare had at some point in his life read "The Office and Duetie of an Husband" by Juan Vives, translated into English by Thomas Paynell in 1553. In this piece, Vives advises husbands to avoid resorting to violence as long as their wives are chaste. Using the analogy of horse training, Vives recommends that husbands should purge their wives of vice like, "The breaker of horses...a sharpe wife must be pleased and mitigated with love and ruled with Majestye." Vives' influence on Shakespeare shows up again in Kate's submission speech in Act V. Many of the ideas in the speech can be found in "A Very Fruteful and Pleasant Boke Callyd the Instruction of a Christen Woman," which was translated by Richard Hyrde and appeared in print around 1529.

Other sources that Shakespeare may have used when writing the main plot of *The Taming of the Shrew* include a story told in Gerard Legh's 1562 publication, *Accedens of Armory* that is very similar to the scene with the tailor and the haberdasher. An episode that closely parallels the sun/moon discussion in Act IV can be found in a collection of stories, *El Conde Lucanor,* written by Don Juan Manuel, Infante of Castile sometime between 1335 and 1347.

The scene in Act V where the husbands wager on their wives' obedience might have been taken from the 1372 collection of stories entitled *The Book of the Knight of La Tour-Landry* by the Angevin knight Geoffrey de la Tour-Landry.

In his book *Narrative and Dramatic Sources of Shakespeare,* Geoffrey Bullough speculates that Simon Goulart's *The Sleeper Awakened,* translated by Edward Grimeston, was the source of the Christopher Sly segment of the play while the Bianca/Lucentio sub-plot is thought to have been based on an Italian intrigue entitled, *I Suppositi,* by Ariosto. The story, translated by George Gascoigne, appeared in 1566 as *The Supposes.* As almost all playwrights of the time, Shakespeare used other sources to create his plays, but the difference between Shakespeare and other playwrights is that he intertwined his stories with an alchemy that created a new product infused with a golden wit and insight that to this day has not been equaled.

Performance History of *The Taming of the Shrew*

The Taming of the Shrew has always been considered as a play that is better performed than read, and it has had an interesting history on both the stage and the screen as directors and actors have tried to make sense of this battle of the sexes. There is little evidence to prove the popularity of *The Taming of the Shrew* during Shakespeare's lifetime, but there are enough allusions to the play in other sources that it must have been a recognizable favorite among the masses. Petruchio would seem to be the central character in early performances of *The Shrew* and in 1611, John Fletcher, the chief dramatist for the King's Men at the time, wrote a sequel to Shakespeare's play entitled, *The Woman's Prize; or, The Tamer Tamed.* The play, which misses the point of Shakespeare's play, portraying Petruchio as a wife beater, picks up after the death of Kate. Petruchio remarries and his second wife proves to be much more difficult to tame. She withholds sexual favors, insisting that Petruchio bring her gifts to appease her, and she soon brings Petruchio around to his own capitulation. In 1633, the King's Men performed both plays together at court.

In 1642, the English Civil Wars caused the theatres to be shut down, but when Charles II was restored to the throne in 1660, the theatres were reopened. Many of Shakespeare's plays were performed as revivals but with many changes to the script to meet the sensibilities of this new audience. The first of these adaptations, written by John Lacy, appeared in 1663 at the Drury Lane Theatre under the name, *Sauny the Scot*. This version of *The Taming of the Shrew* was named after Shakespeare's character, Grumio who has now become the stereotypical, comical Scotsman, so popular in plays of the Restoration. Petruchio is a horror who threatens to whip Kate if she doesn't marry him. Petruchio's reign of terror continues in James Worsdale's *A Cure for a Scold*, performed at the Theatre Royal, Drury Lane in 1735. In this play, the wives vow to tame their husbands as soon as possible but the misogynistic humor is still the centerpiece of the play.

David Garrick's version of the play, entitled *Catherine and Petruchio*, first performed in 1754, was without doubt the most popular and enduring adaptation of *The Taming of the Shrew*. Garrick turned Shakespeare's play into a farce in three acts, cutting both the Induction Scenes and the Bianca/Lucentio plot. He also gave Petruchio a whip for a prop and that prop remained a standard accoutrement for all Petruchios for years afterwards. *Catherine and Petruchio* was performed by some of the most famous actors of the Victorian stage, including Henry Irving and Ellen Terry who performed the play in 1867 at the Queen's Theatre while Herbert Beerbohm Tree presented the play in 1897 at Her Majesty's Theatre.

Shakespeare's "original" text did not reappear in the theatre until 1844 when Benjamin Webster and J.R. Planche produced the play at the Haymarket Theatre in London. Augustin Daly staged the first American production of *The Taming of the Shrew*, in 1887, in New York. Ada Rehan gave an impressive performance of Kate on a set designed by the painter Veronese.

Modern performances of *The Taming of the Shrew* must come to grips with what can be viewed as the misogynistic theme in the relationships between the male and female characters. Judgments must be made as to the most effective way to play the taming scenes, and how Kate will deliver her final speech and decisions about including or eliminating the Induction scenes, must all be determined. The answers to these questions have made for some very interesting, amusing, and unnerving evenings in the theatre.

In 1973, Charles Marowitz presented what was termed a collage version of *The Taming of the Shrew* called *The Shrew*. This adaptation, performed at the Open Space in London, confronted the misogynistic issues in the play head on, seeking to infuriate women's attitudes towards Petruchio. In Marowitz's play, all of the men in the play, including Petruchio, came together in a unified attempt to humiliate Kate. When Petruchio asks for the kiss in Act V, Marowitz inserted Sly's lines from the Induction, "Madam, undress you and come now to bed." Marowitz had Kate reply to this request with the page's lines asking Petruchio to postpone their sexual relationship for a few days on doctor's orders. At this, Kate's father, Baptista, and her servants hold her down on a table while Petruchio takes her from the rear. This incorrigible act is one in a long list of travesties so that by the time Kate delivers her final speech she is a crazed and pathetic woman who has been completely traumatized by the men in her life. Yucel Erten's 1986 production of the play also emphasized the effect of the taming on Kate's psyche. In his production, the trip back to Padua becomes the point where Kate suffers a mental breakdown. She attends the banquet wearing a shawl that she takes off at the end of the submission speech to reveal to the audience that she has slit her wrists and is dying.

Michael Bogdanov's 1978 production of *The Taming of the Shrew* for the Royal Shakespeare Company also dealt with the sexism in the play as it is still reflected in the modern world. Jonathan Pryce, who doubled as both Sly and Petruchio, was in the audience when the play began and, pretending to be drunk, he caused a huge scene. Despite the efforts of unsuspecting audience members and an usherette played by Paola Dionisotti who would eventually become Kate, Pryce made his way to the stage where he proceeded to destroy the beautifully idyllic Italian setting. This episode replaced the Induction and the remainder of the play was performed on a stage with the wings exposed and the only set piece was an intricate metal scaffolding. By destroying the illusionary Italian scenery in place before the play began, Bogdonov used the set to underscore his theme. He felt that Shakespeare possibly took a long, hard look at his own sexism while working on *The Taming of the Shrew* and the metal scaffolding and use of modern dress was representative of the cold, hard reality of the existence of that sexism both in Shakespeare's world and our own.

Three versions of the play in the 1980's used the Induction scenes to set the tone and highlight the themes of each production. Peter Dews' 1982 production in Stratford, Ontario, used the framework to play up the meta-theatricality of *The Taming of the Shrew.* Sly and the Lord remained on stage the entire time and the actors playing Kate and Petruchio would bow and curtsy to the Lord and Sly throughout the play. Viewing the taming portion of the play in this way allowed the audience, being constantly reminded that this is a play within a play, to set up a protective filter through which they could more easily interpret and accept the uneasy issues of gender relations. In 1985, The Mediaeval Players used the same actor cast as the Lord in the Induction to play Kate, emphasizing that Kate's submission was a man's dream created by a male author for a boy actor to play. The play was done in the broad style of Commedia dell'arte, giving the audience permission to laugh at the often uncomfortable taming of the shrew. The production of *The Taming of the Shrew* directed in 1985 by Di Trevis for the Royal Shakespeare Company used the Induction to call attention to the often overlooked issues of class and status in the play. The production opened with the entrance of a group of worn-down players dressed in rags. Pulling a very large prop basket on wheels was a haggard young woman, looking very much like Brecht's Mother Courage, carrying a small child in her arms. A very drunk Sly curses, urinates, and vomits before falling asleep and being dressed in a white tuxedo with a black top hat. Sly, and the players, become merely pawns used for the entertainment of the idle rich. After the capitulation scene, Sly is so caught up in the action of the play that he tries to tame the person he has been told is his wife. At this point, the page removes the wig to reveal that he is a young man, not a woman, and that the joke has been on Sly all along. All of the Lords and Ladies laugh at Sly as they leave the stage, tossing coins at him as they leave. When a few of the players return to the stage to clean up, Sly offers a coin to the woman with the baby who had played Kate in the play.

Two film versions of *The Taming of the Shrew* are important to include in any performance history of the play. The first, filmed in 1929, starring Douglas Fairbanks and Mary Pickford, was the first "talkie" film made of a Shakespeare play. The script was a very shortened adaptation of Garrick's play and contained only about 500 lines of Shakespeare's script. The interesting moment in this film occurs after Kate's submission speech. At that point, she turns to the women in the room, winks, and then sits on the lap of the unsuspecting Petruchio. In 1966, Richard Burton and Elizabeth Taylor, directed by Franco Zeffirelli, filmed a version of the play that seemed to reflect the real life relationship of these two volatile actors. As Kate and Petruchio, Burton and Taylor fell in love at first sight but the chase and the ensuing fights were all part of the courting dance.

Even at the end of the film, Kate forces Petruchio to run after her to claim his marital reward. The film suggests that Petruchio needs some taming of his own and that he has met his match in Kate.

In a made-for-TV production of the play, the BBC cast the usually comic John Cleese as a very Calvanistic and sober Petruchio. There was no physical comedy as is usually seen in the play, and Kate was not tamed as much as she was taught to love by a quiet, intense Petruchio. Cole Porter wrote a musical adaptation of the play in 1948 entitled *Kiss Me Kate*, and the musical continues to delight audiences even today. In 1998, the trend of adapting Shakespeare into films that appeal to a younger audience brought forth a teen-age version of the play called *10 Things I Hate About You.*

Criticism

In the past 400 years, each generation has attempted to make Shakespeare "our contemporary" and as the cultural and societal awareness changes throughout the years, so does our take on Shakespeare and his plays. The obvious sexism in the play has for years been the focus of most of the criticism surrounding the play, and as the feminist movement began in earnest, two trains of thought dominated modern examinations of the text. Critics divide themselves into two camps: One supports the theory that Shakespeare was misogynist and that his play reflects the Elizabethan idea of male supremacy, while the other tries to defend Shakespeare, acknowledging his more humanitarian ideas within the play.

Falling into the first camp is Shirley Nelson Garner. In her article included in Maurice Charney's 1988 book, *"Bad" Shakespeare: Revaluations of the Shakespeare Canon,* Garner argues that the play was written by a man for the enjoyment of men and that you would have to be a man to find any humor in the play. Penny Gay, writing in her book, *As She Likes It: Shakespeare's Unruly Women* (1994) finds

little to commend in this play that "enacts the defeat of the threat of a woman's revolt" and allows an audience the opportunity to "reinforce their misogyny while at the same time feeling good."

Germaine Greer, a founder of the current feminist movement, writing about *The Taming of the Shrew* in her groundbreaking book, *The Female Eunuch* (1970), supports Shakespeare's play arguing that "The submission of a woman like Kate is genuine and exciting because she has something to lay down, her virgin pride and individuality..." Greer goes on to say that "There is no romanticism in Shakespeare's view of marriage. He recognized it as a difficult state of life, requiring discipline, sexual energy, mutual respect and forbearance." Other critics who feel Shakespeare was very aware of the power of women and that Petruchio was more a teacher than a vicious tamer include Irene Dash in *Wooing, Wedding and Power: Women in Shakespeare's Plays* (1981) and J.A. Bryant, Jr. in *Shakespeare and the Uses of Comedy* (1986).

Characters in the Induction

Characters in the Play within the Play

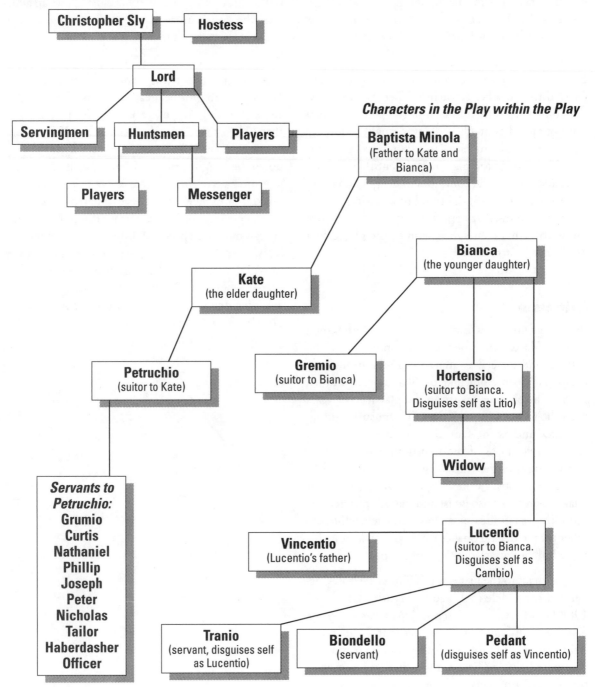

THE TAMING OF THE SHREW

INDUCTION

Sly *Am I a lord? And have I such a lady?*
Or do I dream? Or have I dream'd till now?
I do not sleep: I see, I hear, I speak,
I smell sweet savours, and I feel soft things.
Upon my life, I am a lord indeed
And not a tinker, nor Christopher Sly.
Well, bring our lady hither to our sight,
And once again, a pot o' the smallest ale.

Induction 1

The Hostess of an alehouse throws Christopher Sly, a drunken tinker, out of the pub for his rowdy behavior. Sly passes out and while he is in his alcohol-induced sleep, a Lord who has been out hunting stumbles across Sly's body. Upon realizing that Sly is not dead, the Lord, determined to play a joke on the poor drunk, orders his men to take Sly to his manor, dress him in the Lord's finest clothes, and put him to bed. A group of traveling players comes along and the Lord persuades them to take part in the joke being played on Sly.

INDUCTION, SCENE 1
Before an alehouse on a heath.

[Enter CHRISTOPHER SLY and the HOSTESS]

Sly I'll pheeze you, in faith. 1

Hostess A pair of stocks, you rogue!

Sly Y'are a baggage, the Slys are no rogues. Look in the
Chronicles. We came in with Richard Conqueror.
Therefore, paucas Pallabris, let the world slide. Sessa! 5

Hostess You will not pay for the glasses you have burst?

Sly No, not a denier. Go by, Saint Jeronimy! Go to thy cold
bed and warm thee.

Hostess I know my remedy. I must go fetch the thirdborough.
[Exit]

Sly Third, or fourth, or fifth borough,
I'll answer him by law. 10
I'll not budge an inch, boy. Let him come, and kindly.
[Lies down on the ground, and falls asleep]
[Wind horns. Enter a LORD from hunting, with his TRAIN]

Lord Huntsman, I charge thee, tender well my hounds.
Breathe Merriman (the poor cur is emboss'd)
And couple Clowder with the deep-mouth'd brach.
Saw'st thou not, boy, how Silver made it good 15
At the hedge-corner, in the coldest fault?
I would not lose the dog for twenty pound.

First Huntsman Why, Bellman is as good as he, my lord.
He cried upon it at the merest loss,
And twice to-day pick'd out the dullest scent. 20
Trust me, I take him for the better dog.

NOTES

1. *pheeze you:* fix you, beat, flog.

2. *stocks:* a device used to punish criminals. Usually a wooden frame with holes for the ankles.

4. *Chronicles:* histories.

   Richard Conqueror: Sly confuses William the Conqueror and Richard Coeur-de-Lion.

5. *paucas Pallabris:* Spanish for "few words."

   slide: go by.

   Sessa: either the Spanish "cesa" or the French "cessez," both meaning "stop" or "be silent."

6. *burst:* broken.

7. *denier:* small copper coin with little value.

   Saint Jeronimy: possibly a reference to Hieronimo, the hero of Thomas Kyd's play *The Spanish Tragedy.*

9. *Third . . . borough:* Thirdborough was another term for constable.

   boy: wretch.

11. *kindly:* by all means.

SD. *Wind:* blow.

12. *tender:* look after.

13. *emboss'd:* foaming at the mouth, exhausted.

14. *brach:* hunting bitch.

15. *made it good:* picked up the scent.

16. *the coldest fault:* where the scent is lost.

19. *it:* scent.

   at the merest loss: when scent is completely lost.

Lord Thou art a fool. If Echo were as fleet,
  I would esteem him worth a dozen such.
  But sup them well, and look unto them all.
  To-morrow I intend to hunt again.   25

First Huntsman I will, my lord.

Lord *[Sees Sly]* What's here? One dead, or drunk?
  See, doth he breathe?

Second Huntsman He breathes, my lord. Were he not warm'd with ale,
  This were a bed but cold to sleep so soundly.   30

Lord O monstrous beast! How like a swine he lies!
  Grim death, how foul and loathsome is thine image!
  Sirs, I will practise on this drunken man.
  What think you, if he were convey'd to bed,
  Wrapp'd in sweet clothes, rings put upon his fingers,   35
  A most delicious banquet by his bed,
  And brave attendants near him when he wakes.
  Would not the beggar then forget himself?

First Huntsman Believe me, lord, I think he cannot choose.

Second Huntsman It would seem strange unto him when he wak'd.   40

Lord Even as a flattering dream or worthless fancy.
  Then take him up, and manage well the jest.
  Carry him gently to my fairest chamber,
  And hang it round with all my wanton pictures;
  Balm his foul head in warm distillèd waters,   45
  And burn sweet wood to make the lodging sweet.
  Procure me music ready when he wakes,
  To make a dulcet and a heavenly sound.
  And if he chance to speak, be ready straight
  And, with a low, submissive reverence,   50
  Say 'What is it your honour will command?'
  Let one attend him with a silver basin
  Full of rose-water and bestrew'd with flowers,
  Another bear the ewer, the third a diaper,
  And say 'Will't please your lordship cool your hands?'   55
  Some one be ready with a costly suit,
  And ask him what apparel he will wear.

22.	*fleet:* fast.
24.	*sup:* feed.
32.	*thine image:* death-like sleep.
33.	*practise:* trick.
37.	*brave:* beautifully dressed.
39.	*cannot choose:* will have no other choice.
44.	*wanton:* erotic, sexy.
45.	*Balm:* bathe.
	distilled: concentrated, perfumed.
48.	*dulcet:* sweet.
49.	*straight:* immediately.
50.	*reverence:* bow.
54.	*ewer:* jug.
	diaper: small towel.

Another tell him of his hounds and horse,
And that his lady mourns at his disease.
Persuade him that he hath been lunatic,   60
And, when he says he is, say that he dreams,
For he is nothing but a mighty lord.
This do, and do it kindly, gentle sirs.
It will be pastime passing excellent.
If it be husbanded with modesty.   65

First Huntsman My lord, I warrant you we will play our part
As he shall think by our true diligence
He is no less than what we say he is.

Lord Take him up gently, and to bed with him,
And each one to his office when he wakes.   70
[SLY is carried off] Sound trumpets
Sirrah, go see what trumpet 'tis that sounds.
[Exit SERVINGMAN]
Belike some noble gentleman that means,
Travelling some journey, to repose him here.
[Enter SERVINGMAN]
How now! Who is it?

Servant An't please your Honour, players   75
That offer service to your lordship.

Lord Bid them come near.
[Enter PLAYERS]
Now, fellows, you are welcome.

Players We thank your Honour.

Lord Do you intend to stay with me tonight?   80

FIRST Player So please your Lordship to accept our duty.

Lord With all my heart. This fellow I remember
Since once he play'd a farmer's eldest son.
'Twas where you woo'd the gentlewoman so well.
I have forgot your name, but, sure, that part   85
Was aptly fitted and naturally perform'd.

SECOND Player I think 'twas Soto that your Honour
means.

Lord 'Tis very true; thou didst it excellent.
Well, you are come to me in happy time,

---

61. *when he says he is:* when he says he is now mad.

63. *kindly:* naturally, in a friendly way.

64. *passing:* extremely, exceedingly.

65. *husbanded with modesty:* conducted with moderation and restraint.

67. *As:* so that.

70. *office:* assigned part.

72. *Sirrah:* term of address to a social inferior.

73. *Belike:* probably.
     means: intends.

75. *an't:* if it.
     players: actors.

81. *So please:* if it please.
     duty: respect.

86. *aptly fitted:* well suited.

87. *Soto:* possibly a reference to a character named Soto in *Women Pleased*, John Fletcher's play of 1619.

89. *in happy time:* at just the right time.

The rather for I have some sport in hand   90
Wherein your cunning can assist me much.
There is a lord will hear you play tonight;
But I am doubtful of your modesties,
Lest, over-eying of his odd behaviour
For yet his Honour never heard a play,   95
You break into some merry passion
And so offend him. For I tell you, sirs,
If you should smile, he grows impatient.

FIRST Player Fear not, my lord, we can contain ourselves
Were he the veriest antick in the world.   100

Lord *[to a servingman]* Go, sirrah, take them to the buttery
And give them friendly welcome every one.
Let them want nothing that my house affords.
[Exit one with the PLAYERS]
[to another servingman] Sirrah, go you to Barthol'mew my
    page,
And see him dress'd in all suits like a lady.   105
That done, conduct him to the drunkard's chamber,
And call him 'madam,' do him obeisance.
Tell him from me, as he will win my love,
He bear himself with honourable action,
Such as he hath observ'd in noble ladies   110
Unto their lords, by them accomplishèd.
Such duty to the drunkard let him do
With soft low tongue and lowly courtesy,
And say 'What is't your Honour will command,
Wherein your lady and your humble wife   115
May show her duty and make known her love?'
And then with kind embracements, tempting kisses,
And with declining head into his bosom,
Bid him shed tears, as being overjoy'd
To see her noble lord restor'd to health,   120
Who, for this seven years hath, esteemed him
No better than a poor and loathsome beggar.
And if the boy have not a woman's gift
To rain a shower of commanded tears,
An onion will do well for such a shift,   125

90.   *The rather for:* especially because.

91.   *cunning:* skill, art, talent.

93.   *doubtful of your modesties:* unsure of your self-restraint.

94.   *over-eying of:* observing or over playing.

96.   *merry passion:* hilarity.

100.   *veriest antick:* the oddest person, a buffoon.

101.   *buttery:* a food storage room.

103.   *want:* lack.
      affords: can provide.

104.   *Barthol'mew:* pronounced "Bartelmy."

106.   *him:* the page.

108.   *as he will:* if he wishes.

109.   *He bear:* he should conduct.

111.   *accomplishèd:* performed.

113.   *low tongue:* gentle voice.

118.   *with declining head into his bosom:* with the page's head lowered on Sly's chest.

119.   *him:* the page.
      as being: as if he were.

121.   *esteemed him:* thought himself to be.

124.   *commanded:* forced.

125.   *shift:* purpose, trick.

Which, in a napkin being close convey'd,
Shall in despite enforce a watery eye.
See this dispatch'd with all the haste thou canst.
Anon I'll give thee more instructions.
[Exit a SERVINGMAN]
I know the boy will well usurp the grace,   130
Voice, gait, and action, of a gentlewoman.
I long to hear him call the drunkard "husband"!
And how my men will stay themselves from laughter
When they do homage to this simple peasant.
I'll in to counsel them. Haply my presence   135
May well abate the over-merry spleen
Which otherwise would grow into extremes.   137
[Exeunt]

126.   *napkin:* handkerchief.

     close convey'd: carried secretly.

127.   *Shall in despite enforce a watery eye:* he will force his eyes to water despite his inability to cry.

129.   *Anon:* then, soon.

130.   *usurp:* assume, take on.

133.   *stay:* keep, stop.

134.   *do homage:* show respect.

135.   *Haply:* perhaps.

136.   *abate:* control.

     over-merry spleen: excessive laughter. The spleen was thought to be the seat of strong emotions including laughter.

COMMENTARY

The Taming of the Shrew does not begin with the usual Prologue that most Elizabethan audiences had grown to expect. Instead of a character coming forward to give an overview of what would be happening in the play, the audience is immediately thrown off guard by the off-stage sounds of a loud argument between a man and a woman accompanied by the sound of glass breaking. Soon, Christopher Sly, a drunken tinker explodes on to the stage, followed by the equally loud Hostess. The Hostess of the tavern, or *alewife* as they were often called, became a stock figure in the comedy of the Renaissance. Because she was employed in one of the few jobs that women were still allowed to hold, the alewife became symbolic of the attempt by certain women to maintain some semblance of independence while exhibiting a voluble rebelliousness. A "proper" woman was not rebellious or out-spoken but was expected to adopt the qualities that were required of model Elizabethan women. In both Shakespeare's play and the world in which he lived, most men expected a woman to show "obeisance," or respect, and an attitude of submission towards the males in her life. Women were instructed at an early age to speak with a "soft low tongue" and exhibit "lowly courtesy." As a wife, the woman was expected to "make known her love" by honoring her husband which meant obeying his commands. The Hostess's vociferous and violent behavior, although frowned upon, will be mirrored in the women characters in the play within the play.

The argument between Sly and the Hostess continues until the man passes out and the Hostess runs off to summon the police. Not only has Shakespeare shocked an unsuspecting audience into a sense of imbalance and established the frenzied nature of the play, but he has also introduced the first of the major themes to be found in the play: the battle of the sexes.

The second of the major themes important to the play is that of the struggle between the classes. Christopher Sly is described in the stage directions as a tinker. Tinkers were itinerant workers who moved from village to village repairing household items such as pots and kettles. Tinkers were, for the most part, not trusted and were often perceived to be scoundrels and rogues; definitely members of the lower class. The Hostess, despite being a commoner herself, can claim a higher status than Sly because she has a job and thus a position of power and authority over the drunken tinker who is trying to get out of paying his bill. Sly attempts to regain some status over the Hostess by telling her that he is descended from "Richard Conqueror." Instead of reclaiming any status by trying to establish his family as an honorable one, Sly jumbles up William the Conqueror and Richard the Lion-Hearted, proving his ignorance as well as his tendency towards posturing.

"A pair of stocks, you rogue!" (In. 2)
Mary Evans Picture Library

the "lead actor." Shakespeare is deftly setting up the theme of deception along with the theme of illusion versus reality. He is also theorizing that "All the world's a stage, /And all the men and women merely players." (*As You Like It* II.7) In one form or another, Shakespeare will continue to explore these ideas in most of his existing plays.

Just as Sly is carried away, a group of players enter the scene and agree to join the Lord's "cast" in the duping of the tinker. Groups of traveling players were common in England during Shakespeare's time. The troupes often consisted of six members, although some may have had as many as twenty and usually contained at least one boy who could play the young female parts. The players traveled to places where they knew they would be welcome and performed in town halls and in the yards of inns or pubs. The players would need about ten to fourteen shillings a day to pay for their expenses, such as housing and food for both the horses and the actors. Shakespeare's company, the Lord Chamberlain's Men, toured four of the nine years that they were under the sponsorship of Lord Chamberlain from 1594 to 1603. Under the patronage of James I, they toured every season from 1603 to 1615. In this chaotic world of social inversion, the actors performing *The Taming of the Shrew* are players performing players playing players.

The entrance of the wealthy Lord provides a skillful staging of class rank as he uses his aristocratic privileges to humiliate and manipulate the lowest of classes represented by Christopher Sly. With too much time and money on his hands, the Lord highlights Shakespeare's emphasis on the hierarchal class order as it is represented in *The Taming of the Shrew*. Along with his servants, the Lord has been out hunting, an image that along with the imagery of animals associated with the hunt will pervade much of the play. The Lord stumbles upon Sly who has passed out in the street and after determining that he is not dead, the Lord decides to play a trick on the unsuspecting Sly. A trick played for the entertainment of some regularly includes the humiliation of another who is weaker and less able to defend himself or eventually retaliate. The Lord shows no sympathy or compassion for Sly nor does he want to help him. He sees Sly as merely a plaything, something he can toy with and "practice" on with no thought to the confusion, embarrassment, and pain it might bring to his victim when the fun is over.

At this point, the Lord effectively becomes the "director" of a play of his own making, assigning parts to his servants and giving them directions on how to turn his bedchamber into a theatre, dress the "stage" and costume

The issue of transformation is another idea that Shakespeare explored in most of his plays and *The Taming of the Shrew* is no exception. Beginning with Sly, who has gone from a drunken tinker to what the Lord describes as a "monstrous beast," he will now be transformed once again into a "wealthy Lord." The Lord will become a servant; his male page will become a wife, and the players, professional shape-shifters, will become whatever they are required to be. Nothing or no one is as he or she seems. Thus the question becomes: What is real, and are the transformations permanent or merely the impermanent illusions of trickery?

Induction 2

Christopher Sly awakens to find himself surrounded by luxury. Servants proceed to meet his every need and the Lord, disguised as a servant, tells Sly that he has been delirious for the past fifteen years and that everyone is thrilled at his sudden recovery. At first Sly cannot believe that this is real but soon accepts the words of the servant/Lord as true and begins to enjoy his new station in life. The page, dressed as a woman, pretends to be Sly's wife. Sly asks her to undress and join him in bed but the page/wife says that will have to wait . . . doctor's orders. A messenger enters with the news that the players are ready to perform and Sly and the others prepare to watch the play.

INDUCTION, SCENE 2
A bedchamber in the LORD'S house.

[Enter aloft SLY with ATTENDANTS; some with apparel, basin, and ewer, and other appurtenances; and LORD, disguised as a servant]

Sly For God's sake, a pot of small ale.   1

First Servant Will't please your Lordship drink a cup of sack?

Second Servant Will't please your Honour taste of these conserves?

Third Servant What raiment will your Honour wear today?

Sly I am Christophero Sly! Call not me "Honour" nor "Lord-ship". I   5
ne'er drank sack in my life. And if you give me any conserves,
give me conserves of beef. Ne'er ask me what raiment I'll wear,
for I have no more doublets than backs, no more stockings than
legs, nor no more shoes than feet, nay, sometime more feet than
shoes, or such shoes as my toes look through the over-leather.   10

Lord *[as servant]* Heaven cease this idle humour in your Honour!
O, that a mighty man of such descent,
Of such possessions, and so high esteem
Should be infusèd with so foul a spirit!

Sly What! would you make me mad? Am not I Christopher Sly, old   15

NOTES

1. *small:* weak, cheap.

2. *sack:* an expensive dry, white Spanish wine.

3. *conserves:* candied fruit.

4. *raiment:* outfit.

7. *conserves of beef:* salted beef.

8. *doublets:* jackets.

10. *over-leather:* leather uppers.

11. *idle humour:* foolish fantasy.

14. *infusèd:* imbued.

Sly's son of Burton-Heath, by birth a peddler, by education a
cardmaker, by transmutation a bearherd, and now by present
profession a tinker? Ask Marian Hacket, the fat ale-wife of
Wincot, if she know me not! If she say I am not fourteen
   pence on the score for sheer ale, score me up for the
   lyingest knave in   20
Christendom. *[servant returns with a pot of ale]* What! I am
   not bestraught. Here's — *[Sly drinks]*

Third Servant O! This it is that makes your lady mourn.

Second Servant O! This is it that makes your servants droop.

Lord Hence comes it that your kindred shuns your house,
   As beaten hence by your strange lunacy.   25
   O noble lord, bethink thee of thy birth,
   Call home thy ancient thoughts from banishment,
   And banish hence these abject lowly dreams.
   Look how thy servants do attend on thee,
   Each in his office ready at thy beck.   30
   Wilt thou have music? Hark! Apollo plays,
   [Music]
   And twenty cagèd nightingales do sing.
   Or wilt thou sleep? We'll have thee to a couch
   Softer and sweeter than the lustful bed
   On purpose trimm'd up for Semiramis.   35
   Say thou wilt walk, we will bestrew the ground.
   Or wilt thou ride? Thy horses shall be trapp'd,
   Their harness studded all with gold and pearl.
   Dost thou love hawking? Thou hast hawks will soar
   Above the morning lark. Or wilt thou hunt?   40
   Thy hounds shall make the welkin answer them
   And fetch shrill echoes from the hollow earth.

First Servant Say thou wilt course. Thy greyhounds are as
   swift
   As breathèd stags, ay, fleeter than the roe.

Second Servant Dost thou love pictures? We will fetch thee
   straight   45
   Adonis painted by a running brook,
   And Cytherea all in sedges hid,

16. *Burton-Heath:* possibly Barton-on-Heath, a small village about 16 miles south of Stratford, Shakespeare's birthplace.

17. *cardmaker:* maker of the cards used to comb wool.

   bearherd: keeper of tame or performing bears.

18. *ale-wife:* female alehouse keeper.

19. *Wincot:* another village near Stratford.

   on the score: on account (pub workers kept track of the number of drinks ordered by cutting or scoring a stick or tally.

21. *bestraught:* mad, distracted, crazy.

26. *bethink:* consider.

27. *ancient:* former.

30. *office:* assignment.

   beck: summons.

   Apollo: god of music.

34. *lustful:* provoking sexual desire.

35. *trimm'd:* dressed up.

   Semiramis: queen of Assyria who was noted for her sexual prowess.

36. *bestrew:* cover with flowers or rushes.

37. *trapp'd:* decorated.

39. *hawking:* hunting for birds with trained hawks.

41. *welkin:* the sky.

43. *course:* hunt the rabbit.

44. *breathèd stags:* healthy stags.

   roe: small deer.

45. *pictures:* the "wanton pictures" discussed by the Lord in Induction Scene 1. These lines describe images of seductions and rapes based on the stories told in Ovid's *Metamorphoses*.

46. *Adonis:* a mortal loved by Cytherea.

47. *Cytherea:* Venus.

Which seem to move and wanton with her breath
Even as the waving sedges play with wind.

Lord We'll show thee Io as she was a maid 50
And how she was beguilèd and surpris'd,
As lively painted as the deed was done.

Third Servant Or Daphne roaming through a thorny wood,
Scratching her legs, that one shall swear she bleeds,
And at that sight shall sad Apollo weep, 55
So workmanly the blood and tears are drawn.

Lord Thou art a lord, and nothing but a lord;
Thou hast a lady far more beautiful
Than any woman in this waning age.

First Servant And, till the tears that she hath shed for thee 60
Like envious floods o'errun her lovely face,
She was the fairest creature in the world-
And yet she is inferior to none.

Sly Am I a lord? And have I such a lady?
Or do I dream? Or have I dream'd till now? 65
I do not sleep: I see, I hear, I speak,
I smell sweet savours, and I feel soft things.
Upon my life, I am a lord indeed
And not a tinker, nor Christopher Sly.
Well, bring our lady hither to our sight, 70
And once again, a pot o' the smallest ale.

Second Servant Will't please your mightiness to wash your
  hands?
[Servants present a ewer, basin, and napkin]
O, how we joy to see your wit restor'd!
O, that once more you knew but what you are!
These fifteen years you have been in a dream, 75
Or, when you wak'd, so wak'd as if you slept.

Sly These fifteen years! By my fay, a goodly nap.
But did I never speak of all that time?

First Servant O, yes, my lord, but very idle words.
For though you lay here in this goodly chamber, 80
Yet would you say you were beaten out of door,
And rail upon the hostess of the house,

48.	*wanton:* move sensually.
49.	*sedges:* marsh grass.
50.	*Io:* a maiden raped by Jove and transformed into a heifer.
51.	*beguilèd and surpris'd:* tricked and captured.
52.	*As lively painted as the deed was done:* lifelike.
53.	*Daphne:* a maiden desired and pursued by Apollo.
56.	*workmanly:* expertly.
59.	*waning age:* a reference to the history of man seen as a steady decline from the perfection of Eden.
61.	*envious:* malicious.
	o'errun: over flowed.
63.	*yet:* still.
67.	*savours:* odors.
70.	*our:* Sly begins using the royal "we".
71.	*smallest:* thinnest, weakest.
73.	*wit:* mental powers.
74.	*knew but:* only knew.
75.	*These:* these last.
77.	*fay:* faith.
78.	*of:* during.
79.	*idle:* meaningless, silly.
82.	*house:* inn, pub.

And say you would present her at the leet
Because she brought stone jugs and no seal'd quarts.
Sometimes you would call out for Cicely Hacket.   85

Sly Ay, the woman's maid of the house.

Third Servant Why, sir, you know no house nor no such
    maid,
Nor no such men as you have reckon'd up,
As Stephen Sly, and old John Naps of Greete,
And Peter Turf, and Henry Pimpernell,   90
And twenty more such names and men as these,
Which never were, nor no man ever saw.

Sly Now, Lord be thanked for my good amends!

All Amen.

Sly I thank thee. Thou shalt not lose by it.   95
[Enter the PAGE, as a lady, with ATTENDANTS]

Page *[as a lady]* How fares my noble lord?

Sly Marry, I fare well, for here is cheer enough.
    Where is my wife?

Page Here, noble lord. What is thy will with her?

Sly Are you my wife, and will not call me "husband"?   100
    My men should call me "lord". I am your goodman.

Page My husband and my lord, my lord and husband,
    I am your wife in all obedience.

Sly I know it well. What must I call her?

Lord "Madam".   105

Sly "Alice Madam", or "Joan Madam"?

Lord "Madam", and nothing else. So lords call ladies.

Sly Madam wife, they say that I have dream'd
    And slept above some fifteen year or more.

Page Ay, and the time seems thirty unto me,   110
    Being all this time abandon'd from your bed.

Sly 'Tis much. Servants, leave me and her alone.
    Madam, undress you, and come now to bed.

Page Thrice noble lord, let me entreat of you
    To pardon me yet for a night or two;   115

---

83. *present her at the leet:* bring her to trial before the court of the lord of the manor.

84. *stone jugs and no seal'd quarts:* sealed quarts, bearing official stamps and guaranteeing the quantity they contained, were preferable to stone jugs that held indeterminate quantities.

86. *Ay:* yes.

    The woman's ...house: the landlady's maid.

88. *reckon'd up:* enumerated.

89. *Stephen Sly, John Naps, Peter Turf, Henry Pimpernell:* possibly the names of real people. A Stephen Sly did live in Stratford in January of 1615.

93. *amends:* recovery.

97. *Marry:* an oath on the name of the Virgin Mary.

    cheer: food and drink.

101. *goodman:* the form in which a lower class wife addressed her husband.

109. *above:* more than.

111. *abandon'd:* excluded, banished.

Or, if not so, until the sun be set.
For your physicians have expressly charg'd,
In peril to incur your former malady,
That I should yet absent me from your bed.
I hope this reason stands for my excuse.   120

Sly Ay, it stands so that I may hardly tarry so long; but I
  would
  be loath to fall into my dreams again. I will therefore tarry in
  despite of the flesh and the blood.
  [Enter a servant as a Messenger]

Messenger Your Honour's players, hearing your amendment,
  Are come to play a pleasant comedy   125
  For so your doctors hold it very meet,
  Seeing too much sadness hath congeal'd your blood,
  And melancholy is the nurse of frenzy.
  Therefore they thought it good you hear a play
  And frame your mind to mirth and merriment,   130
  Which bars a thousand harms and lengthens life.

Sly Marry, I will. Let them play it. Is not a comonty a
  Christmas gambold or a tumbling-trick?

Page No, my good lord; it is more pleasing stuff.

Sly What! Household stuff?   135

Page It is a kind of history.

Sly Well, we'll see't. Come, madam wife, sit by my side and
  let
  the world slip. We shall ne'er be younger.   138
  [They sit]

---

118. *In peril . . . malady:* at risk to fall ill again.

120. *reason:* pronounced "raisin", a bawdy reference.
      stands: will serve, is acceptable.

121. *stands:* erect (a bawdy reference to the penis).
      tarry: wait.

124. *players:* actors.
      amendment: recovery.

125. *pleasant:* merry.

126. *hold it very meet:* consider it to be most appropriate.

128. *melancholy:* sad.
      nurse: nourish.
      frenzy: mental illness.

131. *bars:* prevents.

132. *comonty:* comedy.

133. *gambold:* frolic.

135. *Household stuff:* goods belonging to a household such as dishes, etc., "stuff" also has a sexual connotation.

136. *history:* narrative or story.

COMMENTARY

Christopher Sly awakes to find himself ensconced in the unrecognizable lap of luxury. He immediately calls for a "small ale" but is told he can have the more expensive "sack" if he chooses. Sly does not accept that he is a Lord and swears he has never had a sack in his life. Thinking he has lost his mind, Sly tests his own sanity by trying to recall facts about himself, thus he recalls his home and all of his former jobs. However, the Lord, disguised as a servant, admonishes Sly to "banish hence

these abject lowly dreams" and urges him to accept the fact that he is a man who has everything anyone could ever wish for. The Lord negates the validity of Sly's former life, assuming that the life and history of an aristocrat is always preferable to that of a poor man.

Looking at both the positive and fraudulent aspects of learning, the effect of education on people and society is explored throughout the play. In addition to being the "director" of this charade, put on to fool Sly, the Lord

The character Christopher Sly in an engraving by C.W. Sharpe after a painting by W.Q. Orchardson.
Mary Evans Picture Library

form. Daphne was a nymph sworn to virginity. Apollo fell madly in love with her and was determined to claim her virginity. He had almost succeeded when Daphne's mother turned her into a laurel tree. It was no coincidence that each of these figures represents the transformation of one thing into another and that the stories of Venus and Adonis, Io and Jove, and Daphne and Apollo are among the stories of rapes and seductions found in Ovid's *Metamorphoses*.

While Sly is mesmerized by the seductive paintings of strong women who have undergone major transformations, the Lord, still disguised as a servant, informs the tinker that he has a magnificent wife who has spent all the years of his illness mourning for him. At that moment, upon the discovery that he has a beautiful woman of his own, Sly finally becomes convinced that he is truly a Lord, and along with the rich clothing and fine food, takes on the speech of the upper class. Shakespeare often assigned prose to his characters of the lower class and as Sly is "transformed" into a wealthy Lord he begins speaking the poetry assigned to Kings and the aristocracy.

also becomes Sly's teacher, introducing him to art and music as well as instructing him on choosing the appropriate food, entertainment, and sport to be considered a proper aristocrat. As part of his instruction, Sly is offered his choice of entertainments and the words and images take on a sensual tone, meant specifically to seduce Sly through his base nature into believing he is truly a man of wealth and power.

Sly is offered music played by Apollo. He is enticed into a "lustful bed" and the Lord references Semiramis to reinforce the sexuality implied in the offer. Semiramis was the Queen of Assyria and according to Greek legend, she fulfilled her insatiable craving for lust and luxury with countless lovers. Next, Sly is shown a group of pictures including one of Venus and Adonis, possibly a reference to Shakespeare's published poem *Venus and Adonis*. Continuing the onslaught of "wanton pictures," Sly is shown pictures of both Io and Daphne. Io was one of Jupiter's lovers who Jupiter turned in to a heifer to conceal her from Juno. Juno enlisted the support of Argus, the fifty-eyed monster, to thwart Jupiter from turning Io back into human form. Mercury came to the aid of Jupiter by causing Argus to fall asleep and then cutting off his head. Juno then placed Argus' eyes into the tail of a peacock and Io was returned to her human

The acceptance that he is a Lord causes Sly to question whether he is now dreaming or if his previous life had been merely a dream. Again, the reader is asked to call into question what is real and what is illusion. To underscore that question, the male page enters disguised as Sly's wife, and although both the Lord and the reader know that his wife is certainly not what she seems, Sly is fooled and eager to get "her" into bed to make up for the time lost in the past fifteen years. The page convinces Sly that his physicians have insisted that for medical reasons she should remain absent from his bed. Noticing Sly's obvious arousal, the page, playing on the pronunciation of "reason" as "raisin" adds to Sly's ultimate humiliation by asking, "I hope this reason stands for my excuse."

A messenger enters with the news that the players have arrived and are prepared to perform. As the spectators settle in to watch the performance, another series of transformations will occur. The Induction is obviously set in Shakespeare's native Warwickshire. The places mentioned are all well within a short radius of Stratford, Shakespeare's home, and the people mentioned are the names of people actually listed on the town's registers. With the beginning of the play within the play, the setting will become Padua, a town in northern Italy near Venice known for its University. By choosing Padua as the setting for the upcoming "Shrew" play, Shakespeare intends for the readers to separate themselves from what would have been home to the original Elizabethan audience. By doing so, they must recognize that the action that begins in Act I is a play or theatrical event done for the amusement of the Lord, his staff, and Sly and that everything that transpires in the inner play is nothing more than dramatic illusion. Shakespeare also wants to establish the connection of Padua, a center of learning, and the educational process that will continue to occur in the remainder of the play. The tone of the play will also become more farcical. In the genre of Farce, the human character is without depth and is not hampered by thinking or the examination of conscience. Working within this genre, Shakespeare is not content with formulaic play writing and includes much more character complexity than is usually seen in stock Farce, but the overall effect of Farce is to simplify life by making it not only painless but automatic.

Although the inner play is much different in tone and style from the Induction, the play within the play underscores the dreamlike quality of life and reflects many of the themes first introduced in the Induction including the battle of the sexes, class struggles, education, illusion versus reality, and transformation. As Sly and the reader will be prompted to "mind the play" in the following scene, *The Taming of the Shrew* reminds the reader that comedy should both amuse and instruct.

Notes

THE TAMING OF THE SHREW
ACT I

Tranio *Nay, then, 'tis time to stir him from his trance.*
I pray, awake, sir! If you love the maid,
Bend thoughts and wits to achieve her. Thus it stands:
Her elder sister is so curst and shrewd
That till the father rid his hands of her,
Master, your love must live a maid at home,
And therefore has he closely mew'd her up,
Because she will not be annoy'd with suitors.

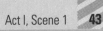

Act I, Scene 1

Lucentio, the son of a wealthy merchant, arrives in Padua accompanied by his servant Tranio, to study at the university. The two men overhear Baptista Minola telling two men, Gremio and Hortensio, that no one will be allowed to marry his younger daughter, the beautiful Bianca, until a suitable husband has been found for his shrewish older daughter Kate. Baptista also mentions to Gremio and Hortensio that he is looking for a tutor for Bianca. Lucentio has fallen in love at first sight with Bianca and decides to change identities with Tranio so that he may pretend to be a tutor to get closer to Bianca, while Tranio, posing as Lucentio, will make himself a third suitor to Bianca. Biondello, Lucentio's other servant, arrives to find Lucentio and Tranio in each other's clothes and is very confused. The two explain that Lucentio accidentally killed someone in a fight and they have exchanged clothes to save his life.

ACT I, SCENE 1

Padua. A public place.

[Flourish. Enter LUCENTIO and his man TRANIO]

Lucentio Tranio, since for the great desire I had   1
   To see fair Padua, nursery of arts,
   I am arriv'd for fruitful Lombardy,
   The pleasant garden of great Italy,
   And by my father's love and leave am arm'd   5
   With his good will and thy good company.
   My trusty servant well approv'd in all,
   Here let us breathe and haply institute
   A course of learning and ingenious studies.
   Pisa, renowned for grave citizens,   10
   Gave me my being and my father first,
   A merchant of great traffic through the world,
   Vincentio, come of the Bentivolii.
   Vincentio's son, brought up in Florence,
   It shall become to serve all hopes conceiv'd,   15
   To deck his fortune with his virtuous deeds:
   And therefore, Tranio, for the time I study
   Virtue, and that part of philosophy
   Will I apply that treats of happiness
   By virtue specially to be achiev'd.   20
   Tell me thy mind, for I have Pisa left
   And am to Padua come, as he that leaves

NOTES

SD.   *Flourish:* a trumpet fanfare.

    man: servant.

1.   *for:* because of.

2.   *nursery of arts:* Padua, famous for its university, was the center of Aristotelianism.

3.   *am arriv'd for:* have arrived in.

5.   *leave:* permission.

7.   *well approv'd:* found to be perfectly reliable.

8.   *breathe:* rest, remain, pause.

    haply: perhaps.

    institute: begin.

9.   *ingenious:* appropriate, highly intellectual.

10.   *grave:* worthy, serious.

11.   *my father first:* my father before me.

12.   *of great traffic:* business, extensive trading.

13.   *come of:* descended from.

    Bentivolii: leading family of Bologna, one of power and political force.

15.   *serve:* work for.

16.   *deck:* embellish.

A shallow plash to plunge him in the deep
And with satiety seeks to quench his thirst.

Tranio Mi perdonato, gentle master mine.   25
I am in all affected as yourself,
Glad that you thus continue your resolve
To suck the sweets of sweet philosophy.
Only, good master, while we do admire
This virtue and this moral discipline,   30
Let's be no stoics nor no stocks, I pray,
Or so devote to Aristotle's checks
As Ovid be an outcast quite abjur'd.
Balk logic with acquaintance that you have,
And practise rhetoric in your common talk;   35
Music and poesy use to quicken you;
The mathematics and the metaphysics,
Fall to them as you find your stomach serves you.
No profit grows where is no pleasure ta'en.
In brief, sir, study what you most affect.   40

Lucentio Gramercies, Tranio, well dost thou advise.
If, Biondello, thou wert come ashore,
We could at once put us in readiness
And take a lodging fit to entertain
Such friends as time in Padua shall beget.   45
[*Enter BAPTISTA with his two daughters, KATHERINA and
BIANCA; GREMIO, a pantaloon, and HORTENSIO, suit-
ors to Bianca*]
But stay awhile! What company is this?

Tranio Master, some show to welcome us to town.
[*Lucentio and Tranio stand by*]

Baptista [*to Gremio and Hortensio*] Gentlemen, importune
    me no further,
For how I firmly am resolv'd you know:
That is, not to bestow my youngest daughter   50
Before I have a husband for the elder.
If either of you both love Katherina,
Because I know you well and love you well,
Leave shall you have to court her at your pleasure.

23.	*plash:* pool, puddle.
25.	*Mi perdonato:* excuse me.
26.	*affected:* inclined, of the same feeling.
30.	*discipline:* philosophy.
31.	*stoics:* a philosophy in which the followers put aside all pleasure, refusing to give in to emotion and desire.
	stocks: blockheads, unfeeling people.
32.	*devote:* devoted.
	Aristotle's checks: the moral self-restraint advocated by Aristotle.
33.	*Ovid:* Rome love poet.
	abjur'd: rejected.
34.	*Balk logic:* bandy words, avoid study of logic.
35.	*rhetoric:* the art of using words effectively.
36.	*poesy:* poetry.
	quicken: make alive.
37.	*metaphysics:* philosophy.
38.	*stomach:* preference, taste.
39.	*ta'en:* taken.
40.	*affect:* like.
41.	*Gramercies:* many thanks.
SD.	*pantaloon:* ridiculous old man.
47.	*show:* spectacle, entertainment.
48.	*importune me:* try to persuade.
50.	*bestow:* give in marriage.
54.	*Leave:* permission.

Gremio To cart her rather. She's too rough for me.   55
There, there, Hortensio, will you any wife?

Kate *[To Baptista]* I pray you, sir, is it your will
To make a stale of me amongst these mates?

Hortensio "Mates", maid! How mean you that? No mates
for you,
Unless you were of gentler, milder mould.   60

Kate I' faith, sir, you shall never need to fear.
Iwis it is not halfway to her heart.
But if it were, doubt not her care should be
To comb your noddle with a three-legg'd stool
And paint your face and use you like a fool.   65

Hortensio From all such devils, good Lord deliver us!

Gremio And me, too, good Lord!

Tranio *[to Lucentio]* Husht, master! Here's some good pastime toward;
That wench is stark mad or wonderful froward.

Lucentio But in the other's silence do I see   70
Maid's mild behaviour and sobriety.
Peace, Tranio!

Tranio Well said, master. Mum, and gaze your fill.

Baptista *[to Hortensio and Gremio]* Gentlemen, that I may
soon make good
What I have said—Bianca, get you in,   75
And let it not displease thee, good Bianca,
For I will love thee ne'er the less, my girl.

Kate A pretty peat! It is best
Put finger in the eye, an she knew why.

Bianca Sister, content you in my discontent.   80
Sir, to your pleasure humbly I subscribe.
My books and instruments shall be my company,
On them to look, and practice by myself.

Lucentio Hark, Tranio! Thou mayst hear Minerva speak.

Hortensio Signior Baptista, will you be so strange?   85
Sorry am I that our good will effects
Bianca's grief.

---

55. *cart:* bawds and whores who violated community regulations were often punished by being paraded through the streets in open carts.

58. *stale:* prostitute, laughingstock.

    mates: fellows.

59. *Mates:* spouses.

62. *Iwis:* certainly.

    it: marriage.

    her: Kate's.

64. *noddle:* head.

65. *paint:* scratch until it bleeds.

68. *Husht:* Be quiet.

    pastime toward: entertainment coming up.

69. *froward:* willful, ungovernable.

73. *Mum:* Hush!

78. *peat:* spoiled child, pet, favorite.

79. *Put finger in the eye:* cry.

81. *subscribe:* submit.

82. *instruments:* musical instruments.

84. *Minerva:* goddess of wisdom.

85. *strange:* rigid, unfriendly.

86. *effects:* brings about.

Gremio Why will you mew her up,
Signior Baptista, for this fiend of hell,
And make her bear the penance of her tongue?   90

Baptista Gentlemen, content you. I am resolv'd.
Go in, Bianca.
[Exit Bianca]
And for I know she taketh most delight
In music, instruments, and poetry,
Schoolmasters will I keep within my house   95
Fit to instruct her youth. If you, Hortensio,
Or, Signior Gremio, you, know any such,
Prefer them hither. For to cunning men
I will be very kind, and liberal
To mine own children in good bringing up.   100
And so, farewell. Katherina, you may stay,
For I have more to commune with Bianca.
[Exit]

Kate Why, and I trust I may go too, may I not?
What! Shall I be appointed hours, as though, belike,
I knew not what to take and what to leave? Ha!   105
[Exit]

Gremio You may go to the devil's dam! Your gifts are so good
here's none will hold you. Their love is not so great,
Hortensio, but we may blow our nails together, and fast it
fairly
out. Our cake's dough on both sides. Farewell. Yet, for the
love I
bear my sweet Bianca, if I can by any means light on a fit
man to   110
teach her that wherein she delights, I will wish him to her
father.

Hortensio So will I, Signior Gremio. But a word, I pray.
Though
the nature of our quarrel yet never brooked parle, know now
upon
advice, it toucheth us both (that we may yet again have
access to   115
our fair mistress, and be happy rivals in Bianca's love) to
labour
and effect one thing specially.

88.	*mew her up:* confine her, lock her up.
89.	*for:* because of.
90.	*her:* Bianca.
	her: Katherine.
98.	*Prefer:* recommend.
	cunning: talented, learned.
102.	*commune:* discuss.
104.	*appointed hours:* told when to stay or go.
	belike: seems likely.
106.	*devil's dam:* mother of the devil.
107.	*hold:* restrain.
	great: important.
108.	*blow our nails:* wait patiently.
	fast it fairly out: survive.
109.	*Our cake's . . . sides:* proverbial for we have lost or failed.
111.	*wish:* recommend.
114.	*brooked parle:* allowed us to discuss.
115.	*advice:* careful deliberation.
	toucheth: concerns.
116.	*labour and effect:* strive to bring about.

Gremio What's that, I pray?

Hortensio Marry, sir, to get a husband for her sister.

Gremio A husband? A devil!   120

Hortensio I say, "a husband".

Gremio I say, "a devil." Thinkest thou, Hortensio, though her
Father be very rich, any man is so very a fool to be married to
hell?

Hortensio Tush, Gremio! Though it pass your patience and mine to   125
endure her loud alarums, why, man, there be good fellows in the
world, an a man could light on them, would take her with all
faults, and money enough.

Gremio I cannot tell. But I had as lief take her dowry with this
condition: to be whipp'd at the
high cross every morning.   130

Hortensio Faith, as you say, there's small choice in rotten
apples. But, come, since this bar in law makes us friends, it
shall be so far forth friendly maintained till by helping
Baptista's eldest daughter to a husband, we set his youngest free
for a husband, and then have to't afresh. Sweet
Bianca! Happy man   135
be his dole! He that runs fastest gets the ring. How say you,
Signior Gremio?

Gremio I am agreed; and would I had given him the best horse in
Padua to begin his wooing, that would thoroughly woo her, wed
her, and bed her, and rid the house of her. Come on.   140

[Exeunt Gremio and Hortensio]

Tranio I pray, sir, tell me, is it possible
That love should of a sudden take such hold?

126.	*alarums:* outcries, brawlings.
127.	*light on:* find.
128.	*and:* if there was.
129.	*as lief:* as willingly.
130.	*high cross:* prominent spot in the town, market cross.
132.	*bar in law:* legal obstruction.
135.	*have to't afresh:* begin again.
136.	*dole:* destiny.

Lucentio O Tranio! Till I found it to be true,
  I never thought it possible or likely. But see, while idly I
    stood looking on,   145
  I found the effect of love in idleness,
  And now in plainness do confess to thee
  That art to me as secret and as dear
  As Anna to the Queen of Carthage was:
  Tranio, I burn, I pine! I perish, Tranio,   150
  If I achieve not this young modest girl.
  Counsel me, Tranio, for I know thou canst:
  Assist me, Tranio, for I know thou wilt.

Tranio Master, it is no time to chide you now.
  Affection is not rated from the heart.   155
  If love have touch'd you, naught remains but so:
  Redime te captum quam queas minimo.

Lucentio Gramercies, lad. Go forward. This contents;
  The rest will comfort, for thy counsel's sound.

Tranio Master, you look'd so longly on the maid,   160
  Perhaps you mark'd not what's the pith of all.

Lucentio O, yes, I saw sweet beauty in her face,
  Such as the daughter of Agenor had,
  That made great Jove to humble him to her hand
  When with his knees he kiss'd the Cretan strand.   165

Tranio Saw you no more? Mark'd you not how her sister
  Began to scold and raise up such a storm
  That mortal ears might hardly endure the din?

Lucentio Tranio, I saw her coral lips to move,
  And with her breath she did perfume the air.   170
  Sacred and sweet was all I saw in her.

Tranio Nay, then, 'tis time to stir him from his trance.
  I pray, awake, sir! If you love the maid,
  Bend thoughts and wits to achieve her. Thus it stands:
  Her elder sister is so curst and shrewd   175
  That till the father rid his hands of her,
  Master, your love must live a maid at home,
  And therefore has he closely mew'd her up,
  Because she will not be annoy'd with suitors.

---

146. *Love in idleness:* a pansy thought to be an aphrodisiac.

147. *plainness:* openly.

149. *Anna to the Queen of Carthage:* In Virgil's *Aenid*, Dido, the queen of Carthage, has a sister Anna to whom the queen reveals her love for Aeneas.

155. *rated:* scolded, chided.

157. *Redime . . . minimo:* now that you have been captured, ransom yourself for the least possible price.

158. *Gramercies:* thanks.

    contents: makes me content.

160. *longly:* long, longingly.

161. *mark'd not:* did not notice.

    pith of all: heart of the matter.

163. *daughter of Agenor:* Europa, whom Jove loved and in the form of a bull, took to Crete.

165. *strand:* shore.

169. *her:* Bianca's.

175. *curst and shrewd:* loud and ill tempered.

178. *mew'd:* caged.

179. *Because:* so that.

Lucentio Ah, Tranio, what a cruel father's he!   180
   But art thou not advis'd he took some care
   To get her cunning schoolmasters to instruct her?

Tranio Ay, marry, am I, sir, and now 'tis plotted.

Lucentio I have it, Tranio!

Tranio Master, for my hand,   185
   Both our inventions meet and jump in one.

Lucentio Tell me thine first.

Tranio You will be schoolmaster
   And undertake the teaching of the maid:
   That's your device.   190

Lucentio It is. May it be done?

Tranio Not possible. For who shall bear your part
   And be in Padua here Vincentio's son,
   Keep house and ply his book, welcome his friends,
   Visit his countrymen, and banquet them?   195

Lucentio Basta, content thee, for I have it full.
   We have not yet been seen in any house,
   Nor can we be distinguish'd by our faces
   For man or master. Then it follows thus:
   Thou shalt be master, Tranio, in my stead,   200
   Keep house and port and servants, as I should.
   I will some other be, some Florentine,
   Some Neapolitan, or meaner man of Pisa.
   'Tis hatch'd, and shall be so. Tranio, at once
   Uncase thee. Take my colour'd hat and cloak.   205
   [They exchange habits]
   When Biondello comes, he waits on thee,
      But I will charm him first to keep his tongue.

Tranio So had you need.
   In brief, sir, sith it your pleasure is,
   And I am tied to be obedient   210
   (For so your father charg'd me at our parting:
   'Be serviceable to my son,' quoth he,
   Although I think 'twas in another sense),
   I am content to be Lucentio,
   Because so well I love Lucentio.   215

181.	*advis'd:* informed.
182.	*cunning:* knowing.
183.	*'tis plotted:* I have a plan.
185.	*for my hand:* I'll wager my part.
186.	*inventions:* schemes.
	meet and jump in one: identical, coincide perfectly.
190.	*device:* plan.
194.	*Keep house:* entertain.
	ply his book: study.
196.	*Basta:* Italian for "enough."
	have it full: worked out a scheme.
201.	*port:* style, lifestyle.
203.	*meaner:* poorer, less socially acceptable.
205.	*Uncase:* undress.
206.	*waits:* serves.
209.	*sith:* since.
210.	*tied:* obligated.
212.	*serviceable:* eager to serve.
	quoth: said.

Lucentio Tranio, be so, because Lucentio loves,
And let me be a slave, to achieve that maid
Whose sudden sight hath thrall'd my wounded eye.   218.   *thrall'd:* enthralled.
[Enter BIONDELLO]
Here comes the rogue. — Sirrah, where have you been?

Biondello Where have I been? Nay, how now!
  Where are you?   220
Master, has my fellow Tranio stol'n your clothes?
Or you stol'n his? Or both? Pray, what's the news?

Lucentio Sirrah, come hither. 'Tis no time to jest,
And therefore frame your manners to the time.   224.   *frame:* adjust.
Your fellow Tranio here, to save my life,   225
Puts my apparel and my count'nance on,   226.   *count'nance:* manner, appearance.
And I for my escape have put on his;
For in a quarrel since I came ashore
I kill'd a man and fear I was descried.   229.   *descried:* observed, identified.
Wait you on him, I charge you, as becomes,   230   230.   *becomes:* appropriate.
While I make way from hence to save my life.
You understand me?

Biondello I, sir! Ne'er a whit.   233.   *Ne'er a whit:* not in the least.

Lucentio And not a jot of Tranio in your mouth.
Tranio is changed to Lucentio.   235

Biondello The better for him. Would I were so too!

Tranio So could I, faith, boy, to have the next wish after,
That Lucentio indeed had Baptista's youngest daughter.
But, sirrah, not for my sake but your master's, I advise   239.   *use your manners:* behave.
You use your manners discreetly
  in all kind of companies.   240
When I am alone, why, then I am Tranio;
But in all places else, your master, Lucentio.

Lucentio Tranio, let's go. One thing more rests, that thyself   243.   *rests:* remains.
  execute,   *execute:* carry out.
to make one among these wooers. If thou ask me why,   244.   *make:* become.
sufficeth my reasons are both good and weighty.   245   245.   *sufficeth:* I need only say.
[Exeunt]
[The Presenters above speak]   SD.   *Presenters:* players from the Induction.

First Servant My lord, you nod. You do not mind the play.

Sly Yes, by Saint Anne, do I. A good matter, surely. Comes
　　there any more of it?

Page My lord, 'tis but begun.

Sly 'Tis a very excellent piece of work,
　　madam lady. Would 'twere done!   250

[They sit and mark]

246.	*nod:* sleep.
	mind: pay attention to.
247.	*Saint Anne:* mother of the Virgin Mary.
250.	*would:* I wish.
SD.	*mark:* watch.

COMMENTARY

The play within the play, or the "Shrew" play, begins with a flourish and the locale is transformed from a Warwickshire-like England into the University town of Padua, Italy. Accompanied by his servant Tranio, a wealthy young man named Lucentio has come to Padua to study philosophy, hoping that studying Aristotle will transform him from a schoolboy into a scholar.

The character of Tranio closely resembles a stock character taken from classical Roman Comedy—the faithful servant who is far superior to his master. Tranio understands Aristotle and can refer to Ovid with obvious confidence in his knowledge of the subject matter. The reference to Ovid both informs the reader that the two young men, Lucentio and Tranio, are romantics who feed on the poetry of the Roman love poet and reminds the reader that, as in Ovid's *Metamorphoses,* there are still transformations to come. Shakespeare also establishes Tranio as more than a mere servant by allowing him to speak poetry rather than the prose usually relegated to the common servant.

The Italian Setting

Because of the number of Shakespeare's plays set in Italy, 12 out of 36, his knowledge of Italy and Italian has often been called into question. Speculation has it that Shakespeare either visited Italy at some length during his lifetime or that he read extensively about the country. However, some scholars use Lucentio's line, "If, Biondello, thou wert come ashore" to prove that Shakespeare had no firsthand knowledge of Italy and was terribly mistaken in believing that Padua was a port city. Padua is in fact not a port city, but during the time

Shakespeare was writing, Northern Italy was indeed a network of canals and waterways where it was possible to hire a boat that left from Venice and arrive seven hours later on a canal behind the University in Padua. Thus, the line is geographically correct. In writing his Roman plays, Shakespeare borrowed story lines from different sources such as myths and poetry. When writing *The Taming of the Shrew,* Shakespeare used some Italian sources that had not at that time been translated into English. This fact leads some scholars to believe that Shakespeare could read Italian, although no absolute proof exists that Shakespeare visited Italy or could speak Italian.

Characterization

As Lucentio and Tranio are discussing the importance of finding time to enjoy the pleasures of Padua as well as the education to be obtained there, Baptista Minola makes his entrance with his two daughters, Bianca and Katherine, as well as two of Bianca's suitors, Hortensio and Gremio. Gremio is another character whose origin could be traced to the Italian form of comedy known as *Commedia dell'arte.* Known as a *pantaloon,* the character would be expected to be a ridiculous old man dressed in baggy pantaloons and perhaps slippers and spectacles. He would appear to be stupid as well as boring. As discussed in the Introduction, Commedia dell'arte is a form of comedy that is played for laughs with broad characters of no complexity. The characters, so familiar to that genre of theatre, reinforce the farcical aspects of the *Shrew* play and remind the reader that this play within a play is not intended to be taken completely seriously, but rather it is to incite laughter with its overstated, implausible situations and its humor resulting from its absurdities and vulgar wit.

Background of the Word "Shrew"

Baptista, surrounded by his daughters and Bianca's suitors, makes it clear that Bianca will not be married until a husband has been found for the eldest daughter, Katherine. Baptista is not as concerned with finding a good husband for Kate as he is with removing the obstacle to Bianca's happiness and advancement. Baptista suggests that Gremio would have his permission to "court" Katherine, but Gremio replies that Baptista must have meant "cart" her. Katherine, or Kate as she is often called, is the shrew that men will attempt to tame in this play. Women identified as shrews (also known as *scolds*) and whores who were accused of breaking the laws of the community were often paraded through the streets in an open cart. This particular punishment provided more humiliation than pain but there were other, more horrible punishments for these women when the occasion demanded it (see the Introduction to the Play).

In the sixteenth and seventeenth centuries, *shrews* were defined as bossy women whose angry, loud, and often public words were considered inappropriate for a proper lady. In court records from the time, it has been noted that Shrews would often force the men in their lives to do what was termed "woman's work," often beating their husbands into submission. They would further humiliate their husbands by drinking in pubs, withholding sex, and taking lovers. Not surprisingly, many of these same women would be accused of witchcraft. Of course the men who allowed their wives to treat them in this manner were considered weak and ineffectual and suffered as much humiliation as their wives did.

From the perspective of the twenty-first century, a shrew would be a woman who refused to acquiesce to a man's authority and assertively maintained her independence. This was not however the perspective that people living in the 1500's and 1600's adopted. In many instances, women labeled as shrews where forced to wear the *scold's bridle,* a metal contraption that fit over the woman's head. Attached to the bridle was a metal prong that, when inserted into the mouth of the shrew,

depressed her tongue and made it impossible for her to speak. *Cucking* was another form of punishment for women accused of being shrews. They would be strapped onto a stool and would then be dunked into water. In addition to the fear and humiliation associated with cucking, it was possible for the woman to be dipped too low causing her mouth and throat to be filled with mud, resulting in suffocation.

Almost all of Shakespeare's women are agents of delight and order in the comedies, but an obvious exception is Kate, who creates fear and a sense of disorder in those around her, especially the men. Her words become her weapons against the abuse she has suffered at the hands of domineering men and conniving women, but she has become proficient at being defensive and thus, not vulnerable. She has made herself intolerable. Her self-defeating behavior not only defines her but also drives others away from her. No man is likely to be inclined to marry a woman who publicly declares that if she had a husband she would keep him in line by hitting him over the head with a stool, scratching his face, and treating him like a fool. Instead of endearing people to her, comments such as this cause them, like Hortensio with his public humiliation of her, to exclude her from society. Even her father, leaving her in the street while he goes in to talk to Bianca, symbolically excludes Kate from her own family. She is a product of the society in which she exists and the topsy-turvy world of comedy that gives her life. Despite Kate's angry words and violent threats, it is impossible not to feel sympathy for this neglected, frustrated, and unhappy woman.

In his 1987 production of *The Taming of the Shrew* for the Royal Shakespeare Company (RSC), Jonathan Miller explored this sad but empathetic view of Kate by having her make her first entrance onto a set that involved a walkway with a very steep angle. On one side of the entrance was the town of Padua and on the other, a very sharp drop-off. This gave the image of a Kate who was walking a very dangerous path, on the brink of tumbling into the abyss. Kate, played by Fiona Shaw, carried a pair of embroidery scissors with which she vandalized the set by carving her initials into the wall and chopping off hunks of her own hair. In *Clamorous*

Voices (1994), by Carol Rutter, Fiona Shaw is quoted as saying that in this production, she "wanted to give the effect of a woman mutilating herself . . . I thought about women in crisis who, far from being aggressive towards other people, are very often aggressive towards themselves."

Bianca—not the gentle sister

Meanwhile, Lucentio, observing the scene between Baptista and the others, has fallen in love at first sight with the beautiful Bianca, whose name, perhaps appropriately, means white, colorless, or blank. He is immediately transformed from a potential scholar into a

"*Hark Tranio, thou mayest hear Minerva speak.*" (1.1)
Mary Evans Picture Library

hopeful lover. In her silence and seeming obedience, Bianca is perceived as the feminine ideal of loveliness, charm, and humility. She seems to possess all of the qualities that the Lord asked the page to assume and is a woman of "gentler, milder mold" that Hortensio prefers. In the character of Bianca, Shakespeare again deftly draws that fine line that exists between appearance and reality. On the surface, Bianca gives the impression of being the epitome of the male fantasy of the perfect woman. Her behavior however speaks another story. In reality, she is spoiled and overly indulged. For example, her father, Baptista, while publicly humiliating Kate, tells Bianca publicly that he will love her "ne'er the less." He also attempts to lessen her "grief" at not being able to marry until Kate is out of the way by indulging her delight in music and poetry with in-house schoolmasters. Nothing is done to relieve Kate's anguish at her own situation. Bianca also shamelessly manipulates others with her tears and beauty. Instead of the obedient young daughter her father thinks she is, Bianca must be told twice to go into the house but manages to tell her father what he wants to hear and wring his sympathy from what she plays as her miserable circumstances.

Bianca's self-pitying words also fool Lucentio who naively likens her to Minerva, the Roman Goddess of Wisdom. Obviously, Lucentio, only "seeing" the outward appearance of Bianca has not, as Tranio says, "marked . . . the pith of all." Lucentio has entirely missed the point of what has just transpired. In this case, love has not struck Lucentio blind, but deaf. He has not really heard what Bianca has said, he has not listened to the angry tongue of Kate, nor has he heard that Bianca must not be married until a husband can be found for Kate. Instead, Lucentio, merely "saw her coral lips to move."

In comparing Bianca's beauty to the daughter of Agenor, Shakespeare foreshadows the upcoming plot to win Bianca's love. Drawing once more from Ovid's *Metamorphoses,* Shakespeare uses the story of Europa, the daughter of the mythical King of Tyre. In this story, Zeus transforms himself into a bull and swims away with Europa, carrying her away to Crete. Lucentio, seeing no other way to win Bianca, hatches a plot with Tranio where Lucentio will be transformed into the schoolmaster, Cambio, and Tranio will be transformed into the master, Lucentio. Disguised as Cambio, Lucentio will attempt to convince Baptista to hire him as a tutor for

"...I saw sweet beauty in her face,/Such as [Europa] the daughter of Agenor had..." (1.1)
Mary Evans Picture Library

a man do not identify the reality of that man or truly distinguish him from another. Although Tranio, dressed in Lucentio's clothes, appears to be the son of a wealthy merchant, he is, in reality, the same man he was before. Tying in directly to the transformation of Christopher Sly, Tranio takes on the illusion of wealth and social importance without really possessing it, but these illusions will be enough to convince many others that he is something other than who he really is.

Back to "reality"

Act I, Scene 1 ends with the final appearance of Christopher Sly and the others watching the Shrew play. Sly has fallen asleep during the performance and although he is nudged awake by a servant, the play within the play, in addition to being a farcical comedy, takes on a dream-like quality that further distances the reader from the reality of what is happening in the "Shrew" play.

Bianca, allowing him easier access to woo the woman of his dreams. Tranio agrees to the deception and the men exchange clothes. Not only is Lucentio transformed into Tranio and Tranio into Cambio, but Shakespeare also makes the point that the clothes or outward trappings of

Act I, Scene 2

Accompanied by his servant Grumio, Petruchio, having traveled to Padua from Verona, arrives at Hortensio's house. Petruchio is in Padua to find a wealthy woman to marry and Hortensio offers to introduce him to Kate. Despite Hortensio's description of Kate's temper, Petruchio agrees to meet Kate and insists that Hortensio take him to Baptista's home immediately. Hortensio decides to disguise himself as a tutor, hoping that Baptista will hire him to instruct Bianca. In the meantime, Lucentio, disguised as Cambio, enters with Gremio, who has agreed to introduce Lucentio to Baptista on the grounds that Cambio will help convince Bianca that she should love Gremio. Hortensio returns with the good news that a possible husband has been found for Kate. Tranio, disguised as Lucentio, enters with Biondello. Seeing the group of men discussing the news of Petruchio and Kate, Tranio asks directions to Baptista's house and indicates he is on his way to woo Bianca. Gremio is upset that there is another competitor for Bianca's love but the news that Kate may soon be married gives joy to all.

ACT I, SCENE 2

Padua. Before HORTENSIO'S house.

[Enter PETRUCHIO and his man GRUMIO]

Petruchio Verona, for a while I take my leave,	1	
To see my friends in Padua, but of all		
My best beloved and approvèd friend,		
Hortensio. And I trow this is his house.		
Here, sirrah Grumio, knock, I say.	5	

Grumio Knock, sir? Whom should I knock? Is there any man has rebused your Worship?

Petruchio Villain, I say, knock me here soundly.

Grumio Knock you here, sir? Why, sir, what am I, sir, that I should knock you here, sir? 10

Petruchio Villain, I say, knock me at this gate
And rap me well, or I'll knock your knave's pate.

Grumio My master is grown quarrelsome. I should knock you first,
And then I know after who comes by the worst.

Petruchio Will it not be? 15
Faith, sirrah, an you'll not knock, I'll ring it.

NOTES

SD. *man:* servant.

2. *all:* especially.

3. *approvèd:* evaluated, tested.

4. *trow:* believe, think.

6. *rebused:* Grumio's error. He means "abused."

8. *knock me hear:* Knock for me. Grumio hears, "knock me ear."

12. *pate:* head.

16. *ring:* pun on "wring."

I'll try how you can sol, fa, and sing it.
[He wrings Grumio by the ears]

Grumio   Help, masters, help! My master is mad.

Petruchio   Now, knock when I bid you, sirrah villain!
[Enter HORTENSIO]

Hortensio   How now! What's the matter? My old friend
  Grumio and my   20
good friend Petruchio! How do you all at Verona?

Petruchio   Signior Hortensio, come you to part the fray?
  Con tutto il cuore ben trovato, may I say.

Hortensio   Alla nostra casa ben venuto; molto honorato
  signor mio Petruchio.
Rise, Grumio, rise. We will compound this quarrel.   25

Grumio   Nay, 'tis no matter, sir, what he 'leges in Latin.
  If thisbe not a lawful cause for me to leave his service, look
    you, sir:
  he bid me knock him and rap him soundly, sir. Well, was it
    fit for
  a servant to use his master so, being perhaps, for aught I see,
  two-and-thirty, a pip out?   30
  Whom, would to God, I had well knock'd at first,
  Then had not Grumio come by the worst.

Petruchio   A senseless villain! Good Hortensio,
  I bade the rascal knock upon your gate
  And could not get him for my heart to do it.   35

Grumio   Knock at the gate? O heavens! Spake you not these
    words
  plain: 'Sirrah knock me here, rap me here, knock me well,
    and
  knock me soundly'? And come you now with 'knocking at
    the gate'?

Petruchio   Sirrah, be gone, or talk not, I advise you.

Hortensio   Petruchio, patience. I am Grumio's pledge.   40
  Why, this's a heavy chance 'twixt him and you,
  Your ancient, trusty, pleasant servant Grumio.
  And tell me now, sweet friend, what happy gale
  Blows you to Padua here from old Verona?

---

17.   *sol, fa:* notes on the scale.

  sing it: wail.

22.   *part the fray:* stop the fight.

23.   *Con tutto il cuore ben trovato:* Italian for "Welcome with all my heart."

24.   *Alla nostra casa [ben] venuto [molto honorato] signor mio Petruchio:* Italian for "Welcome to our house, my much honored Signior Petruchio."

25.   *compound:* settle.

26.   *'leges:* alleges.

30.   *two-and-thirty, a pip out:* a bit crazy, a term from a card game.

35.   *my heart:* my life.

40.   *pledge:* guarantee.

41.   *heavy chance:* sad misfortune.

42.   *ancient:* long time.

Petruchio　Such wind as scatters young men through the
　world　　　　　　　　　　　　　　　　　　　　　45
　To seek their fortunes farther than at home,
　Where small experience grows. But in a few,
　Signior Hortensio, thus it stands with me:
　Antonio, my father, is deceas'd,
　And I have thrust myself into this maze,　　　50
　Happily to wive and thrive as best I may.
　Crowns in my purse I have, and goods at home,
　And so am come abroad to see the world.

Hortensio　Petruchio, shall I then come roundly to thee
　And wish thee to a shrewd ill-favour'd wife?　　55
　Thou'dst thank me but a little for my counsel;
　And yet I'll promise thee she shall be rich,
　And very rich. But th'art too much my friend,
　And I'll not wish thee to her.

Petruchio　Signior Hortensio, 'twixt such friends as we　60
　Few words suffice. And therefore, if thou know
　One rich enough to be Petruchio's wife
　(As wealth is burden of my wooing dance)
　Be she as foul as was Florentius' love,
　As old as Sibyl, and as curst and shrewd　　　65
　As Socrates' Xanthippe or a worse,
　She moves me not, or not removes, at least,
　Affection's edge in me, were she as rough
　As are the swelling Adriatic seas.
　I come to wive it wealthily in Padua;　　　　70
　If wealthily, then happily in Padua.

Grumio　Nay, look you, sir, he tells you flatly what his mind
　is. Why,
　give him gold enough and marry him to a puppet or an
　aglet-baby, or an old trot with ne'er a tooth in her head,
　though
　she have as many diseases as two-and-fifty horses. Why,
　nothing　　　　　　　　　　　　　　　　　　　75
　comes amiss, so money comes withal.

Hortensio　Petruchio, since we are stepp'd thus far in,
　I will continue that I broach'd in jest.

47.　*in a few:* in a few words.

50.　*maze:* uncertain course, complicated puzzle.
51.　*Happily:* perchance, with pleasure.
52.　*Crowns:* coins.

54.　*come roundly:* speak candidly.

55.　*shrewd:* shrewish.

　ill-favour'd: poorly qualified, unattractive due to bad temper.

63.　*burden:* musical refrain.
64.　*foul:* ugly.

　Florentius: a knight who agrees to marry an old hag to save his life. The hag is later transformed into a beautiful, young woman.

65.　*Sibyl:* a prophetess in Greek and Roman mythology who is granted as many years of life as there are grains of sand.

　curst and shrewd: ill tempered.

66.　*Xanthippe:* the bad-tempered wife of Socrates.

67.　*moves:* disturbs.

74.　*aglet-baby:* small carved doll decorated with spangles.

　trot: hag.

76.　*withal:* with it.

78.　*that:* what.

I can, Petruchio, help thee to a wife
With wealth enough, and young and beauteous,   80
Brought up as best becomes a gentlewoman.
Her only fault, and that is faults enough,
Is that she is intolerable curst
And shrewd and froward, so beyond all measure
That, were my state far worser than it is,   85
I would not wed her for a mine of gold.

Petruchio Hortensio, peace! Thou know'st not gold's effect.
Tell me her father's name, and 'tis enough;
For I will board her, though she chide as loud
As thunder when the clouds in autumn crack.   90

Hortensio Her father is Baptista Minola,
An affable and courteous gentleman. Her name is Katherina
  Minola,
Renown'd in Padua for her scolding tongue.

Petruchio I know her father, though I know not her;   95
And he knew my deceased father well.
I will not sleep, Hortensio, till I see her;
And therefore let me be thus bold with you
To give you over at this first encounter,
Unless you will accompany me thither.   100

Grumio *[to Hortensio]* I pray you, sir, let him go while the
  humour lasts. O' my
word, an she knew him as well as I do, she would think
  scolding
would do little good upon him. She may perhaps call him
  half a
score knaves or so. Why, that's nothing; and he begin once,
  he'll
rail in his rope-tricks. I'll tell you what,
  sir, an she stand him   105
but a little, he will throw a figure in her face and so disfigure
her with it that she shall have no more eyes to see withal
  than a
cat. You know him not, sir.

Hortensio Tarry, Petruchio, I must go with thee,
For in Baptista's keep my treasure is.   110
He hath the jewel of my life in hold,

83. *intolerable curst:* impossibly short tempered.

84. *froward:* willful, contrary.

85. *state:* estate, financial status.

89. *board:* woo, seduce.

99. *give you over:* leave you.

101. *humour:* mood.

103. *half a score:* ten.

105. *rail in his rope-tricks:* scold in an shocking way.

      stand: challenge, withstand (with a bawdy meaning as well).

106. *throw a figure:* hurl words.

109. *Tarry:* wait.

110. *keep:* the heavily fortified inner tower of a castle, custody.

111. *hold:* stronghold.

His youngest daughter, beautiful Bianca,
And her withholds from me and other more,
Suitors to her and rivals in my love,
Supposing it a thing impossible,   115
For those defects I have before rehears'd,
That ever Katherina will be woo'd.
Therefore this order hath Baptista ta'en,
That none shall have access unto Bianca
Till Katherine the curst have got a husband.   120

Grumio "Katherine the curst!"
A title for a maid, of all titles the worst.

Hortensio Now shall my friend Petruchio do me grace
And offer me disguis'd in sober robes
To old Baptista as a schoolmaster   125
Well seen in music, to instruct Bianca,
That so I may, by this device at least,
Have leave and leisure to make love to her
And unsuspected court her by herself.

Grumio Here's no knavery! See, to beguile the old folks, how
the   130
young folks lay their heads together!
*[Enter GREMIO, and LUCENTIO disguised as Cambio the
schoolmaster, with books under his arm]*
Master, master, look about you. Who goes there, ha?

Hortensio Peace, Grumio, 'tis the rival of my love. Petruchio,
stand by awhile.
[Petruchio, Hortensio, and Grumio stand aside]

Grumio A proper stripling, and an amorous!   135

Gremio *[to Lucentio]* O, very well; I have perus'd the note.
Hark you, sir, I'll have them very fairly bound,
All books of love. See that at any hand,
And see you read no other lectures to her.
You understand me. Over and beside   140
Signior Baptista's liberality,
I'll mend it with a largess. Take your papers too.
And let me have them very well perfum'd,
For she is sweeter than perfume itself
To whom they go to. What will you read to her?   145

---

113.   *other more:* other lovers.

116.   *rehears'd:* itemized.

118.   *order:* step.

123.   *grace:* favor.
124.   *offer:* introduce, present.
     sober: dark.
126.   *Well seen:* well trained.
127.   *device:* scheme.
128.   *leave:* opportunity.
     make love: woo her.

135.   *proper stripling:* handsome young man (spoken sarcastically).
136.   *note:* list of books.
137.   *fairly:* finely, attractively.
     bound: in Elizabethan times, books were sold unbound.
138.   *See . . . hand:* see to that in any case.
139.   *lectures:* lessons.
141.   *liberality:* generosity.
142.   *mend:* improve.
     largess: gift of money.
     papers: notes.
143.   *them:* the books.

Lucentio Whate'er I read to her, I'll plead for you

As for my patron, stand you so assur'd,

As firmly as yourself were still in place,

Yea, and perhaps with more successful words

Than you, unless you were a scholar, sir.   150

Gremio Othis learning, what a thing it is!

Grumio Othis woodcock, what an ass it is!

Petruchio Peace, sirrah!

Hortensio Grumio, mum! God save you, Signior Gremio!

Gremio And you are well met, Signior Hortensio.   155

Trow you whither I am going? To Baptista Minola.

I promis'd to enquire carefully

About a schoolmaster for the fair Bianca,

And by good fortune I have lighted well

On this young man, for learning and behaviour   160

Fit for her turn, well read in poetry

And other books, good ones, I warrant you.

Hortensio 'Tis well. And I have met a gentleman

Hath promis'd me to help me to another,

A fine musician to instruct our mistress.   165

So shall I no whit be behind in duty

To fair Bianca, so belov'd of me.

Gremio Belov'd of me, and that my deeds shall prove.

Grumio *[Aside]* And that his bags shall prove.

Hortensio Gremio, 'tis now no time to vent our love.   170

Listen to me, and if you speak me fair

I'll tell you news indifferent good for either.

[introducing Petruchio]

Here is a gentleman whom by chance I met,

Upon agreement from us to his liking,

Will undertake to woo curst Katherine,   175

Yea, and to marry her, if her dowry please.

Gremio So said, so done, is well.

Hortensio, have you told him all her faults?

Petruchio I know she is an irksome brawling scold.

If that be all, masters, I hear no harm.   180

---

147.   *stand:* rest.

148.   *As . . . yourself . . . place:* as if you were there the entire time.

152.   *woodcock:* idiot.

156.   *Trow:* know.

161.   *turn:* situation.

162.   *warrant:* guarantee.

169.   *bags:* money bags.

170.   *vent:* express.

171.   *fair:* courteously.

172.   *indifferent:* equally.

174.   *Upon agreement . . . liking:* if we agree to his terms.

175.   *undertake:* promise.

177.   *So said, . . . well:* if the actions match the words, it is good.

Gremio　No? Say'st me so, friend? What countryman?

Petruchio　Born in Verona, old Antonio's son.
My father dead, my fortune lives for me,
And I do hope good days and long to see.

Gremio　O Sir, such a life with such a wife were strange!　185
But if you have a stomach, to't i' God's name;
You shall have me assisting you in all.
But will you woo this wildcat?

Petruchio　Will I live?

Grumio　Will he woo her? Ay, or I'll hang her.　190

Petruchio　Why came I hither but to that intent?
Think you a little din can daunt mine ears?
Have I not in my time heard lions roar?
Have I not heard the sea, puff'd up with winds,
Rage like an angry boar chafèd with sweat?　195
Have I not heard great ordnance in the field And heaven's
artillery thunder in the skies?
Have I not in a pitched battle heard
Loud 'larums, neighing steeds, and trumpets clang?
And do you tell me of a woman's tongue,　200
That gives not half so great a blow to hear
As will a chestnut in a farmer's fire?
Tush, tush! Fear boys with bugs.

Grumio　*[Aside]* For he fears none.

Gremio　Hortensio, hark.　205
This gentleman is happily arriv'd,
My mind presumes, for his own good and ours.

Hortensio　I promis'd we would be contributors
And bear his charge of wooing, whatsoe'er.

Gremio　And so we will, provided that he win her.　210

Grumio　I would I were as sure of a good dinner.
*[Enter TRANIO brave disguised as Lucentio, and
BIONDELLO]*

Tranio　Gentlemen, God save you! If I may be bold,
Tell me, I beseech you, which is the readiest way
To the house of Signior Baptista Minola?

181.　*Say'st me so:* Is that what you tell me?

What countryman: Where are you from?

186.　*stomach:* desire, preference.

189.　*Will I live:* yes, I certainly will.

195.　*chafèd:* irritated.

196.　*ordnance:* cannon, heavy artillery.

199.　*'larums:* alarums, call to battle.

203.　*Fear boys with bugs:* frighten young boys with fantasies of ghosts or goblins.

206.　*happily:* advantageously.

209.　*bear his charge of:* pay his expenses for.

SD.　*brave:* finely dressed.

213.　*readiest:* shortest, quickest.

Biondello He that has the two fair daughters; is't he you
    mean?   215

Tranio Even he, Biondello!

Gremio Hark you, sir, you mean not her—

Tranio Perhaps him and her, sir. What have you to do?

Petruchio Not her that chides, sir, at any hand, I pray.

Tranio I love no chiders, sir. Biondello, let's away.   220

Lucentio *[Aside]* Well begun, Tranio.

Hortensio Sir, a word ere you go.
    Are you a suitor to the maid you talk of, yea or no?

Tranio And if I be, sir, is it any offence?

Gremio No, if without more words
    you will get you hence.   225

Tranio Why, sir, I pray, are not the streets as free
    For me as for you?

Gremio But so is not she.

Tranio For what reason, I beseech you?

Gremio For this reason, if you'll know: 230
    That she's the choice love of Signior Gremio.

Hortensio That she's the chosen of Signior Hortensio.

Tranio Softly, my masters! If you be gentlemen,
    Do me this right: hear me with patience.
    Baptista is a noble gentleman   235
    To whom my father is not all unknown,
    And were his daughter fairer than she is,
    She may more suitors have, and me for one.
    Fair Leda's daughter had a thousand wooers.
    Then well one more may fair Bianca have.   240
    And so she shall. Lucentio shall make one,
    Though Paris came in hope to speed alone.

Gremio What! This gentleman will out-talk us all.

Lucentio Sir, give him head; I know he'll prove a jade.

Petruchio Hortensio, to what end are all these words?   245

Hortensio Sir, let me be so bold as ask you,
    Did you yet ever see Baptista's daughter?

215. *fair:* beautiful

218. *What . . . do?:* what business is it of yours?

219. *at any hand:* in any case.

222. *ere:* before.

225. *get you hence:* go away.

231. *choice:* chosen.

233. *Softly:* gently.

239. *Leda's daughter:* Helen of Troy, daughter of the god Jove and the mortal Leda.

241. *make one:* be one.

242. *Paris:* Helen of Troy's lover.

      speed: succeed.

244. *give him head:* equestrian term to let a horse run.

      jade: a tired, worn out horse.

Tranio No, sir, but hear I do that he hath two,
The one as famous for a scolding tongue
As is the other for beauteous modesty.   250

Petruchio Sir, sir, the first's for me; let her go by.

Gremio Yea, leave that labour to great Hercules,
And let it be more than Alcides' twelve.

Petruchio Sir, understand you this of me, in sooth:
The youngest daughter, whom you hearken for,   255
Her father keeps from all access of suitors
And will not promise her to any man
Until the elder sister first be wed.
The younger then is free, and not before.

Tranio If it be so, sir, that you are the man   260
Must stead us all, and me amongst the rest,
And if you break the ice and do this feat,
Achieve the elder, set the younger free
For our access, whose hap shall be to have her
Will not so graceless be to be ingrate.   265

Hortensio Sir, you say well, and well you do conceive.
And since you do profess to be a suitor,
You must, as we do, gratify this gentleman,
To whom we all rest generally beholding.

Tranio Sir, I shall not be slack; in sign whereof,   270
Please you we may contrive this afternoon
And quaff carouses to our mistress' health,
    And do as adversaries do in law,
Strive mightily, but eat and drink as friends.

Grumio, Biondello O excellent motion! Fellows, let's be
gone.   275

Hortensio The motion's good indeed, and be it so.
Petruchio, I shall be your ben venuto.
[Exeunt]

252. *Hercules:* also known as Alcides. He was required to take on twelve very difficult tasks.

254. *sooth:* truth.

255. *hearken:* long, ask.

261. *stead:* aid, assist.

264. *hap:* luck, fortune.

265. *graceless:* without grace.
      ingrate: ungrateful.

266. *conceive:* understand.

268. *gratify:* reward, pay.

269. *rest:* remain.
      beholding: indebted.

271. *contrive:* pass.

272. *quaff carouses:* drink liberally.

273. *adversaries:* lawyers.

275. *motion:* proposal.

277. *I . . . venuto:* I will ensure your welcome.

COMMENTARY

Petruchio, accompanied by his servant Grumio, has arrived in Padua from Verona, a town in northern Italy about 40 miles west of Padua. He has come to visit his friend Hortensio and find a wealthy wife. Petruchio's father, Antonio, has died, and although Petruchio has been left with land and a few crowns in his purse, he is still merely a landowner, not a member of the aristocracy. The character of Hortensio provides the link between the main plot concerning Kate and Petruchio and the subplot that revolves around Bianca and Lucentio, while Grumio satisfies the Elizabethan penchant for comic servants. Unlike Lucentio's servant Tranio, who is as smart or smarter than his master, Grumio is the stock servant who takes everything literally and provides much of the bawdy humor while occasionally providing the voice of reason in an upside-down world. Grumio is faithful to his master and like Petruchio, he is witty, rebellious, and unconcerned with the conventions of society.

Pertruchio—comic hero

In his 1981 book, *Shakespeare's Comedies of Play,* J. Dennis Huston compares Petruchio to the conventional hero often found in older comedies such as those written by Aristophanes. Huston cites Cedric Whitman discussing the heroes of Aristophanes:

"The comic hero is a low character who sweeps the world before him, who dominates all society . . . creating the world around him like a god . . . the comic hero himself is wayward, and abides by no rules except his own, his heroism consisting largely in his infallible skill in turning everything to his own advantage, often by a mere trick of language. He is a great talker."

This definition of the comic hero would certainly apply to Shakespeare's Petruchio. He is a rebel who dominates and controls the world around him and his verbal skills allow him to shape the perceptions of others to conform to his own perceptions.

Petruchio's verbal skills are immediately evident as he and Grumio launch at once into a verbal duel that gives great insight into Petruchio's character. Petruchio asks Grumio to knock on Hortensio's door. Grumio typically misinterprets Petruchio's request to mean to knock or hit Petruchio and cannot understand why his master would make such an odd and seemingly dangerous demand. In just a few lines, Shakespeare

"I come to wive it wealthily in Padua;/If wealthily, then happily in Padua." (I.2)
Mary Evans Picture Library

reconnects with the theme of education first presented in the Induction and in the previous scene by introducing Petruchio as the teacher who must instruct Grumio about what to knock. His role as a teacher will play a large part in his ability to tame the shrew. The reader is also provided a precursory glimpse of Petruchio's quick wit in the cleverly crafted use of word play. This part of the scene with its verbal play and physical knockabout is indicative of the comedic genre of farce.

Petruchio also reflects the animal and hunting images begun in the Induction and continued throughout the play. His nature is base and much like an animal driven purely by his senses, Petruchio has very little regard for etiquette or respectability. He enjoys good food, good drink, and his knowledge of falconry and horses suggests the sportive hunter who is now on a quest for a mate and a large fortune. Petruchio is a straightforward man with a no-nonsense attitude. He is raucous and often threatens violence. If he were a woman, Petruchio would perhaps be defined as a shrew himself.

Petruchio and Hortensio

Hortensio, overhearing the argument between Petruchio and Grumio, comes out to investigate and is delighted to see his old friend Petruchio. The two men greet each other in Italian. This exchange is the longest Italian passage in all of Shakespeare's plays and many of these phrases can be found in the opening chapters of *Firste Fruites* by John Florio. Florio was a well-known Italian tutor in the Southampton household who published two Italian/English manuals. *Firste Fruites,* published in 1578, includes a 108-page appendix entitled, "Necessarie Rules, for Englishmen to learne to reade, speak and write true Italian." Shakespeare was a close friend of the Earl of Southampton, dedicating both *The Rape of Lucrece* and *Venus and Adonis* to him. There is also some speculation that the Earl was the young man referred to in many of Shakespeare's sonnets. Given the close relationship between the Earl of Southampton and William Shakespeare, it is quite probable that Shakespeare would have had access to a copy of *Firste Fruites.*

Looking for a wife

Hortensio is thrilled to hear that Petruchio has come to Padua to find a wife, realizing that if Petruchio marries Kate, Bianca will then be free to be married. Petruchio makes it clear that he has come to find a wealthy wife and that the woman's beauty and temperament are of no concern. She could be "an old trot with ne'er a tooth in her head, though she have as many diseases as two-and-fifty horses." The image of horses resounds throughout the play. They are often spirited animals of great value, but until their spirits have been broken and their natures tamed, they cannot take their place in an organized civilization. This image is often applied to women in this play to suggest the men's need to control and dominate them to make them useful to their male masters.

In making his point that wealth is the only requirement for his prospective wife, Petruchio makes several references to historic and mythological characters. Xanthippe, the wife of Socrates, was reputed to be a curst and shrewish woman while Sibyl, loved by Apollo, promised herself to him if he would grant her the gift of prophecy and as many years of life as there are grains of sand. Apollo granted Sibyl's wishes but when she betrayed him, the angry Apollo reminded Sibyl that she had asked for years, not youth, and so she kept getting older and older.

These references underscore Petruchio's intellect and knowledge of classical literature while an allusion to Florentius's love foreshadows the conclusion of the play. Florentius was the name of a knight found in *Confessio Amantis* by the fourteenth-century poet, John Gower. To save his own life by finding the answer to a particular riddle, the knight Florentius agreed to marry an old hag. As a reward for marrying her, the old hag was transformed into a beautiful young woman. Despite Petruchio's academic knowledge, his methods remain grounded in the practical and straightforward.

Although he did not especially like *The Taming of the Shrew,* George Bernard Shaw, writing about the play in 1897, commended the character of Petruchio saying:

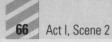

De A. Theuet, Liure II. 78

SOCRATES PHILOSOPHE.
Chap. 36.

Socrates, the Athenian philosopher and teacher.
Mary Evans Picture Library

"Petruchio is worth fifty Orlandos *As You Like It* as a human study. The preliminary scenes in which he shows character by pricking up his ears at the news that there is a fortune to be got by any man who will take an ugly and ill-tempered woman off her father's hands, and hurrying off to strike the bargain before somebody else picks it up, are not romantic; but they give an honest and masterly picture of a real man, whose like we have all met."

Even though Hortensio stands to lose Petruchio as a possible suitor for Kate, he does not want to lose his friendship. Therefore, Hortensio does not hold back from Petruchio what he feels is the truth about Kate, telling him that she is "intolerable curst" and "shrewd and forward." As long as "Katherine the curst" is Katherine the wealthy, Petruchio is not fazed. He is self-assured and confident enough to convince Hortensio that he can easily conquer the dreaded shrew. At first

glance, Petruchio's motives seem very mercenary, but they are actually extraordinarily practical. He is determined to get married and settle down right away and this means he will not know the woman very well. Recognizing that women are often not what they seem when they are being courted, Petruchio is wise enough to insist on the one thing that can be proven: her dowry. Petruchio is older and perhaps more realistic than the romantic and naive young Lucentio and the contrast between the two is a striking commentary on the nature of love and marriage. As the play progresses, this issue is seen more clearly and as Petruchio's financial concerns turn to love, Lucentio's love proves to be empty and insincere.

Plans in motion

Upon learning that Baptista Minola was well acquainted with his father, Petruchio, not one to procrastinate, insists that Hortensio take him to the Minola household right away. Hortensio also sees this as an opportunity for him to get closer to Bianca. He will disguise himself and have Petruchio introduce him as a music teacher named Litio so that he may have time alone with Bianca.

après la IX-Pl. d.

SOCRATE ET SA FEMME

1.

"Be she...as curst and shrewd as Socrates' Xanthippe..." (I.2)
Mary Evans Picture Library

The plot moves quickly forward as, at this moment, Gremio enters with Lucentio, who is disguised as the schoolmaster, Cambio. (It is interesting to note that *cambio* means "changes" in Italian.) Gremio has agreed to introduce Lucentio/Cambio to Baptista as a Latin tutor for Bianca. Explaining to the disguised Lucentio what he should "teach" to Bianca, the foolish old man has no idea that Lucentio/Cambio has no intention of pleading any one's case except his own. Lucentio's deception goes well beyond a physical disguise. He is willing to lie and cheat to obtain the object of his desires, calling into question his ethics and sense of morality.

Some scholars have speculated that Shakespeare may have collaborated with another author on the Lucentio/Bianca sub-plot. Citing the lack of spirit in this scene following the entrance of Gremio and Lucentio as well as the rhyming lines and incorrect stress, the scene has often been called "un-Shakespearean." This point has never been proven nor has the question of authentic authorship been settled.

Hortensio comes forward to inquire about his rival Gremio's business and to learn the identity of the strange young man. He also reports to Gremio that he has also found a tutor for Bianca and even more importantly, a possible husband for Kate. Although Gremio wholeheartedly desires to find a suitable husband for Kate, he joins the other men in warning Petruchio that Kate is a "wildcat." In discussing Kate's unacceptable conduct, the men embellish what has been evidenced so far in the text making her into a monster that only a Hercules could conquer. Petruchio, unperturbed, confidently reviews his qualifications, listing many of the problematic things he has already conquered in his life and assures them there is nothing to worry about. In addition to his desire to marry a wealthy woman, Petruchio is now intrigued by the prospect of taming Kate. He could easily make his move to woo Bianca. Besides being beautiful and soft-spoken, she is as potentially wealthy as Kate and Petruchio would surely be smart enough to out-maneuver the other suitors, but the challenge and sport of taming Kate stimulates Petruchio's adventuresome interest in her rather than the bland Bianca.

The masquerade continues as Tranio, accompanied by Biondello, enters disguised as Lucentio. Tranio/Lucentio overtly asks for directions to the Minola household, indicating that he is on his way to woo Baptista's youngest daughter. Tranio is playing his part so well that Hortensio and Gremio are fooled, and Lucentio compliments him on his performance. Neither suitor suspects that Lucentio/Cambio is plotting to win the love of Bianca and with all suspicions directed towards Tranio/Lucentio, Lucentio is free to pursue his goal of winning Bianca. Despite the fear that Tranio as Lucentio will be a third rival for Bianca's love, the men decide to join forces, paying Petruchio for his troubles, to ensure that Kate, the obstacle to Bianca's advancement, is married and out of the way.

Notes

Notes

Notes

THE TAMING OF THE SHREW
ACT II

Petruchio *Why, that is nothing. For I tell you, father,*
I am as peremptory as she proud-minded;
And where two raging fires meet together,
They do consume the thing that feeds their fury.
Though little fire grows great with little wind,
Yet extreme gusts will blow out fire and all.
So I to her and so she yields to me,
For I am rough and woo not like a babe.

Act II, Scene 1

Petruchio, accompanied by Biondello, Hortensio, Gremio, Lucentio, and Tranio arrives at Baptista's home. Petruchio introduces the disguised Hortensio as a music teacher for Bianca and declares his desire to marry Kate. Baptista recognizes Petruchio as the son of an old friend and is happy to see him. Gremio introduces Lucentio/Cambio as another tutor for Bianca and Tranio/Lucentio announces his desire to woo Bianca. The two new "tutors" leave to instruct their pupil while Petruchio and Baptista discuss Kate's dowry. Kate is introduced to Petruchio and the attraction between the two is immediate. Petruchio announces he will marry Kate on Sunday and Baptista agrees. Now that Kate has been engaged, Gremio and Tranio ask Baptista for Bianca's hand. Baptista tells the men that the one with the greatest wealth will be given permission to marry Bianca. Tranio and Gremio proceed to list their assets and Tranio wins based on proof of his (Lucentio's) wealth.

ACT II, SCENE 1

Padua. A room in BAPTISTA'S house.

[Enter KATE and BIANCA with her hands bound]

Bianca　Good sister, wrong me not, nor wrong yourself,　1
　To make a bondmaid and a slave of me.
　That I disdain. But for these other gawds,
　Unbind my hands, I'll pull them off myself,
　Yea, all my raiment, to my petticoat,　5
　Or what you will command me will I do,
　So well I know my duty to my elders.

Kate　Of all thy suitors here I charge thee tell
　Whom thou lov'st best. See thou dissemble not.

Bianca　Believe me, sister, of all the men alive　10
　I never yet beheld that special face
　Which I could fancy more than any other.

Kate　Minion, thou liest. Is't not Hortensio?

Bianca　If you affect him, sister, here I swear
　I'll plead for you myself, but you shall have him.　15

Kate　O, then belike you fancy riches more.
　You will have Gremio to keep you fair.

Bianca　Is it for him you do envy me so?
　Nay, then you jest, and now I well perceive

NOTES

2.　*bondmaid:* slave.

3.　*gawds:* adornments, finery.

8.　*charge:* command.

13.　*Minion:* impertinent creature, hussy.

14.　*affect:* like, love.

16.　*belike:* probably, perhaps.

17.　*fair:* well-dressed.

18.　*envy:* hate.

You have but jested with me all this while.   20
I prithee, sister Kate, untie my hands.

Kate If that be jest, then an the rest was so.
[Strikes her]
[Enter BAPTISTA]

Baptista Why, how now, dame! Whence grows this
    insolence?
Bianca, stand aside. Poor girl, she weeps! *[unties her hands]*
[to Bianca] Go ply thy needle; meddle not with her.   25
[to Kate] For shame, thou hilding of a devilish spirit!
Why dost thou wrong her that did ne'er wrong thee?
When did she cross thee with a bitter word?

Kate Her silence flouts me, and I'll be reveng'd.
[Flies after Bianca]

Baptista What, in my sight? Bianca, get thee in.   30
[Exit Bianca]

Kate What, will you not suffer me? Nay, now I see
She is your treasure, she must have a husband,
I must dance bare-foot on her wedding-day
And, for your love to her, lead apes in hell.
Talk not to me: I will go sit and weep   35
Till I can find occasion of revenge.
[Exit]

Baptista Was ever gentleman thus griev'd as I?
But who comes here?
[Enter GREMIO, LUCENTIO [disguised as Cambio] in the
    habit of a mean man;
PETRUCHIO, with HORTENSIO [disguised as Litio]; and
    TRANIO[disguised as Lucentio], with his boy
    [BIONDELLO], bearing a lute and books]

Gremio Good morrow, neighbour Baptista.

Baptista Good morrow, neighbour Gremio. God save you,
    gentlemen!   40

Petruchio And you, good sir! Pray, have you not a daughter
Call'd Katherina, fair and virtuous?

Baptista I have a daughter, sir, call'd Katherina.

Gremio You are too blunt. Go to it orderly.

---

23.   *dame:* madam, term of reproach.

26.   *hilding:* base wretch, beast.

28.   *cross:* contradict, annoy.

29.   *flouts:* insults.

31.   *suffer me:* allow me to.

33.   *dance...day:* the proverbial fate of older, single women.

34.   *for:* because of.

      lead apes in hell: proverbial misfortune of an unmarried woman who has no children to lead her into heaven.

SD.   *mean:* lower class.

44.   *orderly:* properly, in due order.

Petruchio You wrong me, Signior Gremio. Give me leave. 45
I am a gentleman of Verona, sir,
That hearing of her beauty and her wit,
Her affability and bashful modesty,
Her wondrous qualities and mild behaviour,
Am bold to show myself a forward guest 50
Within your house, to make mine eye the witness
Of that report which I so oft have heard.
And, for an entrance to my entertainment,
I do present you with a man of mine,
[Presents Hortensio, disguised as Litio]
Cunning in music and the mathematics, 55
To instruct her fully in those sciences,
Whereof I know she is not ignorant.
Accept of him, or else you do me wrong.
His name is Litio, born in Mantua.

Baptista You're welcome, sir, and he for your good sake. 60
But for my daughter Katherine, this I know,
She is not for your turn, the more my grief.

Petruchio I see you do not mean to part with her;
Or else you like not of my company.

Baptista Mistake me not. I speak but as I find. 65
Whence are you, sir? What may I call your name?

Petruchio Petruchio is my name. Antonio's son,
A man well known throughout all Italy.

Baptista I know him well. You are welcome for his sake.

Gremio Saving your tale, Petruchio, I pray 70
Let us that are poor petitioners speak too.
Bacare, you are marvelous forward.

Petruchio O, pardon me, Signior Gremio, I would fain be
doing.

Gremio I doubt it not, sir. But you will curse your wooing.
[to Baptista] Neighbour, this is a gift very grateful, I am sure
of it. 75
To express the like kindness, myself, that have been more
kindly
beholding to you than any, freely give unto you this young
scholar,

45.	*Give me leave:* allow me to continue.
50.	*forward:* eager.
53.	*entrance:* price of admission.
	entertainment: reception as a guest.
56.	*sciences:* branches of knowledge.
58.	*Accept of:* accept.
62.	*is not for your turn:* is not right for you.
64.	*like not of:* do not like.
70.	*Saving:* with all respect to.
72.	*Bacare:* Latin for "stand back."
	marvelous: very.
73.	*fain:* rather.
	be doing: a sexual reference.
75.	*gift:* Litio (given by Petruchio to Baptista).
	very grateful: quite acceptable.

[Presents Lucentio, disguised as Cambio]
that hath been long studying at Rheims, as cunning in
  Greek,
Latin, and other languages, as the other in music and   80
mathematics. His name is Cambio. Pray accept his service.

Baptista A thousand thanks, Signior Gremio. Welcome,
  good Cambio.
[To Tranio as Lucentio]
But, gentle sir, methinks you walk like a stranger. May
I be so bold to know the cause of your coming?

Tranio Pardon me, sir, the boldness is mine own,   85
That being a stranger in this city here
Do make myself a suitor to your daughter,
Unto Bianca, fair and virtuous.
Nor is your firm resolve unknown to me,
In the preferment of the eldest sister.   90
This liberty is all that I request,
That, upon knowledge of my parentage,
I may have welcome 'mongst the rest that woo
And free access and favour as the rest.
And, toward the education of your daughters,   95
I here bestow a simple instrument
And this small packet of Greek and Latin books.
[Biondello offers the gifts to Baptista]
If you accept them, then their worth is great.

Baptista Lucentio is your name. Of whence, I pray?

Tranio Of Pisa, sir; son to Vincentio.   100

Baptista A mighty man of Pisa. By report
I know him well. You are very welcome, sir.
[To Hortensio as Litio] Take you the lute,
[To Lucentio as Cambio] and you the set of books.
You shall go see your pupils presently.   105
Holla, within!
[Enter a SERVANT]
Sirrah, lead these gentlemen
To my two daughters, and tell them both
These are their tutors. Bid them use them well.
[Exit Servant, with Hortensio, Lucentio, and Biondello]

80.   *the other:* Litio.

91.   *In the preferment of:* granting priority or preference to.

94.   *favour:* countenance, acceptance.

96.   *instrument:* the lute.

105.   *presently:* at once, immediately.

108.   *them both:* Kate and Bianca.

We will go walk a little in the orchard,   110
And then to dinner. You are passing welcome,
And so I pray you all to think yourselves.

Petruchio   Signior Baptista, my business asketh haste,
And every day I cannot come to woo.
You knew my father well, and in him me,   115
Left solely heir to all his lands and goods,
Which I have bettered rather than decreas'd.
Then tell me, if I get your daughter's love,
What dowry shall I have with her to wife?

Baptista   After my death, the one half of my lands,   120
And in possession twenty thousand crowns.

Petruchio   And, for that dowry, I'll assure her of
Her widowhood, be it that she survive me,
In all my lands and leases whatsoever.
Let specialities be therefore drawn between us,   125
That covenants may be kept on either hand.

Baptista   Ay, when the special thing is well obtain'd,
That is, her love, for that is all in all.

Petruchio   Why, that is nothing. For I tell you, father,
I am as peremptory as she proud-minded;   130
And where two raging fires meet together,
They do consume the thing that feeds their fury.
Though little fire grows great with little wind,
Yet extreme gusts will blow out fire and all.
So I to her and so she yields to me,   135
For I am rough and woo not like a babe.

Baptista   Well mayst thou woo, and happy be thy speed!
But be thou arm'd for some unhappy words.

Petruchio   Ay, to the proof, as mountains are for winds,
That shakes not, though they blow perpetually.   140
[Enter HORTENSIO, as Litio, with his head broke]

Baptista   How now, my friend! Why dost thou look so pale?

Hortensio   For fear, I promise you, if I look pale.

Baptista   What, will my daughter prove a good musician?

Hortensio   I think she'll sooner prove a soldier.
Iron may hold with her, but never lutes.   145

---

110.   *orchard:* garden.

111.   *dinner:* main meal of the day, served around noon.

       passing: very.

121.   *in possession:* at the moment of marriage.

123.   *widowhood:* the estate settled upon a widow at the time of her marriage.

125.   *specialties:* explicit contracts.

126.   *on either hand:* on both sides.

130.   *peremptory:* resolved.

137.   *happy:* fortunate.

       speed: progress.

139.   *proof:* test.

143.   *prove:* become.

145.   *hold with her:* withstand her use.

Baptista Why, then thou canst not break her to the lute?

Hortensio Why, no, for she hath broke the lute to me.
I did but tell her she mistook her frets,
And bow'd her hand to teach her fingering.
When, with a most impatient devilish spirit,   150
"Frets, call you these?" quoth she. "I'll fume with them!"
And with that word she struck me on the head,
And through the instrument my pate made way,
And there I stood amazèd for a while,
As on a pillory, looking through the lute,   155
While she did call me "rascal fiddler,"
And "twangling Jack," with twenty such vile terms,
As she had studied to misuse me so.

Petruchio Now, by the world, it is a lusty wench!
I love her ten times more than e'er I did.   160
O, how I long to have some chat with her!

Baptista *[To Hortensio, as Litio]* Well, go with me, and be not
so discomfited.
Proceed in practice with my younger daughter.
She's apt to learn, and thankful for good turns.
Signior Petruchio, will you go with us,   165
Or shall I send my daughter Kate to you?

Petruchio I pray you do. I will attend her here.
[Exeunt all but Petruchio. . .]
And woo her with some spirit when she comes.
Say that she rail, why, then I'll tell her plain
She sings as sweetly as a nightingale.   170
Say that she frown, I'll say she looks as clear
As morning roses newly wash'd with dew.
Say she be mute, and will not speak a word,
Then I'll commend her volubility
And say she uttereth piercing eloquence.   175
If she do bid me pack, I'll give her thanks
As though she bid me stay by her a week.
If she deny to wed, I'll crave the day
When I shall ask the banns, and when be married.
But here she comes, and now, Petruchio, speak.   180
[Enter KATE]
Good morrow, Kate, for that's your name, I hear.

146. *break:* discipline, tame.

147. *to me:* on my head.

148. *mistook her frets:* placed her fingers the wrong way on the neck of the lute.
      frets: the bars on the neck of the lute; also, a pun on "frets" meaning vexed or irritated.

149. *bow'd:* bent.

151. *fume:* rage.

153. *pate:* head.

154. *amazèd:* astonished.

155. *pillory:* stocks for head and arms.

157. *Jack:* rascal.

159. *lusty:* vigorous.

161. *chat:* conversation.

162. *discomfited:* discouraged.

163. *Proceed in practice:* continue your lessons.

164. *apt:* inclined.

167. *attend:* await.

169. *rail:* scold.
      plain: simply.

176. *pack:* leave.

178. *deny:* refuse.
      crave the day: entreat her to name the wedding day.

179. *banns:* a public announcement in church of the intent to marry.

Kate Well have you heard, but something hard of hearing.
  They call me Katherine that do talk of me.

Petruchio You lie, in faith, for you are call'd plain Kate,
  And bonny Kate, and sometimes Kate the curst.   185
  But Kate, the prettiest Kate in Christendom,
  Kate of Kate Hall, my super-dainty Kate,
  For dainties are all Kates: and therefore, Kate,
  Take this of me, Kate of my consolation:
  Hearing thy mildness prais'd in every town,   190
  Thy virtues spoke of, and thy beauty sounded
  Yet not so deeply as to thee belongs,
  Myself am mov'd to woo thee for my wife.

Kate "Mov'd!" In good time! Let him that mov'd you hither
  Remove you hence. I knew you at the first   195
  You were a moveable.

Petruchio Why, what's a moveable?

Kate A joint-stool.

Petruchio Thou hast hit it. Come, sit on me.

Kate Asses are made to bear, and so are you.   200

Petruchio Women are made to bear, and so are you.

Kate No such jade as you, if me you mean.

Petruchio Alas, good Kate, I will not burden thee,
  For, knowing thee to be but young and light—

Kate Too light for such a swain as you to catch;   205
  And yet as heavy as my weight should be.

Petruchio Should be! Should buzz!

Kate Well ta'en, and like a buzzard.

Petruchio O, slow-wing'd turtle, shall a buzzard take thee?

Kate Ay, for a turtle, as he takes a buzzard.   210

Petruchio Come, come, you wasp! I' faith, you are too angry.

Kate If I be waspish, best beware my sting.

Petruchio My remedy is then to pluck it out.

Kate Ay, if the fool could find it where it lies.

Petruchio Who knows not where a wasp does wear his sting?215
  In his tail.

---

185. *bonny:* big, stout.

    curst: ill-tempered.

187. *super-dainty:* precious.

188. *dainties:* eatable delicacies, sometimes called "cates."

189. *consolation:* comfort.

191. *sounded:* spoken of, measured for depth (thus "deeply" in following line).

193. *mov'd:* inspired.

194. *In good time:* indeed.

196. *moveable:* piece of furniture, a quirky person.

198. *joint-stool:* a low stool made of parts that are jointed together.

200. *bear:* to have children, with pun on bearing the weight of a man during sexual intercourse.

202. *jade:* a worthless horse that lacks endurance.

204. *light:* frivolous, lusty.

205. *light:* quick.

    swain: person of low class.

207. *buzz:* sound of a stinging bee with pun on "buzz" as rumor or scandal.

208. *ta'en:* taken, understood.

    buzzard: an unteachable hawk, hence an idiot.

209. *take:* capture.

Kate In his tongue.

Petruchio Whose tongue?

Kate Yours, if you talk of tales, and so farewell.

Petruchio What, with my tongue in your tail? Nay, come again,   220
   Good Kate. I am a gentleman.

Kate That I'll try.
[She strikes him]

222. *try:* test.

Petruchio I swear I'll cuff you if you strike again.

Kate So may you lose your arms.
   If you strike me, you are no gentleman,   225
   And if no gentleman, why then no arms.

224. *arms:* coat of arms.

Petruchio A herald, Kate? O! put me in thy books.

227. *herald:* an officer who determined who had the right to bear a coat of arms.

in thy books: in the herald's books, in your favor.

Kate What is your crest? A coxcomb?

228. *crest:* a device placed on a wreath and displayed above the shield and helmet in a coat of arms, the comb on a rooster or cock.

coxcomb: The traditional fool's cap.

Petruchio A combless cock, so Kate will be my hen.

229. *A combless cock:* an unaggressive rooster.

Kate No cock of mine. You crow too like a craven.   230

230. *craven:* a coward, a defeated cock.

Petruchio Nay, come, Kate, come. You must not look so sour.

Kate It is my fashion when I see a crab.

232. *crab:* crab apple or sour-faced person.

Petruchio Why, here's no crab, and therefore look not sour.

Kate There is, there is.

Petruchio Then show it me.   235

Kate Had I a glass I would.

236. *glass:* mirror.

Petruchio What, you mean my face?

Kate Well aim'd of such a young one.

238. *aim'd:* guessed.

Petruchio Now, by Saint George, I am too young for you.

Kate Yet you are wither'd.   240

Petruchio 'Tis with cares.

Kate I care not.

Petruchio Nay, hear you, Kate: in sooth, you 'scape not so.

243. *sooth:* truth.
'scape: escape.

Kate I chafe you if I tarry. Let me go.

244. *chafe:* excite you, irritate, inflame feelings.
tarry: stay.

Petruchio No, not a whit. I find you passing gentle.   245
   'Twas told me you were rough, and coy, and sullen,
   And now I find report a very liar.
   For thou art pleasant, gamesome, passing courteous,

245. *whit:* bit.
passing: very.
246. *coy:* distant, aloof.
247. *a very:* an utter.
248. *gamesome:* playful.

But slow in speech, yet sweet as springtime flowers.
Thou canst not frown, thou canst not look askance,   250
Nor bite the lip as angry wenches will,
Nor hast thou pleasure to be cross in talk.
But thou with mildness entertain'st thy wooers,
With gentle conference, soft and affable.
Why does the world report that Kate doth limp?   255
O sland'rous world! Kate like the hazeltwig
Is straight and slender, and as brown in hue
As hazelnuts, and sweeter than the kernels.
O, let me see thee walk! Thou dost not halt.

Kate Go, fool, and whom thou keep'st command.   260

Petruchio Did ever Dian so become a grove
As Kate this chamber with her princely gait?
O! be thou Dian, and let her be Kate,
And then let Kate be chaste, and Dian sportful!

Kate Where did you study all this goodly speech?   265

Petruchio It is extempore, from my motherwit.

Kate A witty mother, witless else her son.

Petruchio Am I not wise?

Kate Yes, keep you warm.

Petruchio Marry, so I mean, sweet Katherine, in thy bed. 270
And therefore, setting all this chat aside,
Thus in plain terms: your father hath consented
That you shall be my wife, your dowry 'greed on,
And, will you, nill you, I will marry you.
Now, Kate, I am a husband for your turn,   275
For by this light, whereby I see thy beauty,
Thy beauty that doth make me like thee well,
Thou must be married to no man but me.
For I am he am born to tame you, Kate,
And bring you from a wild Kate to a Kate   280
Conformable as other household Kates.
[Enter BAPTISTA, GREMIO, TRANIO (as Lucentio)]
Here comes your father. Never make denial.
I must and will have Katherine to my wife.

Baptista Now, Signior Petruchio, how speed you with my
daughter?

---

249. *slow in speech:* not sharp tongued.

250. *askance:* turn aside.

252. *cross:* prone to oppose or contradict.

253. *entertain'st:* treat.

254. *conference:* conversation.

259. *halt:* limp.

260. *whom thou keep'st command:* your servants.

261. *Dian:* Diana, goddess of the moon and the hunt.

264. *sportful:* lustful.

265. *study:* memorize, prepare.

266. *motherwit:* natural intelligence.

267. *else:* otherwise.

269. *keep you warm:* proverbial: "He is wise enough that can keep himself warm."

274. *will you, nill you:* whether you like it or not.

275. *for your turn:* for your advantage, with sexual pun on "turn" as copulation.

280. *wild Kate:* pun on "wildcat."

281. *Conformable:* submissive.

284. *speed:* succeed, prosper.

Petruchio How but well, sir? How but well?   285
It were impossible I should speed amiss.

Baptista Why, how now, daughter Katherine? In your dumps?

Kate Call you me daughter? Now I promise you
You have show'd a tender fatherly regard,
To wish me wed to one half lunatic,   290
A madcap ruffian and a swearing Jack,
That thinks with oaths to face the matter out.

Petruchio Father, 'tis thus: yourself and all the world
That talk'd of her have talk'd amiss of her.
If she be curst, it is for policy,   295
For she's not froward, but modest as the dove;
She is not hot, but temperate as the morn.
For patience she will prove a second Grissel,
And Roman Lucrece for her chastity.
And to conclude, we have 'greed so well together   300
That upon Sunday is the wedding day.

Kate I'll see thee hang'd on Sunday first.

Gremio Hark, Petruchio, she says she'll see thee hang'd first.

Tranio Is this your speeding? Nay, then, goodnight our part!

Petruchio Be patient, gentlemen. I choose her for myself.   305
If she and I be pleas'd, what's that to you?
'Tis bargain'd 'twixt us twain, being alone,
That she shall still be curst in company.
I tell you, 'tis incredible to believe
How much she loves me. O, the kindest Kate!   310
She hung about my neck, and kiss on kiss
She vied so fast, protesting oath on oath,
That in a twink she won me to her love.
O, you are novices! 'Tis a world to see
How tame, when men and women are alone,   315
A meacock wretch can make the curstest shrew.
Give me thy hand, Kate. I will unto Venice
To buy apparel 'gainst the wedding-day.
Provide the feast, father, and bid the guests.
I will be sure my Katherine shall be fine.   320

287. *In your dumps:* depressed.

288. *promise:* tell, assure.

292. *face:* brave, brazen.

295. *curst:* quarrelsome.
      policy: tactical advantage.

296. *froward:* strong-willed.

297. *hot:* angry, passionate.
      temperate: chaste, mild.

298. *Grissel:* Griselda, the wife from Chaucer's *The Clerk's Tale*, who, with great patience, remained submissive to her brutal husband.

299. *Lucrece:* Roman woman who committed suicide after being raped by Tarquin.

304. *speeding:* success.
      goodnight our part: goodbye to our suits to Bianca.

307. *bargain'd:* agreed.
      twixt: between.

308. *still:* always.

312. *vied:* made higher bids, increased in number, repeated.

313. *twink:* instant, twinkling of an eye.

314. *world:* wonder.

316. *meacock:* timid, tame, meek.

318. *'gainst:* in preparation for.

319. *bid:* invite.

320. *fine:* beautifully dressed.

Baptista I know not what to say, but give me your hands.
God send you joy, Petruchio! 'Tis a match.

Gremio, Tranio Amen, say we. We will be witnesses.

Petruchio Father, and wife, and gentlemen, adieu.
I will to Venice; Sunday comes apace.   325
We will have rings, and things, and fine array,
And kiss me, Kate. We will be married o' Sunday.
[Exeunt PETRUCHIO and KATE, severally]

Gremio Was ever match clapp'd up so suddenly?

Baptista Faith, gentlemen, now I play a merchant's part
And venture madly on a desperate mart.   330

Tranio 'Twas a commodity lay fretting by you.
'Twill bring you gain, or perish on the seas.

Baptista The gain I seek is quiet in the match.

Gremio No doubt but he hath got a quiet catch.
But now, Baptista, to your younger daughter.   335
Now is the day we long have looked for.
I am your neighbour and was suitor first.

Tranio And I am one that love Bianca more
Than words can witness or your thoughts can guess.   340

Gremio Youngling, thou canst not love so dear as I.

Tranio Greybeard, thy love doth freeze.

Gremio But thine doth fry.
Skipper, stand back. 'Tis age that nourisheth.

Tranio But youth in ladies' eyes that flourisheth.   345

Baptista Content you, gentlemen. I will compound this strife.
'Tis deeds must win the prize, and he of both
That can assure my daughter greatest dower
Shall have my Bianca's love.
Say, Signior Gremio, what can you assure her?   350

Gremio First, as you know, my house within the city
Is richly furnished with plate and gold,
Basins and ewers to lave her dainty hands;
My hangings all of Tyrian tapestry;
In ivory coffers I have stuff'd my crowns,   355
In cypress chests my arras counterpoints,

---

325. *apace:* quickly.

SD. *severally:* separately.

328. *clapp'd up:* fixed, rapidly arranged.

330. *desperate mart:* risky business.

331. *commodity:* goods, convenience, also reference to woman as male possession for sexual pleasure.
fretting: rotting, decaying.

334. *he:* Petruchio.

341. *Youngling:* novice.

344. *Skipper:* term of content for someone young enough to skip, to be light brained.

346. *compound:* settle.

347. *deeds:* actions, also legal documents.
he of both: one of you two.

348. *dower:* husband's gifts to his wife.

353. *lave:* wash.
354. *hangings:* wall hangings.
Tyrian: from Tyre: famous for scarlet and purple dyes.
355. *crowns:* gold coins.
356. *arras counterpoints:* counterpanes of Arras tapestry.

Costly apparel, tents, and canopies,
Fine linen, Turkey cushions boss'd with pearl,
Valance of Venice gold in needlework,
Pewter and brass, and all things that belongs   360
To house or housekeeping. Then, at my farm
I have a hundred milch-kine to the pail,
Six score fat oxen standing in my stalls,
And all things answerable to this portion.
Myself am struck in years, I must confess;   365
And if I die tomorrow this is hers,
If whilst I live she will be only mine.

Tranio That "only" came well in. *[To Baptista]* Sir, list to me:
I am my father's heir and only son.
If I may have your daughter to my wife,   370
I'll leave her houses three or four as good,
Within rich Pisa's walls, as any one
Old Signior Gremio has in Padua,
Besides two thousand ducats by the year
Of fruitful land, all which shall be her jointure.   375
What, have I pinch'd you, Signior Gremio?

Gremio Two thousand ducats by the year of land?
[aside] My land amounts not to so much in all.
That she shall have, besides an argosy
That now is lying in Marseilles' road.   380
[to Tranio] What, have I chok'd you with an argosy?

Tranio Gremio, 'tis known my father hath no less
Than three great argosies, besides two galliasses
And twelve tight galleys. These I will assure her,
And twice as much, whate'er thou offer'st next.   385

Gremio Nay, I have offer'd all. I have no more,
And she can have no more than all I have.
[to Baptista] If you like me, she shall have me and mine.

Tranio Why, then, the maid is mine from all the world,
By your firm promise. Gremio is outvied.   390

Baptista I must confess your offer is the best,
And, let your father make her the assurance,
She is your own; else, you must pardon me.
If you should die before him, where's her dower?

357. *tents:* canopies, bed curtains.

358. *Turkey:* Turkish.

boss'd: embroidered.

359. *Valance:* drapery.

gold: gold thread.

362. *milch-kine to the pail:* cows providing milk.

363. *Six score:* one hundred twenty.

364. *answerable:* consistent.

portion: estate.

365. *struck:* advanced.

368. *list:* listen.

374. *ducats:* gold coins.

by the: per.

375. *Of:* from.

fruitful: fertile.

jointure: estate to be inherited on the death of the husband.

376. *pinch'd you:* put you in a tight spot.

379. *argosy:* largest of trading ships.

380. *Marseilles' road:* a sheltered anchorage outside the harbor at Marseilles.

383. *galliasses:* large galleys.

384. *tight:* sound, watertight.

assure: promise.

390. *outvied:* outbid.

Tranio That's but a cavil. He is old, I young.   395

Gremio And may not young men die as well as old?

Baptista Well, gentlemen,
I am thus resolv'd: On Sunday next, you know,
My daughter Katherine is to be married.
[to Tranio] Now, on the Sunday following, shall Bianca   400
Be bride to you, if you make this assurance.
If not, to Signior Gremio.
And so I take my leave, and thank you both.

Gremio Adieu, good neighbour.
[Exit Baptista]
Now, I fear thee not.   405
Sirrah young gamester, your father were a fool
To give thee all and in his waning age
Set foot under thy table. Tut, a toy!
An old Italian fox is not so kind, my boy.
[Exit Gremio]

Tranio A vengeance on your crafty wither'd hide!   410
Yet I have fac'd it with a card of ten.
'Tis in my head to do my master good.
I see no reason but suppos'd Lucentio
Must get a father, call'd 'suppos'd Vincentio'—
And that's a wonder. Fathers commonly   415
Do get their children. But in this case of wooing,
A child shall get a sire, if I fail not of my cunning.   417
[Exit]

395. *cavil:* meaningless objection.

406. *Sirrah:* form of address to inferiors.
      gamester: gambler.

408. *Set foot under thy table:* be forced to be a guest in
      your house.
      toy: joke.

410. *A vengeance on:* I will be avenged on.

411. *fac'd it . . . ten:* bluffed it without a face card.

416. *get:* beget.

417. *sire:* father.

COMMENTARY

The opening of Act II gives the reader a much closer look at the two Minola sisters. Kate has bound Bianca's hands and is demanding that Bianca tell her the truth about which suitor she prefers. Kate's irascible temper is out of control and she is determined to make Bianca endure a measure of physical pain to compensate for the emotional pain of neglect that Kate constantly feels. Kate's furious interest in Bianca's love life indicates that Kate is not only generally jealous of her sister but she is specifically jealous of the fact that her sister is being courted and will soon be married. To protect herself from rejection and its consequent public and private humiliation, Kate pretends to shun the idea of marriage, but despite her protestations, she is very interested in the prospect of marriage and desperately desires someone to love her. Marriage will not only provide Kate with a partner but it will imbue her with a social acceptance that she presently does not have and give her the perfect opportunity to escape her father's home.

The real shrew?

Alone with her sister, Bianca reveals her true character. In her first speech, she makes a point of mentioning the fact that Kate is older than Bianca when she says,

"... I know my duty to my elders." Bianca says this line with the intent of both hurting and angering her sister. Despite Bianca's coy, flirtatious behavior in the first act, the reader now learns that she does not care for either Hortensio or Gremio. Bianca even offers Hortensio to her sister if she will unbind her, perhaps choosing to keep Gremio because he is not only the wealthier of the two but also the older and most likely to leave Bianca a wealthy widow sooner than later. Frustrated by Bianca's lies and hypocrisy, Kate slaps her. Despite Kate's angry response, it is not impossible to feel empathy for Kate's reactions. Bianca knows how to trigger Kate's anger and does so purposely to reinforce her own position as the favored daughter.

The source of much of Kate's anger clearly stems from her father's obvious preference for his "treasure" Bianca and what she feels is the inequity of it all. Bianca is protected and coddled while Kate is neglected, excluded, and termed a monster. The only way she can get her father's attention is by causing him embarrassment with her unruly behavior. Unfortunately, this behavior serves only to push her father farther away.

Baptista enters to investigate the fray only to find Bianca in tears with her hands bound. To incense her father even more against Kate, Bianca turns up the volume of her cries. He immediately assumes that Kate is solely to blame, comforts Bianca, and sends her out of the room, but Bianca does not obey her father. Instead, she stays in the room specifically to see what punishment Kate will receive and to torment her behind her father's back. Baptista turns on Kate, his own daughter, calling her a beast and child of the devil.

Like everyone, Kate wants to love and be loved but she has been shown and told so often that she is unlovable that she believes it. She has been taught that she has no worth and she has learned her lesson all too well. Kate also realizes that she is an obstacle to her sister's prospective marriage and is embarrassed and humiliated by that fact. That shame is revealed in Kate's reference to the adage that the elder, unmarried sister was forced to dance barefoot at her younger sister's marriage. Her despair, loneliness, and fear are exposed in her mention of leading apes into hell, the traditional fate of spinsters who die with no children to lead them to heaven. Kate is so full of pain, rage, fear, and uncertainty that she has no recourse but to "go sit and weep." She will weep until she can figure out some sort of revenge.

Enter Petruchio

Baptista is upset by Kate's behavior but his grief is quickly interrupted by the arrival of the disguised suitors along with Gremio, Petruchio, and Biondello. Lucentio is disguised as the schoolmaster Cambio, while Hortensio is disguised as the music teacher Litio and Tranio is disguised as Lucentio. However, before the suitors can make their move, Petruchio introduces himself to Baptista, informing him that he is the son of Antonio, a man Baptista knew well. He characteristically wastes no time getting to the point of his being there: He wants permission to court Kate. Baptista is stunned, but despite what would seem his obvious desire to find a suitable husband for Kate, he warns Petruchio that Kate is a difficult woman and that it might be impossible for him to woo her much less win her.

Katherine and Bianca in an engraving by F. Engleheart after a painting by F.P. Stephanoff. Mary Evans Picture Library

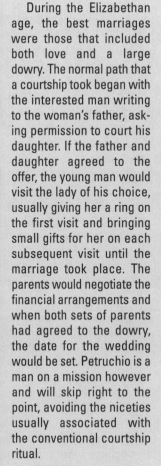

Kate and Petruchio in a production of The Taming of the Shrew, Old Vic, 1954.
The Raymond Mander and Joe Mitchenson Theatre Collection

During the Elizabethan age, the best marriages were those that included both love and a large dowry. The normal path that a courtship took began with the interested man writing to the woman's father, asking permission to court his daughter. If the father and daughter agreed to the offer, the young man would visit the lady of his choice, usually giving her a ring on the first visit and bringing small gifts for her on each subsequent visit until the marriage took place. The parents would negotiate the financial arrangements and when both sets of parents had agreed to the dowry, the date for the wedding would be set. Petruchio is a man on a mission however and will skip right to the point, avoiding the niceties usually associated with the conventional courtship ritual.

A dowry, money, or property brought into a marriage was a very serious consideration in the choice of a marriage partner. In *The Taming of the Shrew*, the granting of the dowry exemplifies the economics involved in the transaction. Baptista is a businessman both professionally and parentally. He makes the decision to withhold his better merchandise, Bianca, until he has unloaded his less desirable goods, Kate. To make a marriage to Kate more attractive, Baptista will reverse the normal payment of the dowry by offering a large settlement to the man who agrees to marry the inferior Kate rather than expecting her potential husband to provide the financial settlement. In the meantime, withholding the more desirable Bianca will make

Bianca's disguised suitors are introduced to Baptista as Gremio accuses Petruchio of being too blunt and "marvelous forward," words that have also been used in Act I, Scene 1 to describe Kate. However, with three of the characters on stage in disguise, it appears that it is not Petrucio's refusal to put on the mask of manners that is duplicitous. The deceptions work, however, and Baptista accepts them as tutors for his daughters. As they go off to "teach" their new pupils, Petruchio immediately begins the negotiations required for his marriage to Kate.

her seem even more valuable and raise the price she will receive as her dowry. To marry Kate, Petruchio is offered, upon Baptista's death, half of his lands with 20,000 crowns to be paid immediately. Crowns were gold coins that were first issued in 1526 and were worth approximately 5 shillings. To make clear the worth of 20,000 crowns, one can look at the pay that a soldier in the sixteenth century received. A soldier was paid approximately a sixpence, or one-tenth of a crown, per day. Therefore, Petruchio's 20,000 crowns could have paid the wages of 200,000 soldiers for one day. Petruchio then counters with his own bargain, agreeing to provide her with all of his "lands and leases" upon his own death. The two men agree to the deal, leaving only one hurdle left to be crossed: Is Petruchio man enough to convince the irascible Kate to marry him? Baptista is not sure that Petruchio is up to the task and says that no contract will be valid unless Petruchio can obtain Kate's love, something that no other man has ever been able to do.

Baptista's fatherly concern for Kate has always been debated. On the surface, he seems magnanimous for wanting his oldest daughter married before his youngest daughter, but he humiliates her publicly because she does not have a suitor and tells potential suitors that she isn't for "your turn." The concern consequently takes on a look of financial maneuvering rather than worry for Kate's future or her feelings. In this scene, Baptista informs Petruchio that he cannot marry Kate unless he has obtained "her love, for that is all in all." Again, this takes on the appearance of a father who is adamant that his daughter loves the man she will spend the rest of her life with. In reality, Baptista feels that Petruchio will not be able to convince Kate to marry him. After Petruchio's meeting with Kate, her verbal protests make it very clear that she is not ready or willing to marry Petruchio at this time. Baptista ignores Kate's complaints, obviously not concerned with Kate's feelings, and continues with plans for a wedding on Sunday.

Shrew Taming: Lesson One

Prefacing Petruchio's first meeting with Kate, Hortensio enters looking very pale. Kate, frustrated with Hortensio's attempt to teach her music, has broken the lute over his head. Baptista asks Hortensio if he could not "break" Kate to the lute. Baptista's reference is to the breaking of wild horses, metaphorically comparing his daughter to a feral animal that needs to be controlled.

This attitude towards Kate may give more evidence as to why she is so angry and reticent to behave the way she has been expected to.

Instead of frightening Petruchio, the lute incident merely fuels his curiosity concerning this "lusty wench" and he is determined to meet her as soon as possible. Baptista exits to find Kate, leaving Petruchio unaccompanied in the room. In his time alone, Petruchio clues the reader in to what his plans are regarding the taming of this wealthy shrew. In a sense, Petruchio is rehearsing his game plan and reassuring himself that he is up to the task. Instead of breaking her by beating her into submission, he plans to begin taming Kate by flattering her and contradicting every negative thing she says with something positive.

What follows is one of the most cleverly written and interesting scenes in all of Shakespeare. The scene is full of wit, energy, and bawdy puns and illustrates the first meeting of two very equally matched individuals. *Puns,* a play on words that are spelled or sound the same but have different meanings, have often been called the lowest form of humor, but Elizabethan audiences delighted in them. These two non-conventional people immediately recognize themselves in each other, sensing their similarities. It is at least lust at first sight if not actually love. Kate and Petruchio are both rebellious against the constraints placed on them by society and they each take a mischievous amusement in flouting convention. Despite the immediate attraction to each other, Kate is frightened and untrusting and resorts to her usual unruly and overbearing behavior. Instead of running from her like Hortensio or scolding her like Baptista, Petruchio stands firm. As he promised, he contradicts everything she says. He criticizes her for the things in her character she is most proud of and tells her that she possesses traits that she doesn't believe she has. Petruchio's speeches are full of metaphors and similes comparing Kate to nature and things of great beauty. The verbal exchange between the two is not only witty and intelligent but it is sexually charged as well. Both Petruchio and Kate give as good as they get and, despite the insults and verbal sparring, both characters seem to be genuinely amused by the game and each other.

Beneath the banter, Petruchio has begun his role as teacher and in this first lesson Petruchio gives Kate a glimpse of not only what he wants her to be but also who she is capable of becoming. He declares that she

A representation of Petruchio and Kate in an unattributed engraving.
Mary Evans Picture Library

is gentle, pleasant, gamesome, courteous, and he truly sees a beauty in her that no one, including Kate, has ever acknowledged before. He treats her with more gentleness than her behavior requires and when she slaps him, he does not run away or hit back but sincerely warns her that she must never strike him again. Kate is touched by Petruchio's tenderness but does not know how to trust or even acknowledge his kindness.

Much like the Lord in the Induction scenes, Petruchio becomes an actor in a play he has written and will be directing. He casts himself as the hero and Kate becomes the princess who must be saved from her self. Petruchio begins by calling Katherine, "Kate." She reminds him that her name is "Katherine" but by changing her name, Petruchio is assigning her another role to play. He directs her to play this new role as someone who is mild, virtuous, and beautiful. She is to take on the role of one who is loving and loveable; someone who can be desired and married to a man who is her equal. Kate grasps the power of Petruchio's wit and verbal skills, encouraging her to ask, "Where did you study

all this goodly speech?" Admitting he is role-playing, Petruchio answers, "It is extempore." With this answer, Petruchio gives Kate the first real clue that he feels that life is a stage and if you know how to play the game, you can make any audience happy by giving them the play they want to see. He will continue to teach this game to Kate until she learns to play it on her own.

The performance choices made by a director in this interesting scene can set the entire tone for the rest of the play. In 1978, Michael Bodganov directed *The Taming of the Shrew* for the Royal Shakespeare Theatre, envisioning the play as a male dream about taking revenge on women. In this scene, Jonathan Pryce, who played Petruchio to Paola Dionisotti's Kate, was very violent, pinning down Kate's wrists and throwing her to the ground. Barry Kyle's production in Stratford-upon-Avon in 1982 made Kate the violent one. Sinead Cusak played Kate to Alun Armstrong's Petruchio, and as Kate, she threw punches, fell off the stage, pushed Petruchio into a pool, tried to strangle him, and kicked him in the genitals. In direct contrast to these two stage productions is Jonathan Miller's production of the play for the BBC. In this production, John Cleese, the comic genius of *Monty Python* fame, played an almost Puritan version of Petruchio. The scene took place in a drawing room as Petruchio talked very softly and businesslike to Kate. There was none of the loud verbal exchanges or physical assaults usually associated with this scene. In Franco Zeffirelli's 1966 film version of the play, Petruchio, played by Richard Burton, chases Elizabeth Taylor's Kate around rooms and over rooftops. The scene is full of sexual chemistry between the two characters but the violence is replaced by what seems like rowdy play. When Kate twists her ankle towards the end of the scene, Petruchio, in a very telling moment in the film, puts his arm around Kate to support her and helps her out the door.

When Baptista checks in to see how things are going between his daughter and Petruchio, Kate complains that her father could wish her "wed to one half lunatic" but she does not throw a tantrum, break anything over anyone's head, nor does she leave the room. She is intrigued by Petruchio and attracted to him on many levels but she only knows how to react belligerently. When Petruchio announces that they will be married on Sunday, Kate says she will see him hanged first but she does not say she will not marry him. The men in the room ignore her comment, but instead of using her tongue and violent temper to ensure she is not ignored, Kate remains silent until she exits the scene. Very often the things not said by Shakespeare's characters are more important than what is said, and Kate's silence at this moment speaks volumes about her true feelings.

Instead of boasting to Gremio, Tranio, and Baptista about how he bent Kate to his will, or interpreting the "I'll see thee hanged on Sunday first" as a sexual reference, Petruchio defends Kate, telling the others of her loving kindness. He declares that based on an agreement between the two of them, her shrewishness will occur only in public. Petruchio compares Kate to Grissel and in doing so Shakespeare gives the reader a clearer insight into Petruchio's plans for reforming the petulant Kate. Grissel or Griselda was a heroine in Boccaccio's *Decameron*, a tale adapted by Chaucer and included in *The Canterbury Tales.* In the story, an Italian nobleman marries a lovely, moral maiden named Griselda who was from a lower class family. The nobleman decides he will test his wife's love so he pretends to kill their two children and acts as if he has been married to a younger woman. Despite the horrible things done to her, Griselda remained patient, finally being rewarded by being restored to her children and her husband. The key word in this story is of course "pretend." Petruchio will "pretend" to be harsh and put Kate through many trials but it is not his true nature and once he has managed to tame Kate he will restore order to his own life and household.

Petruchio's mention of Lucrece is also an interesting choice on the part of Shakespeare. The story of Lucrece includes a group of Roman aristocrats away at war. They begin discussing their wives, exclaiming their virtue and faithfulness. The men decide to place a wager on their wives and return to Rome to check on their activities only to find all of their wives dancing, feasting, and gossiping. The exception was Lucrece who was at home alone with her maids doing her household chores. The story of Lucrece certainly serves to foreshadow certain events in the last Act of the play.

With the wedding day set, Petruchio leaves for Venice, one of Italy's richest cities, to buy his wedding clothes. As he leaves, Petruchio asks Kate for a kiss, which of course she denies. At this moment however, the reader realizes that Petruchio's desire for money has taken second place to winning Kate as a true wife in every sense. He wants her to accept him, and the kiss would prove a willingness to do this. If he only wanted money, he would have no reason or desire to explore the physical aspects of the relationship.

The business of marriage

During the sixteenth century, five steps were required to achieve a lawful marriage, and each step took a certain amount of time. The first step was the written contract establishing the bride's dowry. Next, the betrothal ceremony occurred where the couple would formally exchange oral promises before witnesses. For the next three weeks, the banns, the announcement of an upcoming marriage, were proclaimed publicly in the church. This allowed anyone who knew of reasons why the couple should not be married to come forward. The fourth step was the wedding in the church and the fifth was the consummation. It was difficult but not impossible to skip right from the proposal to the wedding. The church would recognize any exchange of vows

OLLON

Versaille

A sculpture of Apollo at Versailles in Roman Antiquities.
Mary Evans Picture Library

Balon.

A sixteenth century engraving of a jester by A. Kohl.
Mary Evans Picture Library

or state, and Baptista, hoping to get rid of Kate before Petruchio can change his mind, does not object.

Now that Kate has unexpectedly become engaged, Baptista is free to deal with the more pleasant prospect of marrying off Bianca. The economics of marriage again become the focus as Baptista resumes playing the "merchant's part." The suitors are informed that Bianca will be given permission to marry the man who can provide the greatest dowry. In effect, Baptista is auctioning off his daughter to the highest bidder. With Hortensio and Cambio/Lucentio inside teaching Bianca, Gremio and Tranio, disguised as Lucentio, are left to compete for the hand of Bianca. Tranio, bidding as Lucentio, continues to outbid Gremio until Gremio can go no higher. Baptista agrees that Tranio/Lucentio may marry Bianca but he must first have his father, Vincentio, confirm that he actually has the money and property that he has offered. It is ironic that the highest bidder is actually a poor servant who is only pretending to be a man of affluence and status. As the themes of role-playing and appearance versus reality first established in the Induction continue, Tranio is now faced with the prospect of finding someone to pretend to be Vincentio.

before witnesses as a valid marriage but it would not necessarily ensure that the wife would have any legal rights to the husband's property after his death. Petruchio, however, intends to be married on Sunday and he is not one to conform to the conventional laws of church

Notes

Notes

Notes

THE TAMING OF THE SHREW

ACT III

Kate *No shame but mine. I must, forsooth, be forc'd*
To give my hand, oppos'd against my heart,
Unto a mad-brain rudesby, full of spleen,
Who woo'd in haste and means to wed at leisure.
I told you, I, he was a frantic fool,
Hiding his bitter jests in blunt behaviour,
And, to be noted for a merry man,
He'll woo a thousand, 'point the day of marriage,
Make feast, invite friends, and proclaim the banns,
Yet never means to wed where he hath woo'd.
Now must the world point at poor Katherine,
And say 'Lo, there is mad Petruchio's wife,
If it would please him come and marry her.'

Act III, Scene 1

The two "tutors" make their play for Bianca. Cambio/Lucentio reveals his true identity to Bianca in the midst of reading Ovid. Bianca offers Cambio/Lucentio a glimmer of hope when she rejects Litio/Hortensio. Bianca is called away to help prepare for Kate's upcoming wedding and the two suitors take their leave.

ACT III, SCENE 1

Padua. A room in BAPTISTA'S house.

[Enter LUCENTIO [as Cambio], HORTENSIO [as Litio], and BIANCA]

Lucentio Fiddler, forbear. You grow too forward, sir.   1
Have you so soon forgot the entertainment
Her sister Katherine welcome'd you withal?

Hortensio But, wrangling pedant, this is
The patroness of heavenly harmony.   5
Then give me leave to have prerogative,
And when in music we have spent an hour,
Your lecture shall have leisure for as much.

Lucentio Preposterous ass, that never read so far
To know the cause why music was ordain'd!   10
Was it not to refresh the mind of man
After his studies or his usual pain?
Then give me leave to read philosophy,
And, while I pause, serve in your harmony.

Hortensio Sirrah, I will not bear these braves of thine.   15

Bianca Why, gentlemen, you do me double wrong
To strive for that which resteth in my choice.
I am no breeching scholar in the schools.
I'll not be tied to hours nor 'pointed times,
But learn my lessons as I please myself.   20
And, to cut off all strife, here sit we down.
[to Hortensio] Take you your instrument, play you the whiles;
His lecture will be done ere you have tun'd.

Hortensio You'll leave his lecture when I am in tune?

Lucentio That will be never. Tune your instrument.   25

[Hortensio stands aside, tunig his lute]

Bianca Where left we last?

NOTES

1.   *forbear:* stop.

2.   *entertainment:* hitting him with the lute.

3.   *withal:* with.

4.   *this:* Bianca.

6.   *leave:* permission.

    prerogative: priority.

8.   *Your lecture . . . much:* Your instruction will be given equal time.

9.   *Preposterous:* inverting the natural order of things.

10.   *ordain'd:* created.

12.   *usual pain:* daily labor.

13.   *read:* give a lesson in.

14.   *serve in:* serve up, perform, present.

15.   *bear these braves:* endure these taunts.

18.   *breeching scholar:* young student in breeches.

19.   *'pointed:* appointed.

21.   *cut off:* end.

22.   *the whiles:* in the meantime.

Lucentio Here, madam:

[opens the book to show Bianca]

Hic ibat Simois; hic est Sigeia tellus,

Hic steterat Priami regia celsa senis.

Bianca Construe them.　　　　　　　　　　　　　　　30

Lucentio 'Hic ibat,' as I told you before, 'Simois,' I am
　　Lucentio, 'hic

est,' son unto Vincentio of Pisa, 'Sigeia tellus,' disguised thus

to get your love, 'Hic steterat,' and that Lucentio that comes

a-wooing, 'Priami,' is my man Tranio, 'regia,' bearing my
　　port,

'celsa senis,' that we might beguile the old pantaloon.　　35

Hortensio *[Returning]* Madam, my instrument's in tune.

Bianca Let's hear.

[Hortensio plays]

O fie, the treble jars!

Lucentio Spit in the hole, man, and tune again.

[Hortensio returns to tuning his lute]

Bianca Now let me see if I can construe it: 'Hic ibat
　　Simois,' I　　　　　　　　　　　　　　　　　　　40

know you not; 'hic est Sigeia tellus,' I trust you not; 'Hic

steterat Priami,' take heed he hear us not; 'regia,' presume
　　not;

'celsa senis,' despair not.

Hortensio Madam, 'tis now in tune.

[Hortensio plays again]

Lucentio All but the bass.　　　　　　　　　　　　45

Hortensio The bass is right. 'Tis the base knave that jars.

[Aside] How fiery and forward our pedant is!

Now for my life the knave doth court my love!

Pedascule, I'll watch you better yet.

Bianca *[to Lucentio]* In time I may believe, yet I mistrust.　50

Lucentio Mistrust it not; for sure, Aeacides

Was Ajax, call'd so from his grandfather.

Bianca I must believe my master; else, I promise you,

I should be arguing still upon that doubt.

But let it rest. Now, Litio, to you.　　　　　　　55

28–29. *Hic ibat . . . senis:* "Here flowed the Simois; here is the Sigeian land;/Here had stood old Priam's high palace" (Ovid).

30. *Construe:* interpret.

34. *bearing my port:* assuming my social position.

35. *pantaloon:* reference to Gremio.

38. *jars:* is out of tune.

49. *Pedascule:* Latin for "little pedant."

51–52 *Aeacides/Ajax:* Ajax, son of Telamon, was called Aeacides after his grandfather, Aeacus. Possibly referenced in Ovid.

Good master, take it not unkindly, pray,
That I have been thus pleasant with you both.

Hortensio *[to Lucentio]* You may go walk and give me leave
awhile.
My lessons make no music in three parts.

Lucentio Are you so formal, sir?   60
Well, I must wait, *[Aside]*
And watch withal, for, but I be deceiv'd,
Our fine musician groweth amorous.
[Lucentio moves aside]

Hortensio Madam, before you touch the instrument,
To learn the order of my fingering   65
I must begin with rudiments of art,
To teach you gamut in a briefer sort,
More pleasant, pithy, and effectual
Than hath been taught by any of my trade.
And there it is in writing fairly drawn.   70

Bianca Why, I am past my gamut long ago.

Hortensio Yet read the gamut of Hortensio.
[Hortensio hands Bianca a paper]

Bianca *[reading]* "Gamut I am, the ground of all accord:
'A re,' to plead Hortensio's passion;
'B mi,' Bianca, take him for thy lord,   75
'C fa ut,' that loves with all affection;
'D sol re,' one clef, two notes have I;
'E la mi,' show pity or I die."
Call you this "gamut"? Tut, I like it not.
Old fashions please me best. I am not so nice   80
To change true rules for odd inventions.
[Enter a SERVANT]

Servant Mistress, your father prays you leave your books
And help to dress your sister's chamber up.
You know tomorrow is the wedding day.

Bianca Farewell, sweet masters, both. I must be gone.   85
[Exeunt Bianca and Servant]

Lucentio Faith, mistress, then I have no cause to stay.
[Exit]

---

57.   *pleasant:* merry.

58.   *give me leave:* leave me alone.

59.   *three parts:* three voices.

60.   *formal:* socially correct.

62.   *withal:* as well.
      but: unless.

67.   *gamut:* the musical scale.
      briefer sort: quicker way.

70.   *drawn:* set out.

73.   *ground:* beginning, first note.
      accord: harmony.

80.   *nice:* whimsical, difficult to please.

81.   *odd inventions:* bizarre plans.

Hortensio But I have cause to pry into this pedant.
Methinks he looks as though he were in love.
Yet if thy thoughts, Bianca, be so humble
To cast thy wand'ring eyes on every stale,   90
Seize thee that list! If once I find thee ranging,
Hortensio will be quit with thee by changing.   92
[Exit]

88.	*Methinks:* I think.
89.	*humble:* base, common.
90.	*stale:* a term from falconry meaning lure.

COMMENTARY

This scene between Hortensio/Litio, Lucentio/Cambio, and Bianca is in direct contrast to the previous scene. Both scenes deal with wooing, but the differences in the styles of wooing between Kate and Petruchio and Bianca and her suitors are obvious. Petruchio's wooing of Kate was full of bombastic word play and lusty innuendo while Hortensio/Litio and Lucentio/Cambio will use music and poetry to woo Bianca. Their courting is quiet, subtle, and sly compared to the loud, overt, and passionate scene between Kate and Petruchio.

As the scene begins, Hortensio/Litio and Lucentio/Cambio are sparring for the opportunity to be the first to spend time alone with Bianca. During the time that Shakespeare was writing, young women were not permitted to attend grammar school or read the Bible in English.

Grammar schools, similar to modern secondary schools, stressed an education rich in math, Greek, Latin, geography, and composition. Because young women could not attend these schools, wealthier families such as the Minola family would hire tutors for their female children who would then be taught to read and write. Occasionally, the girls would also be instructed in music and language. Keeping with the theme of education and learning, it is interesting to note that teachers with absolutely no credentials surround Bianca. They are pretending to be something they are not; there to woo Bianca with deceit, not to teach her.

Of course Bianca has been deceitful as well. The sweet, innocent young lady that she appears to be has already been exposed in Act II, Scene 1 and the reader is now shown even more of Bianca's true nature.

Irritated by the posturing of Hortensio/Litio and Lucentio/Cambio, Bianca, assuming the dominate position, tells the men that it will be her decision as to which teacher she will work with first. Instead of the teacher setting the rules, Bianca says she will set her own. She will learn what and when she chooses. She is no "breeching scholar." The roles have literally become reversed and Bianca is now the teacher instructing the "tutors" on who and what she really is. Unlike Kate, who so obviously rebels against the constraints placed upon her by her father and society, Bianca can appear to be playing by the rules while ignoring them completely. Unfortunately, her "pupils" are slow to learn, seeing only what they want to see. In their eyes Bianca is not the shrew in sheep's clothing that the reader knows she is but the demure, virtuous maiden they want her to be.

Hortensio/Litio is sent away to tune his instrument, leaving Lucentio/Cambio alone with Bianca. Using Ovid's guide to seduction for young men, *Ars Amatoria (The Art of Love)* as his text, Lucentio/Cambio conceals his own message of love within the words of the poet. He tells Bianca who he really is and why he is there. Instead of teaching her the Latin that he has been hired to teach, he uses words to manipulate Bianca into learning what he wants her to know. As will be revealed later in the play, he does a wonderful job of teaching her the art of deceit and manipulation.

Bianca obviously prefers the young Lucentio/Cambio to the elder Hortensio/Litio but she is coy enough to give him hope but not promises. Hortensio/Litio is suspicious of what is happening between the two young people and intends to make his play for Bianca as soon as possible. Bawdy puns were one of Shakespeare's great strengths and this scene is full of them. For example, Hortensio/Litio tells Bianca that before she can touch his "instrument" to "learn the order of my fingering" that she should read his "gamut." These types of *double entendres*,

"I am no breeching scholar"
The Raymond Meander and Joe Mitchenson Theatre Collection

words or phrases with double meanings that are usually risqué, were very popular with the Elizabethan audience. Horetensio/Litio uses the music scales to intersperse his declarations of love for Bianca, begging her to "show pity or I die." Before she can respond, a servant enters telling Bianca she is needed to help prepare for Kate's wedding day.

Left alone, Hortensio decides that it may not be worth pursuing Bianca any further. He is an older man looking for comfort more than beauty. Despite his flowery words to Bianca, his attitude towards love is basically much more realistic than Lucentio's and perhaps he has glimpsed past Bianca's façade. Comparing her to a hawk, Hortensio believes Bianca is too easily influenced by the flattery of "every stale," colorful decoys with no substance.

Act III, Scene 2

Kate's wedding day has arrived, and Petruchio is nowhere to be found. He finally shows up dressed in an old jacket turned inside out, tattered pants, and boots so worn out that they have been used to hold trash. When the wedding is over, Petruchio refuses to stay for the reception and despite Kate's insistence on being allowed to stay, the newlyweds leave immediately for Verona.

ACT III, SCENE 2

The same. Before BAPTISTA'S house.

[Enter BAPTISTA, GREMIO, TRANIO [as Lucentio], KATE, BIANCA, LUCENTIO [as Cambio], and others, ATTENDANTS]

Baptista *[To Tranio]* Signior Lucentio, this is the 'pointed day	1	
That Katherine and Petruchio should be married,		
And yet we hear not of our son-in-law.		
What will be said? What mockery will it be		
To want the bridegroom when the priest attends	5	
To speak the ceremonial rites of marriage?		
What says Lucentio to this shame of ours?		

Kate No shame but mine. I must, forsooth, be forc'd
To give my hand, oppos'd against my heart,
Unto a mad-brain rudesby, full of spleen, 　　　10
Who woo'd in haste and means to wed at leisure.
I told you, I, he was a frantic fool,
Hiding his bitter jests in blunt behaviour,
And, to be noted for a merry man,
He'll woo a thousand, 'point the day of marriage, 　　15
Make feast, invite friends, and proclaim the banns,
Yet never means to wed where he hath woo'd.
Now must the world point at poor Katherine,
And say 'Lo, there is mad Petruchio's wife,
If it would please him come and marry her.' 　　　20

Tranio Patience, good Katherine, and Baptista too.
Upon my life, Petruchio means but well,
Whatever fortune stays him from his word.
Though he be blunt, I know him passing wise;
Though he be merry, yet withal he's honest. 　　　25

NOTES

1.　　'*pointed:* appointed.

5.　　*want:* lack.
　　　attends: is present.

8.　　*forsooth:* indeed.

10.　　*rudesby:* rude person.
　　　spleen: impulsiveness.

12.　　*frantic:* insane.

13.　　*blunt:* rude.

14.　　*noted for:* reputed, known as.

16.　　*proclaim the banns:* announce the upcoming marriage.

22.　　*means but:* means only.

23.　　*fortune:* chance, accident.

24.　　*passing:* very.

25.　　*merry:* pleasant.

Kate Would Katherine had never seen him though!
[Exit, weeping, followed by Bianca and others]

Baptista Go, girl, I cannot blame thee now to weep,
For such an injury would vex a very saint;
Much more a shrew of thy impatient humour.
[Enter BIONDELLO]

Biondello Master, master! News! And such old   30
news as you never heard of!

Baptista Is it new and old too? How may that be?

Biondello Why, is it not news to hear of Petruchio's coming?

Baptista Is he come?

Biondello Why, no, sir.

Baptista What then?   35

Biondello He is coming.

Baptista When will he be here?

Biondello When he stands where I am and sees you there.

Tranio But, say, what to thine old news?

Biondello Why, Petruchio is coming, in a   40
new hat and an old
Jerkin, a pair of old breeches thrice turned, a pair of boots
that have been candle-cases, one buckled, another laced;
an old
rusty sword ta'en out of the town armoury, with a broken hilt,
and chapeless; with two broken points; his horse hipped,
with an
old mothy saddle and stirrups of no kindred,   45
besides possessed
with the glanders and like to mose in the chine, troubled with
the lampass, infected with the fashions, full of windgalls, sped
with spavins, rayed with the yellows, past cure of the fives,
stark spoiled with the staggers, begnawn with the bots,
swayed in
the back and shoulder-shotten, near-legged   50
before, and with a
half-checked bit and a head-stall of sheep's leather, which,

---

29. *humour:* temperament.

30. *old:* odd, strange.

39. *to:* about.
41. *Jerkin:* short jacket.
     turned: inside out to get more wear from the garment.
42. *candle-cases:* places used to throw the ends of burned candles.
44. *chapeless:* without a chape, the metal plate used to cover the point of a scabbard.
     points: laces used to hold up stockings.
     hipped: dislocated hip.
45. *of no kindred:* that do not match.
46. *glanders:* swollen glands accompanied by nasal discharge.
     like . . . chine: susceptible to glanders or likely to decay in the backbone.
47. *lampass:* swelling in the mouth.
     fashions: correct word: farcins: a disease in horses causing painful ulcerations especially on the legs.
     windgalls: tumors.
     sped with spavins: destroyed by inflamed cartilage.
48. *rayed with the yellows:* disfigured by jaundice.
     fives: avives, a disease causing swelling below the ears.
49. *stark:* entirely.
     the staggers: staggering.
     begnawn: eaten away.
     bots: maggots, intestinal worms.
     swayed: sagging.
50. *shoulder-shotten:* lame in the shoulder.
     near-legged before: with knock kneed forelegs.
51. *half-checked bit:* wrongly adjusted bit.
     head-stall: part of the horse's bridle.
     sheep's leather: inferior leather, not as good as cow hide or pigskin.

being restrained to keep him from stumbling, hath been often
burst, and now repaired with knots; one girth six times pieced,
and a woman's crupper of velure, which hath two letters
  for her
name fairly set down in studs, and here and there pieced
  with pack-thread.   55

Baptista Who comes with him?

Biondello O, sir, his lackey, for all the world caparisoned like
the horse: with a linen stock on one leg and a kersey boot-hose
on the other, gartered with a red and blue list;   60
  an old hat, and
the humour of forty fancies prick'd in't for a feather. A
monster, a very monster in apparel, and not like a Christian
footboy or a gentleman's lackey.

Tranio 'Tis some odd humour pricks him to this fashion,
Yet oftentimes he goes but mean-apparell'd.   65

Baptista I am glad he's come, howsoe'er he comes.

Biondello Why, sir, he comes not.

Baptista Didst thou not say he comes?

Biondello Who? That Petruchio came?

Baptista Ay, that Petruchio came.   70

Biondello No, sir; I say his horse comes with him on his
  back.

Baptista Why, that's all one.

Biondello Nay, by Saint Jamy,
  I hold you a penny,
  A horse and a man   75
  Is more than one,
  And yet not many.
  [Enter PETRUCHIO and GRUMIO]

Petruchio Come, where be these gallants? Who's at home?

Baptista You are welcome, sir.

Petruchio And yet I come not well.   80

Baptista And yet you halt not.

Tranio Not so well apparell'd
  As I wish you were.

---

52. *restrained:* drawn tightly.

53. *girth:* band of leather or cloth around a horse's belly, used to hold the saddle in place.

    pieced: patched, mended, repaired.

54. *crupper:* strap under a horse's tail to keep saddle in place.

    velour: velvet, less sturdy as leather.

55. *studs:* large headed nails of silver or brass.

    pieced with packthread: held together with thread.

57. *lackey:* footman.

    caparisoned: outfitted.

59. *stock:* stocking.

    kersey boot-hose: coarse wool stocking.

60. *list:* cloth border.

61. *humour:* whim.

    fancies: decorations.

    prick'd: fastened with a pin.

62. *monster:* beast.

63. *footboy:* page in livery.

64. *humour:* mood.

    pricks: incites.

65. *mean-apparell'd:* poorly dressed.

72. *all one:* the same thing.

74. *hold:* bet.

78. *gallants:* men of fashion.

81. *halt:* limp.

Petruchio Were it better, I should rush in thus.
  But where is Kate? Where is my lovely bride?   85
  How does my father? Gentles, methinks you frown.
  And wherefore gaze this goodly company
  As if they saw some wondrous monument,
  Some comet or unusual prodigy?

Baptista Why, sir, you know this is your wedding day.   90
  First were we sad, fearing you would not come,
  Now sadder, that you come so unprovided.
  Fie, doff this habit, shame to your estate,
  An eyesore to our solemn festival.

Tranio And tell us what occasion of import   95
  Hath all so long detain'd you from your wife
  And sent you hither so unlike yourself?

Petruchio Tedious it were to tell, and harsh to hear.
  Sufficeth, I am come to keep my word,
  Though in some part enforced to digress,   100
  Which at more leisure I will so excuse
  As you shall well be satisfied withal.
  But where is Kate? I stay too long from her.
  The morning wears. 'Tis time we were at church.

Tranio See not your bride in these unreverent robes.   105
  Go to my chamber, put on clothes of mine.

Petruchio Not I, believe me. Thus I'll visit her.

Baptista But thus, I trust, you will not marry her.

Petruchio Good sooth, even thus. Therefore ha' done with
    words.
  To me she's married, not unto my clothes.   110
  Could I repair what she will wear in me,
  As I can change these poor accoutrements,
  'Twere well for Kate and better for myself.
  But what a fool am I to chat with you
  When I should bid goodmorrow to my bride   115
  And seal the title with a lovely kiss!
  [Exeunt Petruchio and Grumio]

Tranio He hath some meaning in his mad attire.
  We will persuade him, be it possible,

---

86. *Gentles:* gentlemen.

87. *wherefore:* why.

88. *monument:* warning sign, omen.

89. *comet:* usually a bad omen.

     prodigy: marvel, wonder.

92. *unprovided:* unprepared.

93. *habit:* clothes.

     estate: rank, social status.

94. *solemn:* ceremonial.

95. *import:* importance.

99. *Sufficeth:* it is enough that.

100. *in some part:* to some extent.

     enforced to digress: forced to deviate from his promise.

104. *wears:* is passing.

105. *unreverent:* disrespectful.

109. *Good sooth:* yes, indeed; in truth.

111. *wear:* the abrasion of the penis in sexual intercourse.

112. *accoutrements:* clothes.

116. *seal:* sanction.

     title: deed of ownership.

     lovely: loving.

To put on better ere he go to church.

Baptista I'll after him, and see the event of this.   120

[*Exeunt Baptista, Gremio, Biondello, and Attendants*]

Tranio But, sir, to love concerneth us to add
Her father's liking, which to bring to pass,
As I before imparted to your Worship,
I am to get a man—whate'er he be
It skills not much, we'll fit him to our turn,—
And he shall be "Vincentio of Pisa,"   125
And make assurance here in Padua
Of greater sums than I have promised.
So shall you quietly enjoy your hope
And marry sweet Bianca with consent.

Lucentio Were it not that my fellow schoolmaster   130
Doth watch Bianca's steps so narrowly,
'Twere good, methinks, to steal our marriage,
Which, once perform'd, let all the world say no,
I'll keep mine own despite of all the world.

Tranio That by degrees we mean to look into,   135
And watch our vantage in this business.
We'll overreach the greybeard, Gremio,
The narrowprying father, Minola,
The quaint musician, amorous Litio,
All for my master's sake, Lucentio.   140

[*Enter GREMIO*]

Signior Gremio, came you from the church?

Gremio As willingly as e'er I came from school.

Tranio And is the bride and bridegroom coming home?

Gremio A bridegroom, say you? 'Tis a groom indeed,
A grumbling groom, and that the girl shall find.   145

Tranio Curster than she? Why, 'tis impossible.

Gremio Why, he's a devil, a devil, a very fiend.

Tranio Why, she's a devil, a devil, the devil's dam.

Gremio Tut, she's a lamb, a dove, a fool to him.
I'll tell you, Sir Lucentio: when the priest   150
Should ask if Katherine should be his wife,
'Ay, by gogs-wouns' quoth he, and swore so loud

---

120. *event:* outcome.

121. *love:* Bianca's love.

124. *skills:* matters.

     turn: purpose.

126. *make assurance:* to guarantee.

131. *narrowly:* closely.

132. *steal our marriage:* elope.

135. *That:* the marriage.

     by degrees: gradually.

136. *watch our vantage:* look for opportunities.

137. *overreach:* get the better of.

138. *narrowprying:* excessively watchful.

139. *quaint:* skilled, clever.

144. *a groom indeed:* as rough as a serving man.

146. *Curster:* more obstinate.

148. *dam:* mother.

149. *fool:* harmless creature.

151. *Should ask:* asked.

152. *gog's wouns:* God's wounds.

That, all amaz'd, the priest let fall the book,

And as he stoop'd again to take it up,

The mad-brain'd bridegroom took him such a cuff   155

That down fell priest and book, and book and priest.

'Now take them up,' quoth he 'if any list.'

Tranio What said the wench when he rose again?

Gremio Trembled and shook, for why he stamp'd and swore

As if the vicar meant to cozen him.   160

But after many ceremonies done,

He calls for wine: 'A health!' quoth he, as if

He had been aboard, carousing to his mates

After a storm; quaff'd off the muscadel

And threw the sops all in the sexton's face,   165

Having no other reason

But that his beard grew thin and hungerly,

And seem'd to ask him sops as he was drinking.

This done, he took the bride about the neck

And kiss'd her lips with such a clamorous smack   170

That at the parting all the church did echo.

And I, seeing this, came thence for very shame,

And after me I know the rout is coming.

Such a mad marriage never was before!

[Music plays]

Hark, hark! I hear the minstrels play.   175

[Enter PETRUCHIO, KATE, BIANCA, BAPTISTA,
*   HORTENSIO,*
GRUMIO, and ATTENDANTS]

Petruchio Gentlemen and friends, I thank you for your pains.

I know you think to dine with me today

And have prepar'd great store of wedding cheer,

But so it is, my haste doth call me hence,

And therefore here I mean to take my leave.   180

Baptista Is't possible you will away to-night?

Petruchio I must away today, before night come.

Make it no wonder. If you knew my business,

You would entreat me rather go than stay.

And, honest company, I thank you all,   185

That have beheld me give away myself

---

153.   *amaz'd:* flabbergasted.

155.   *took:* gave.

    cuff: blow with his fists.

157.   *he:* Petruchio.

    list: wishes to.

159.   *for why:* because.

160.   *vicar:* priest.

    cozen: cheat.

162.   *health:* toast.

163.   *aboard:* on shipboard.

    carousing: calling "bottoms up."

164.   *quaff'd:* drank.

    muscadel: a strong, sweet wine often served at weddings.

165.   *sops:* cake soaked in wine.

    sexton: church officer.

167.   *hungerly:* scantily.

173.   *rout:* a crowd of guests.

177.   *think:* expect.

178.   *store:* quantities.

    cheer: food and drink.

183.   *Make it no wonder:* Do not be surprised.

To this most patient, sweet, and virtuous wife.
Dine with my father, drink a health to me,
For I must hence, and farewell to you all.

Tranio Let us entreat you stay till after dinner.   190

Petruchio It may not be.

Gremio Let me entreat you.

Petruchio It cannot be.

Kate Let me entreat you.

Petruchio I am content.   195

Kate Are you content to stay?

Petruchio I am content you shall entreat me stay,
But yet not stay, entreat me how you can.

Kate Now, if you love me, stay.

Petruchio Grumio, my horse!   200

Grumio Ay, sir, they be ready; the oats have eaten the horses.

Kate Nay, then,
Do what thou canst, I will not go today,
No, nor to-morrow, not till I please myself.
The door is open, sir. There lies your way.   205
You may be jogging whiles your boots are green.
For me, I'll not be gone till I please myself.
'Tis like you'll prove a jolly surly groom,
That take it on you at the first so roundly.

Petruchio O Kate! content thee. Prithee, be not angry.   210

Kate I will be angry. What hast thou to do?
Father, be quiet. He shall stay my leisure.

Gremio Ay, marry, sir, now it begins to work.

Kate Gentlemen, forward to the bridal dinner.
I see a woman may be made a fool   215
If she had not a spirit to resist.

Petruchio They shall go forward, Kate, at thy command.
Obey the bride, you that attend on her.
Go to the feast, revel and domineer,
Carouse full measure to her maidenhead,   220
Be mad and merry, or go hang yourselves.

---

188. *my father:* Baptista, my father-in-law.

206. *jogging . . . green:* leaving before your new boots become old.

208. *like:* likely.

jolly: domineering.

209. *That . . . roundly:* in that you so readily presume to take complete control.

210. *Prithee:* I pray you.

211. *What . . . do?:* what business is it of yours?

212. *stay my leisure:* wait until I am ready.

213. *marry:* indeed.

219. *domineer:* feast riotously.

220. *maidenhead:* virginity.

But for my bonny Kate, she must with me.
Nay, look not big, nor stamp, nor stare, nor fret;
I will be master of what is mine own.
She is my goods, my chattels; she is my house,   225
My household stuff, my field, my barn,
My horse, my ox, my ass, my anything.
And here she stands, touch her whoever dare.
I'll bring mine action on the proudest he
That stops my way in Padua. Grumio,   230
Draw forth thy weapon. We are beset with thieves.
Rescue thy mistress, if thou be a man!
Fear not, sweet wench, they shall not touch thee, Kate.
I'll buckler thee against a million.
[Exeunt PETRUCHIO, KATE, and GRUMIO]

Baptista Nay, let them go. A couple of quiet ones!   235

Gremio Went they not quickly, I should die with laughing.

Tranio Of all mad matches, never was the like.

Lucentio Mistress, what's your opinion of your sister?

Bianca That, being mad herself, she's madly mated.

Gremio I warrant him, Petruchio is Kated.   240

Baptista Neighbours and friends, though bride and bride-
groom wants
For to supply the places at the table,
You know there wants no junkets at the feast.
Lucentio, you shall supply the bridegroom's place,
And let Bianca take her sister's room.   245

Tranio Shall sweet Bianca practise how to bride it?

Baptista She shall, Lucentio. Come, gentlemen, let's go.   247
[Exeunt]

223.	*big:* defiant.
	stare: swagger.
225.	*chattels:* property.
226.	*stuff:* goods, again a bawdy reference.
229.	*bring mine action:* attack physically; bring legal action.
234.	*buckler:* shield, defend.
239.	*mated:* married.
240.	*Kated:* caught like a disease, the "Kate."
241–242.	*wants . . . supply:* are not here to occupy.
243.	*wants:* are lacking.
	junkets: sweetmeats, confections.
245.	*room:* place.

COMMENTARY

During the sixteenth century, weddings customarily took place on Sundays between 8:00 a.m. and noon before the entire congregation, where the bride, given away by her father, and the groom would be married at the church door. The bride and groom would wear their finest clothes with the bride usually dressed in either white or russet and her hair left to hang loose. The bride would also wear a *chaplet,* a headdress set with gems and *bride's lace,* long blue ribbons binding sprigs of rosemary, tied to her arm. After the ceremony, these ribbons would be pulled off of the bride's arm by the men attending the wedding and worn on their hats.

The first part of the ceremony would include the formal exchange of the dowry. Traditionally a few pennies would then be set-aside for the poor. Next, the vows would be exchanged and the simple gold wedding band would be blessed. The groom would then place the ring on three of the bride's fingers before leaving it on her ring finger. This was thought to protect the bride from evil demons. After the ceremony, a nuptial mass would be said. Following the ceremony, it was traditional for the bride's family to provide a wedding feast.

Baptista would have spared no expense to give Kate the most lavish of weddings and much of Padua would have planned, out of curiosity, on attending this unexpected ceremony. To his great chagrin, the morning of the wedding arrives and Petruchio is nowhere to be found. Baptista is very concerned about what the people of Padua will say about his family if Kate is left standing alone at the altar, and even Kate knows people will talk: "Lo, there is mad Petruchio's wife, /If it would please him come and marry her." It appears that once again, Kate has been excluded from one of society's great rituals. She has been embarrassed and humiliated, reinforcing her own feelings of separation and unworthiness. Kate is understandably distraught and exits the scene weeping. Her tears seem to indicate that she is not only angry with Petruchio but also mourning his absence. He was her last chance for finding some semblance of salvation and now he too is "lost" to her. Like a widow, she is left alone and isolated.

Dressed to shrill

Petruchio eventually makes his way to the wedding, but instead of the beautiful new clothes he said he was going to Venice to purchase, he is horrendously attired and riding a horse that is so old and crippled that it can hardly move. This scene in the play has been performed in many amusing ways in the Theatre. Instead of riding in on an old horse, Petruchio has made his entrance on such things as a motorcycle, a unicycle, and a Volkswagen Beetle and has been dressed in everything from a clown suit to a costume reminiscent of a professional wrestler. Needless to say, his entrance is very funny but, if done correctly, holds a tinge of embarrassment from the audience on behalf of the bride-to-be.

Baptista is certainly not impressed by the way Petruchio looks but is grateful that he has shown up at all.

Although he suggests that Petruchio change his clothes, Baptista's motivations lean more toward getting Kate off his hands than how the groom is dressed and the effect that might have on Kate. Tranio, disguised as Lucentio, is the first to question Petruchio's choice of apparel. Considering that Tranio, a servant, is wearing the fine clothes of his master so as to fool both Baptista and Bianca, his statement not only highlights his own hypocrisy but also calls into question the entire confusion that clothes create. Can Christopher Sly become a Lord by wearing expensive clothes? Is Tranio transformed into a wealthy student by wearing the clothes of his master? Does Petruchio's outlandish wedding apparel make him an unfit husband? Do the clothes make the man? Petruchio answers these questions with his statement, "To me she's married, not unto my clothes." Petruchio understands that it is a person's true nature that matters, not the trappings that so often serve to deceive others. Just as he sees beneath the "costume" of shrewishness that Kate has taken on, he intends for her to see the genuine Petruchio. The wedding could also be another attempt by Petruchio to be actor and director in this script of his own making. Like the Lord in the Induction who takes off his wealthy attire to dress like a servant to make Sly think he is an aristocrat, Petruchio replaces what should have been his wedding finery to wear an outrageous costume, unfitting for a ceremony such as this. Reflecting the actions of the Induction, Petruchio is also tricking Kate. She is not a wife just because she has on wedding garb. She must see past the traditions or expectations of the wedding ceremony to realize that nothing of any real importance has taken place. Transformation does not occur with a change of clothes or religious ritual. It is an inner process that goes much deeper than Kate has been forced to go before.

The wedding

As the wedding party moves into the church, Tranio tells Lucentio that he must find a man to impersonate Lucentio's father. Lucentio worries that something may go wrong and suggest that he and Bianca should just elope.

The wedding takes place off stage, but, from Gremio's description, it was an outrageous event. In addition to being late, Petruchio so loudly cursed the priest that the Bible was dropped. As the priest reaches to pick the Bible up, Petruchio punches the priest so hard that the priest falls down. In the meantime, Petruchio continues stomping and swearing and calls for wine. He then throws the sops into the face of the sexton and kisses Kate so loudly that the smack has echoed throughout the church. In fact, Petruchio's behavior was so obscene that Gremio is totally embarrassed and has left the service before it has ended.

The questions raised in this episode are why does Petruchio behave so outlandishly and why does Kate not object? Based on her former behavior, the reader is aware that Kate is more likely to slap Petruchio and call a loud, violent halt to the wedding rather than endure this humiliation. The fact that she stays indicates that she either sees no way out of this situation or that she truly wants to marry this man.

Beginning at this point in the play, Petruchio's behavior is called into question and can be interpreted as either misogynist or compassionate. Many scholars have suggested that Petruchio is a domineering man who humiliates Kate at the wedding as part of his plan to break her into submission. In keeping with this theory, scholars site Petruchio's desire to "seal the title with a lovely kiss." Sealing the title would indicate that the mercenary Petruchio is still simply interested in making sure the dowry is legal and that when Kate becomes his property, he is free to use her as he wishes. Other scholars see Petruchio's motivations more firmly rooted in a real love for Kate. Along this line of thinking, Petruchio's actions become a mirror where Kate can see herself and her behavior reflected. Nothing that Petruchio does in the church is any worse or any different than any of the things the reader has seen Kate do in the previous scenes. By showing Kate what a shrew really looks like, Petruchio forces her into her first foray of self-examination.

Heading off into the sunset

Traditionally, the newlyweds would enjoy a large feast with family and friends and then spend their first night together in the bride's home. Petruchio, as usual, has his own plans. Immediately after the wedding, Petruchio declares he and Kate must leave without delay. The wedding party is stunned and begs Petruchio to stay. Even Kate breaks her silence to tell her husband that he can go without her.

Petruchio answers the pleas to stay at the banquet with a speech that has spurred much debate. In his monologue, Petrucio declares himself "master of what

is mine own." In the King James Version of the Bible, Exodus 20: 1 –17 states the tenth commandment: "Thou shalt not covet thy neighbour's house, thou shalt not covet thy neighbour's wife, nor his manservant, nor his maidservant, nor his ox, nor his ass, nor any thing that is thy neighbour's." Petruchio references this biblical verse when he declares Kate his "goods . . . his household stuff." Kate now belongs to Petruchio, body and soul. Many feminist scholars use this speech as proof that Petruchio sees Kate as nothing more than a commodity to be disposed of at his own discretion. By ruining the wedding with his horrible behavior and denying Kate the opportunity to enjoy the feast, Petruchio is attempting to break Kate's spirit by controlling her every move and emphatically establishing that nothing will happen in their relationship until and unless he chooses.

The Elizabethans believed in what E.M.W. Tillyard referred to as "The Elizabethan World Picture." In this view of the cosmos, everything from God to the plants exists in a hierarchical order where the fundamental principle of the universe is harmony. This chain of being begins with God as master of the Universe just as a King is the master of his kingdom. In the middle of the chain is man who is master of the household followed by his wife and his children. If any link in this chain is disordered, such as a woman usurping the authority of her husband, harmony is destroyed and chaos reigns. By asserting her own will above the will of the men in her life, Kate has created chaos. Petruchio has taken it upon himself to assert his authority, put Kate in her proper place, and restore harmony to the universe.

Once it is determined that Petruchio will not stay for the banquet, and neither will Kate, Petruchio changes his tone and takes on the role of "white knight." He draws his rusty weapon, dares anyone to try and stop the couple, sweeps Kate onto the horse, and rides off to Verona. This move can be interpreted as either a rescue of Kate from her neglectful and abusive family or as another attempt by Petruchio to deprive her of her dignity with no regard to human kindness. The reader could also choose to interpret Petruchio's actions as those of an actor dedicated to shaping Kate into a woman who knows what role to play and how to play it for the pleasure of her self and the audience. By rescuing Kate from those that have made her into a monster, Petruchio casts himself once more as the play's hero.

Fiona Shaw, who played Kate in Jonathan Miller's production of the play in 1987, had a very interesting

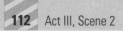
moment at this juncture in the play that explains why, instead of causing a riot and running away, Kate leaves with Petruchio. Instead of throwing Kate over his shoulder as many actors do at this point, Petruchio, played by Brian Cox, handed her a Bible. The Bible became symbolic of the expectations placed on Elizabethan women and Kate realized that the Bible, thought previously to be her protection, was, with its binding laws of patriarchal superiority, actually her trap. She chooses to go with Petruchio because she cannot run. There is no better place to go.

The bewildered wedding guests go into the banquet and, in an ironic foreshadowing of the next wedding feast, Bianca and Lucentio are chosen to sit in the seats that had been earlier reserved for Kate and Petruchio.

Notes

Notes

Notes

Notes

CLIFFSCOMPLETE

THE TAMING OF THE SHREW

ACT IV

Kate *Then God be bless'd, it is the blessed sun.*
But sun it is not when you say it is not,
And the moon changes even as your mind.
What you will have it nam'd, even that it is,
And so it shall be so for Katherine.

Act IV, Scene 1

Kate and Petruchio arrive at his home in the country and Petruchio begins his first lesson in the "taming" of the shrewish Kate. On her wedding night, Kate goes to bed cold, dirty, hungry, and alone. Petruchio lets the audience in on his plan to "tame" Kate like a falconer tames his falcon.

ACT IV, SCENE 1
A hall in PETRUCHIO'S country house.

[Enter GRUMIO]

Grumio Fie, fie on all tired jades, on all mad masters, and all   1
foul ways! Was ever man so beaten? Was ever man so
'ray'd? Was
ever man so weary? I am sent before to make a fire, and
they are
coming after to warm them. Now, were not I a little pot
and soon
hot, my very lips might freeze to my teeth, my tongue to
the roof   5
of my mouth, my heart in my belly, ere I should come by a
fire to
thaw me. But I with blowing the fire shall warm myself. For,
considering the weather, a taller man than I will take cold.
Holla, ho! Curtis!

[Enter CURTIS]

Curtis Who is that calls so coldly?   10

Grumio A piece of ice. If thou doubt it, thou mayst slide
from my
shoulder to my heel with no greater a run but my head
and my
neck. A fire, good Curtis.

Curtis Is my master and his wife coming, Grumio?

Grumio O, ay, Curtis, ay; and therefore fire, fire! Cast on no   15
water.

Curtis Is she so hot a shrew as she's reported?

Grumio She was, good Curtis, before this frost. But thou
knowest
winter tames man, woman, and beast, for it hath tamed
my old
master and my new mistress and myself, fellow Curtis.   20

NOTES

1.   *jades:* useless horses.

2.   *foul ways:* poor, dirty roads.
     'ray'd: betrayed.

5.   *hot:* proverbial: "A small pot is soon hot."

12. *run:* running start.

17. *hot:* violent, angry.

Curtis   Away, you three-inch fool! I am no beast.

Grumio   Am I but three inches? Why, thy horn is a foot, and so long

am I, at the least. But wilt thou make a fire? Or shall I complain

on thee to our mistress, whose hand, (she being now at hand)-

thou shalt soon feel, to thy cold comfort, for being slow in thy   25

hot office?

Curtis   I prithee, good Grumio, tell me, how goes the world?

Grumio   A cold world, Curtis, in every office but thine, and

therefore fire. Do thy duty, and have thy duty, for my master and

mistress are almost frozen to death.   30

Curtis   There's fire ready. And therefore, good Grumio, the news?

Grumio   Why, 'Jack boy, ho, boy!' and as much news as thou wilt.

Curtis   Come, you are so full of cony-catching.

Grumio   Why, therefore fire, for I have caught extreme cold.

Where's the cook? Is supper ready, the house trimmed, rushes   35

strewed, cobwebs swept, the servingmen in their new fustian,

their white stockings, and every officer his weddinggarment on?

Be the Jacks fair within, the Jills fair without, the carpets

laid, and everything in order?

Curtis   All ready. And therefore, I pray thee, news?   40

Grumio   First, know my horse is tired, my master and mistress fallen out.

Curtis   How?

Grumio   Out of their saddles into the dirt, and thereby hangs a tale.

Curtis   Let's ha't, good Grumio.

Grumio   Lend thine ear.   45

Curtis   Here.

---

21.   *three-inch fool:* a reference to Grumio's height.

22.   *Am I but three inches:* a bawdy reference to the size of his genitals.

      horn: symbol of the cuckold (a husband whose wife is unfaithful).

24.   *on:* about.

      at hand: nearby.

26.   *office:* chore (lighting a fire).

29.   *have thy duty:* get what you are owed.

32.   *"Jack boy, ho boy!":* line from a song.

33.   *cony-catching:* a "cony" is a rabbit, in this sense the cony is a victim of deception.

35.   *rushes strewed:* a floor covering put in place for guests.

36.   *fustian:* work clothes made of coarse cloth.

37.   *officer:* servant.

38.   *Jacks:* large leather drinking cups; men servants.

      Jills: small metal drinking cups; women servants.

      carpets: wool table covers.

Grumio *[Striking Curtis]* There.

Curtis This 'tis to feel a tale, not to hear a tale.

Grumio And therefore 'tis called a sensible tale. And this cuff
was but to knock at your ear and beseech listening. Now I
begin:　　　　　　　　　　　　　　　　　　　50
Imprimis, we came down a foul hill, my master riding
behind my
mistress,—

Curtis Both of one horse?

Grumio What's that to thee?

Curtis Why, a horse.　　　　　　　　　　　　　　55

Grumio Tell thou the tale! But hadst thou not crossed me,
thou
shouldst have heard how her horse fell, and she under her
horse;
thou shouldst have heard in how miry a place, how she was
bemoiled, how he left her with the horse upon her, how he
beat me
because her horse stumbled, how she waded through the
dirt to　　　　　　　　　　　　　　　　　　60
pluck him off me, how he swore; how she prayed that never
prayed
before, how I cried, how the horses ran away, how her
bridle was
burst, how I lost my crupper; with many things of worthy
memory
which now shall die in oblivion, and thou return unexperienced to thy grave.　　　　　　　　　　　　　65

Curtis By this reck'ning, he is more shrew than she.

Grumio Ay; and that thou and the proudest of you all shall
find
when he comes home. But what talk I of this? Call forth
Nathaniel, Joseph, Nicholas, Phillip, Walter, Sugarsop, and the
Rest. Let their heads be slickly combed, their blue coats
brush'd,　　　　　　　　　　　　　　　　　70
and their garters of an indifferent knit. Let them curtsy with
their left legs, and not presume to touch a hair of my master's
horse-tail till they kiss their hands. Are they all ready?

49.　*sensible:* rational.

51.　*Imprimis:* Latin for "first."
　　foul: muddy, dirty.

53.　*of:* on.

56.　*crossed:* interrupted.

58.　*miry:* swampy.
　　bemoiled: covered in dirt.

61.　*that:* who.

63.　*burst:* broken.

65.　*unexperienced:* uninformed.

66.　*reck'ning:* account.

68.　*what:* why.

70.　*slickly:* smoothly.
　　blue coats: servants' uniforms.

71.　*indifferent:* appropriate.

Curtis They are.

Grumio Call them forth.   75

Curtis Do you hear, Ho? You must meet my master to countenance my mistress.

76.   *to countenance:* to show respect.

Grumio Why, she hath a face of her own.

Curtis Who knows not that?

Grumio Thou, it seems, that calls for company to countenance her.   80

Curtis I call them forth to credit her.

81.   *credit:* pay respect to.

Grumio Why, she comes to borrow nothing of them.
[Enter four or five SERVINGMEN]

Nathaniel Welcome home, Grumio!

Philip How now, Grumio?

Joseph What, Grumio!   85

Nicholas Fellow Grumio!

Nathaniel How now, old lad?

Grumio Welcome, you! How now, you? What, you!
Fellow, you!
And thus much for greeting. Now, my spruce companions,
is all
ready, and all things neat?   90

89.   *spruce:* well turned-out.

Nathaniel All things is ready. How near is our master?

Grumio E'en at hand, alighted by this. And therefore
be not,—
Cock's passion, silence! I hear my master.
[Enter PETRUCHIO and KATE]

93.   *Cock's:* God or Christ's.

Petruchio Where be these knaves? What, no man at door
To hold my stirrup nor to take my horse?   95
Where is Nathaniel, Gregory, Phillip?—

All Servants Here! Here, sir; here, sir!

Petruchio "Here, sir! Here, sir! Here, sir! Here, sir!"
You loggerheaded and unpolish'd grooms!
What? No attendance? No regard? No duty?   100
Where is the foolish knave I sent before?

99.   *loggerheaded:* stupid.

Grumio Here, sir, as foolish as I was before.

Petruchio   You peasant swain, you whoreson malt-horse
    drudge!
Did I not bid thee meet me in the park
And bring along these rascal knaves with thee?   105

Grumio   Nathaniel's coat, sir, was not fully made,
And Gabriel's pumps were all unpink'd i' the heel.
There was no link to colour Peter's hat,
And Walter's dagger was not come from sheathing.
There were none fine but Adam, Rafe, and Gregory.   110
The rest were ragged, old, and beggarly.
Yet, as they are, here are they come to meet you.

Petruchio   Go, rascals, go, and fetch my supper in.
[Exeunt Servingmen]
[sings] Where is the life that late I led?
Where are those—?   115
Sit down, Kate, and welcome.
[they sit at the table]
Soud, soud, soud, soud!
[Enter SERVANTS with supper]
Why, when, I say?—Nay, good sweet Kate, be merry.—
Off with my boots, you rogues! you villains! When?
[sings] It was the friar of orders grey,   120
As he forth walked on his way—
[servant begins to remove Petruchio's boots]
Out, you rogue! You pluck my foot awry.
Take that! *[striking the servant]* And mend the plucking off
    the other.
Be merry, Kate. Some water, here! What, ho!
[Enter ONE with water]
Where's my spaniel Troilus? Sirrah, get you hence   125
And bid my cousin Ferdinand come hither.
[Exit Servant]
One, Kate, that you must kiss and be acquainted with.
Where are my slippers? Shall I have some water?
Come, Kate, and wash, and welcome heartily.—
[Servant lets the ewer fall]
You whoreson villain! Will you let it fall?   130
    [Petruchio strikes him]

Kate   Patience, I pray you, 'twas a fault unwilling.

---

103.   *peasant:* rascal.

       swain: peasant, person of low rank.

       whoreson: bastard.

       malt-horse drudge: literally a horse attached to a
       treadmill that grinds malt; stupid slave.

104.   *park:* grounds of a country house.

107.   *unpink'd:* undecorated.

108.   *link:* blacking from a torch.

109.   *sheathing:* process of having a sheath made.

117.   *Soud:* noise made by a very tired hungry person.

119.   *When:* How long must I wait?

123.   *mend . . . other:* do more careful when removing the
       other boot.

130.   *it:* the basin of water.

131.   *unwilling:* involuntary.

Petruchio A whoreson, beetle-headed, flap-ear'd knave!
  Come, Kate, sit down. I know you have a stomach.
  Will you give thanks, sweet Kate, or else shall I?—
  What's this? Mutton?   135

First Servant Ay.

Petruchio Who brought it?

Peter I.

Petruchio 'Tis burnt; and so is all the meat.
  What dogs are these? Where is the rascal cook?   140
  How durst you, villains, bring it from the dresser
  And serve it thus to me that love it not?
  [Throws the meat, etc., at them]
  There, take it to you, trenchers, cups, and all!
  [He throws the food and dishes at them]
  You heedless joltheads and unmanner'd slaves!
  What, do you grumble? I'll be with you straight.   145
  [Exeunt Servants]

Kate I pray you, husband, be not so disquiet.
  The meat was well, if you were so contented.

Petruchio I tell thee, Kate, 'twas burnt and dried away,
  And I expressly am forbid to touch it,
  For it engenders choler, planteth anger,   150
  And better 'twere that both of us did fast
  Since, of ourselves, ourselves are choleric,
  Than feed it with such over-roasted flesh.
  Be patient. Tomorrow 't shall be mended,
  And for this night we'll fast for company.   155
  Come, I will bring thee to thy bridal chamber.
  [Exeunt PETRUCHIO, KATE, and CURTIS]
  [Enter SERVANTS severally]

Nathaniel Peter, didst ever see the like?

Peter He kills her in her own humour.
  [Enter CURTIS]

Grumio Where is he?

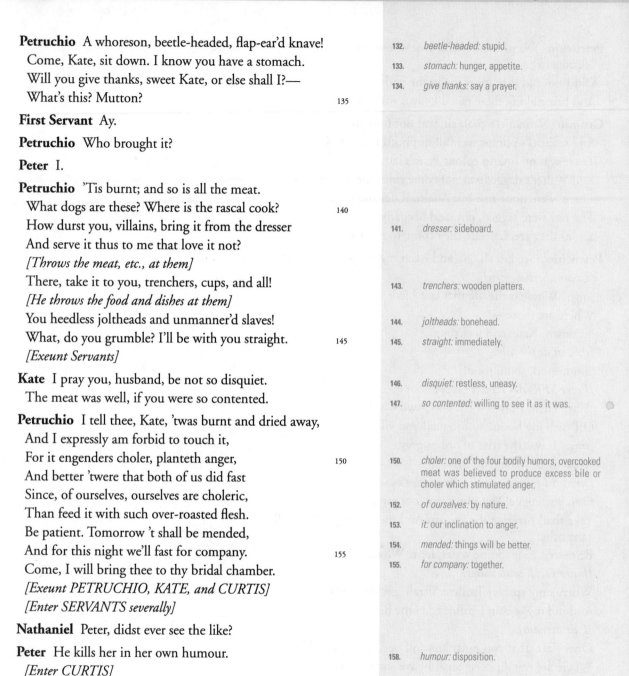

132. *beetle-headed:* stupid.

133. *stomach:* hunger, appetite.

134. *give thanks:* say a prayer.

141. *dresser:* sideboard.

143. *trenchers:* wooden platters.

144. *joltheads:* bonehead.

145. *straight:* immediately.

146. *disquiet:* restless, uneasy.

147. *so contented:* willing to see it as it was.

150. *choler:* one of the four bodily humors, overcooked meat was believed to produce excess bile or choler which stimulated anger.

152. *of ourselves:* by nature.

153. *it:* our inclination to anger.

154. *mended:* things will be better.

155. *for company:* together.

158. *humour:* disposition.

Curtis In her chamber, making a sermon of continency
    to her,   160
And rails and swears and rates, that she, poor soul,
Knows not which way to stand, to look, to speak,
And sits as one new risen from a dream.
Away, away, for he is coming hither!
[Exeunt]
[Enter PETRUCHIO]

Petruchio Thus have I politicly begun my reign,   165
And 'tis my hope to end successfully.
My falcon now is sharp and passing empty.
And till she stoop, she must not be full-gorg'd,
For then she never looks upon her lure.   *UNTRAINED FALCON*
Another way I have to man my haggard,   170
To make her come and know her keeper's call.
That is, to watch her, as we watch these kites
That bate and beat and will not be obedient.
She ate no meat today, nor none shall eat.
Last night she slept not, nor tonight she shall not.   175
As with the meat, some undeserved fault
I'll find about the making of the bed,
And here I'll fling the pillow, there the bolster,
This way the coverlet, another way the sheets.
Ay, and amid this hurly I intend   180
That all is done in reverend care of her.
And, in conclusion, she shall watch all night,
And, if she chance to nod, I'll rail and brawl,
And with the clamour keep her still awake.
This is a way to kill a wife with kindness.   185
And thus I'll curb her mad and headstrong humour.
He that knows better how to tame a shrew,
Now let him speak; 'tis charity to show.   188
[Exit]

160. *continency:* self-restraint.

161. *rails:* scolds.
    rates: berates.

165. *politicly:* with a calculated plan.

167. *falcon:* hawk trained for hunting.
    sharp: hungry.
    passing: extremely, completely.

168. *stoop:* fly directly to the keeper or the prey.
    full-gorg'd: fully fed.

169. *lure:* the bait held by the keeper.

170. *man my haggard:* train my falcon.

172. *watch her:* force her to remain awake.
    kites: small falcons.

173. *bate:* beat their wings.

178. *bolster:* cushion extending the width of the bed as under support for pillows.

180. *hurly:* uproar, commotion.
    intend: profess, propose.

181. *reverend:* respectful.

182. *watch:* kept awake.

183. *brawl:* noisy quarrel.

188. *show:* reveal.

COMMENTARY

Act IV of *The Taming of the Shrew* illustrates the methods used by Petruchio in his attempt to tame Kate. The animal imagery in the play is heavily concentrated in the following scenes, but even the title of the play, which includes the first example of animal imagery, reveals some insight into what is really happening in the play generally and in this Act specifically. Taming is of course what is done to wild animals to bring them under control. A shrew, however, is a small, mouse-like creature with an unmerited reputation as being vicious and venomous. What is the real necessity of taming a shrew? The play on the word "shrew," meaning both a scold and a harmless "mouse," is a way of revealing Kate's true temperament. How others perceive her is not necessarily who she really is and taming is not necessarily what she needs.

Mr. Atkins and Miss Cross, of the Theatre of Royal Birmingham, appear as Grumio and Curtis in this unattributed engraving.
Mary Evans Picture Library

Home sweet home

Act IV, Scene 1 begins with great noise and commotion. Grumio has come before his master to make sure that the house is ready for Petruchio's new bride. All of the servants are interested in their new mistress and press Grumio for details. The trip from Padua to Petruchio's country home has been exceedingly cold and wet. During the trip, Kate's horse fell and Petruchio left her there while he berated Grumio for allowing the horse to stumble. Shakespeare often uses a journey or a trip through a natural setting to indicate not only the passage from one place to the next but also a passage from one life experience to the next. The journey is usually one of enlightenment where the traveler learns important lessons that change his or her life in drastic ways. Note that this particular journey is one taken in the darkness, across slippery ground, and through very harsh weather.

According to Grumio, Petruchio has been uncharacteristically cruel and abrasive on the journey to the country and as his entrance into his home confirms, his temper has not improved. He immediately confronts his servants, criticizing them because of the way they have greeted Kate. When Petruchio's servant fails to remove his boots to his liking, he hits the servant and sends him running. Petruchio is dissatisfied with the dinner that the cook has prepared and despite Kate's enormous hunger, Petruchio, much to Kate's consternation, throws the food and the dishes at his servants. Several other servants feel the wrath of Petruchio's fist and Kate is moved to beg Petruchio to show more patience towards his staff.

Again, Petruchio's actions can be construed in several different ways. One point of view would be that with his own shrewish behavior, Petruchio is continuing what he started at the wedding, illustrating to Kate her own behavior. Even Peter, Petruchio's servant, sees through his master's performance saying, "He kills her in her own humor." By the compassion Kate shows to Petruchio's servants, it would seem that Kate may not only be showing her true nature, but she may also be becoming aware of how her actions affect those around her. By making Kate and his servants the brunt of his fury, Petruchio has been able to break through at least a portion of Kate's defenses by enabling her to recognize herself in his rage. By showing Kate her own behavior, Petruchio appeals to her innate intelligence and Kate can move outside of herself to feel empathy for others and perhaps even see some method in Petruchio's madness. On the other hand, some critics see Petruchio's actions as a declaration of his omnipotent power and authority. His violence is a lesson to Kate that he is master of his household and that she is expected do as he asks, when he asks, or risk the painful consequences.

The Taming of a shrew and a falcon

The Taming of the Shrew has been a difficult play to adapt to the concerns of the twenty-first century. The debate concerning Petruchio's true motivations usually falls into two very distinct camps. Many feel that Petruchio is an abusive manipulator out to break Kate's spirit and force her into submission, while others see Petruchio's taming of Kate in a more humanistic light. Some feminist scholars insist that Petruchio diminishes Kate to an animal or a sub-human, capable of learning only through deprivation of food and rest. On the basis of fear and her husband's complete control of her thoughts and environment, she exists solely for his masculine pleasure. Others argue, based on the fact that Petruchio does not rape Kate or physically abuse her in any other way, that Petruchio sees Kate not as an animal to be used, but a wild spirit that can be taught for her own good how to exist peacefully in a harmonious society. Others see Petruchio as someone who teaches Kate the benefit of play and how to assume the role of conformity when the situation calls for it.

Petruchio's monologue at the end of this scene may shed some light on his true intentions. In the first few lines of his monologue, Petruchio uses the extended metaphor of falconry to explain his methods for transforming Kate from a wild bird into a prize-winning hawk. The art of falconry can be traced back to the Middle East as far as 2000 B.C., but the activity found its way to medieval England where it was a favored sport for well over four centuries.

Hunting with birds was very popular in England and having your own falcon was seen as a status symbol. The birds were trained to catch prey both on the ground and in the air, but the true sport was having the bird catch the prey in the air. While training a falcon, the teacher first went through a process called *manning.*

PETRUCHIO, PRETENDING TO FIND FAULT WITH EVERY DISH, THREW THE MEAT ABOUT THE FLOOR

A painting of Petruchio, 1909.
Mary Evans Picture Library

This process allowed the bird to get used to its master and usually involved withholding food and sleep. During the breaking of a falcon, which could take more than two days, the master would stay with his bird, soothing it, as he also refrained from food and sleep, until the bird no longer attacked him. Writing in *Country Contentments,* published in 1615, Gervase Markham describes the procedure of training a falcon: "All hawks generally are manned after one manner, that is to say, by watching and keeping them from sleep, by a continual carrying of them upon your fist, and by a most familiar stroking and playing with them, with the wing of a dead

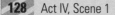

fowl or such like, and by often gazing and looking at them in the face, with a loving and gentle countenance and so making them acquainted with man, Petruchio's taming of Kate will take the same loving diligence of a falconer and will result in an intense emotional attachment between Kate and Petruchio that will enable the two to work together.

Barry Kyle made this point very clearly in his 1982 production of the play for the RST. Alum Armstrong, playing Petruchio, delivered this speech with a real falcon, hooded and perched on his arm. At the end of the speech, Petruchio removed the hood from the falcon and she would gently shake her bells. The imagery is of course to reinforce the fact that Petruchio did not mean to hurt Kate but to rather free her from her anger and brutality.

Petruchio, like a falconer training a new bird, intends to keep Kate hungry and sleepless, not to punish her, but to establish the love and trust necessary between a husband and wife. He says that everything he does is "done in reverend care of her" concluding that "This is a way to kill a wife with kindness." Petruchio will impart to Kate the wisdom that is essential if she is to take a productive position in the existing social order.

Petruchio at the Feast, a painting from Charles Folkard in "The Children's Shakespeare", 1911. Mary Evans Picture Library

Act IV, Scene 2

Tranio, Lucentio, and Bianca are thrilled to hear that Hortensio has decided to marry a wealthy widow. Needing someone to pretend to be Lucentio's father so that they may confirm Lucentio has the money he says he does, Biondello convinces a pedant to pretend to be Lucentio's father, Vincentio.

ACT IV, SCENE 2
Padua. Before BAPTISTA'S house.

[Enter TRANIO and HORTENSIO]

Tranio Is 't possible, friend Litio, that Mistress Bianca   1
Doth fancy any other but Lucentio?
I tell you, sir, she bears me fair in hand.

Hortensio Sir, to satisfy you in what I have said,
Stand by, and mark the manner of his teaching.   5
[They stand aside]
[Enter BIANCA and LUCENTIO, as Cambio]

Lucentio Now mistress, profit you in what you read?

Bianca What, master, read you? First resolve me that.

Lucentio I read that I profess, *the Art to Love*.

Bianca And may you prove, sir, master of your art!

Lucentio While you, sweet dear, prove mistress of my heart. 10
[Bianca and Lucentio move aside, kissing and courting]

Hortensio Quick proceeders, marry! Now tell me, I pray,
You that durst swear that your Mistress Bianca
Lov'd none in the world so well as Lucentio.

Tranio O despiteful love, unconstant womankind!
I tell thee, Litio, this is wonderful!   15

Hortensio Mistake no more. I am not Litio,
Nor a musician as I seem to be,
But one that scorn to live in this disguise
For such a one as leaves a gentleman
And makes a god of such a cullion.   20
Know, sir, that I am call'd Hortensio.

Tranio Signior Hortensio, I have often heard
Of your entire affection to Bianca,
And since mine eyes are witness of her lightness,

I will with you, if you be so contented,   25
Forswear Bianca and her love forever.

Hortensio See, how they kiss and court! Signior Lucentio,
Here is my hand, and here I firmly vow
Never to woo her more, but do forswear her
As one unworthy all the former favours   30
That I have fondly flatter'd her withal.

Tranio And here I take the like unfeigned oath,
Never to marry with her, though she would entreat.
Fie on her! See how beastly she doth court him!

Hortensio Would all the world but he had quite forsworn!35
For me, that I may surely keep mine oath,
I will be married to a wealtlly widow
Ere three days pass, which hath as long lov'd me
As I have lov'd this proud disdainful haggard.
And so farewell, Signior Lucentio.   40
Kindness in women, not their beauteous looks,
Shall win my love, and so I take my leave,
In resolution as I swore before.

[Exit HORTENSIO. LUCENTIO and BIANCA advance]

Tranio Mistress Bianca, bless you with such grace
As 'longeth to a lover's blessed case!   45
Nay, I have ta'en you napping, gentle love,
And have forsworn you with Hortensio.

Bianca Tranio, you jest. But have you both forsworn me?

Tranio Mistress, we have.

Lucentio Then we are rid of Litio.   50

Tranio I' faith, he'll have a lusty widow now
That shall be woo'd and wedded in a day.

Bianca God give him joy!

Tranio Ay, and he'll tame her.

Bianca He says so, Tranio?   55

Tranio Faith, he is gone unto the taming-school.

Bianca The taming-school! What, is there such a place?

26. *Forswear:* swear off.

30. *favours:* marks of esteem.

31. *fondly:* foolishly.
     withal: with.

34. *beastly:* shamelessly.

35. *but he:* except for Cambio.

38. *Ere:* before.
     which: who.

39. *haggard:* a wild female hawk.

43. *In resolution:* firmly determined.

45. *longeth:* belongeth.

46. *ta'en you napping:* caught you, surprised you.

Tranio Ay, mistress, and Petruchio is the master,
That teacheth tricks eleven and twenty long
To tame a shrew and charm her chattering tongue.   60
[Enter BIONDELLO, running]

Biondello O master, master! I have watch'd so long
That I am dog-weary, but at last I spied
An ancient angel coming down the hill
Will serve the turn.

Tranio What is he, Biondello?   65

Biondello Master, a mercantante or a pedant,
I know not what; but formal in apparel,
In gait and countenance surely like a father.

Lucentio And what of him, Tranio?

Tranio If he be credulous, and trust my tale,   70
I'll make him glad to seem Vincentio
And give assurance to Baptista Minola
As if he were the right Vincentio.
Take in your love, and then let me alone.
[Exeunt LUCENTIO and BIANCA]
[Enter a PEDANT]

Pedant God save you, sir!   75

Tranio And you, sir! You are welcome.
Travel you far on, or are you at the farthest?

Pedant Sir, at the farthest for a week or two,
But then up farther, and as far as Rome,
And so to Tripoli, if God lend me life.   80

Tranio What countryman, I pray?

Pedant Of Mantua.

Tranio Of Mantua, sir? Marry, God forbid! And come to
Padua, careless of your life?

Pedant My life, sir? How, I pray? For that goes hard.   85

Tranio 'Tis death for any one in Mantua
To come to Padua. Know you not the cause?
Your ships are stay'd at Venice; and the Duke
For private quarrel 'twixt your duke and him,
Hath publish'd and proclaim'd it openly.   90

---

59. *eleven and twenty long:* allusion to card game "Thirty One," meaning exactly right.

60. *charm:* silence.

62. *dog-weary:* exhausted.

63. *ancient angel:* trustworthy old man.

64. *serve the turn:* suit the purpose.

66. *mercantante:* Italian for merchant.
      pedant: school master, teacher, tutor.

68. *gait and countenance:* bearing and style.

77. *far on:* farther on.
      the farthest: the end of the journey.

81. *What countryman:* what country are you from?

84. *careless:* without regard for.

85. *goes hard:* is serious.

88. *stay'd:* held up, detained.

90. *it:* the death sentence upon citizens of Mantua.

'Tis marvel, but that you are but newly come,
You might have heard it else proclaim'd about.

Pedant Alas, sir, it is worse for me than so,
For I have bills for money by exchange
From Florence, and must here deliver them.   95

Tranio Well, sir, to do you courtesy,
This will I do, and this I will advise you.
First tell me, have you ever been at Pisa?

Pedant Ay, sir, in Pisa have I often been,
Pisa renowned for grave citizens.   100

Tranio Among them know you one Vincentio?

Pedant I know him not, but I have heard of him:
A merchant of incomparable wealth.

Tranio He is my father, sir, and sooth to say,
In countenance somewhat doth resemble you.   105

Biondello *[Aside]* As much as an apple doth an oyster, and
all one.

Tranio To save your life in this extremity,
This favour will I do you for his sake
(And think it not the worst of all your fortunes
That you are like to Sir Vincentio):   110
His name and credit shall you undertake,
And in my house you shall be friendly lodg'd.
Look that you take upon you as you should.
You understand me, sir. So shall you stay
Till you have done your business in the city.   115
If this be courtesy, sir, accept of it.

Pedant O sir, I do, and will repute you ever
The patron of my life and liberty.

Tranio Then go with me, to make the matter good.
This, by the way, I let you understand: 120
My father is here look'd for every day
To pass assurance of a dower in marriage
'Twixt me and one Baptista's daughter here.
In all these circumstances I'll instruct you.
Go with me to clothe you as becomes you.   125

    [Exeunt]

91.	*but . . . but:* except...only.
92.	*else:* otherwise.
94.	*bills:* promissory notes.
97.	*advise:* explain to.
100.	*grave:* worthy.
104.	*sooth:* truth.
106.	*all one:* no difference.
110.	*are like to:* look like.
111.	*credit:* reputation.
	undertake: adopt, assume.
113.	*take . . . should:* play your part, assume your role.
117.	*repute:* value, esteem.
119.	*make . . . good:* execute the plan.
120.	*by the way:* as we walk along.
121.	*look'd for:* expected.
122.	*pass assurance:* formally guarantee.

COMMENTARY

Act IV, Scene 2 and Act IV, Scene 4 are each constructed as *diptychs,* two scenes hinged together with a similar structure. Both scenes deal with two problems or two parts of the same problem. The second problem occurs unpredictably in the middle of the scene, requiring additional resourcefulness on the part of the conspirators. Enforcing the farcical nature of the play within the play, the action advances rapidly and the events are often outrageous and sometimes even unusual.

Identity and deception

The romantic sub-plot continues rapidly, unfolding in this scene as the jealous Hortensio brings Tranio, who is supposedly Lucentio, to see that Bianca is actually in love with Cambio, who is really Lucentio. If that isn't confusing enough, Tranio also needs to find someone who will pretend to be Vincentio, Lucentio's father, to confirm the bid Tranio, disguised as Lucentio, made for Bianca's dowry.

Cambio/Lucentio is again reading to Bianca from Ovid's *The Art of Love.* The book, as described before, is a textbook for seducers rather than a manual for romantically inclined lovers. The choice of reading matter certainly provides an ironic glimpse into Lucentio's wooing techniques and the "innocent" Bianca is enormously interested in his ability to perform the art he so closely studies. Despite his appearance as the romantic young lover, he is as interested in manipulating and conquering Bianca as Petruchio is in taming Kate. Certainly Lucentio's techniques are much calmer and subtler than Petruchio's, but the end result of wooing whether calm or boisterous is to connect with a mate.

Hortensio complains to Tranio/Lucentio about Bianca's fickleness and Tranio, thrilled for his master's sake that Hortensio is taking himself out of the race for Bianca, agrees with him that the woman is too capricious and not worth acquiring. The paradox in this conversation is that both men are hypocritically condemning Bianca for seeming to be something she isn't when the two of them are also masquerading as someone other than who they are. Even though Hortensio reveals his true identity to Tranio/Lucentio, everyone else in the scene is role-playing. Weaving the thematic tapestry that runs through the play, Shakespeare emphasizes that with both Christopher Sly and

An engraving by Kenny Meadows.
Mary Evans Picture Library

the young lovers, fact is irrelevant. Sly is not a Lord anymore than Tranio is a wealthy scholar or Hortensio is a music teacher. Bianca is not the sweet, naïve young innocent she portrays any more than Lucentio is a Latin teacher. The irony is that no one appears to question this widespread use of deceit. Bianca and Lucentio find no moral dilemma in maintaining their disguises even after Lucentio has revealed himself to Bianca and Bianca certainly does not seem to be having a crisis of conscience knowing they are deliberately deceiving her father. They are both content to fall in love with the surface exterior without making any attempt to truly know each other. Whereas Petruchio is determined to break through to what he believes is the true nature of Kate, Bianca and Lucentio are content with the mere trappings of what they think is love. Hortensio has had

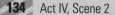

enough of this charade and vows to abandon the pursuit of Bianca to marry a wealthy widow who has loved him for a long time. In a continuation of the animal imagery, Hortensio calls Bianca a "proud disdainful haggard" and leaves for Verona to attend Petruchio's "taming school" before he marries the widow.

Biondello has finally found someone who might be able to pass for Vincentio. Biondello is not sure if the man is a "mercantante" or a pedant but Tranio is only concerned with the man's willingness to pretend to be someone he isn't. Mistaken identity is a staple in many of Shakespeare's comedies. The ruse creates laughter for the reader who knows the true identity of the characters but also adds to the theme of appearance versus reality that held such intrigue for Shakespeare in so many of his plays.

According to the text, the Pedant is traveling from Mantua to Tripoli. If this is indeed the case, he has been traveling for quite a while and still has an extremely long journey before him. He has traveled east from Mantua for 60 miles to arrive in Padua. From Padua he is planning to continue south to Rome, which is approximately 250 miles from Padua. To travel from Rome to Tripoli, the Pedant will be traveling about 600 miles, including a trip across the sea to the North African coast. Because of the nature of this trip, some scholars believe that Shakespeare intended for the pedant to be a merchant instead of a teacher, but the 1623 Folio identifies the character as "Pedant." Some editors choose to emend the text to identify the man as "Merchant."

Act IV, Scene 3

Back in Verona, Petruchio continues his taming of Kate by starving her, depriving her of sleep, and destroying her new clothes. When she continually refuses to accept Petruchio's authority, he cancels their trip back to Padua.

ACT IV, SCENE 3
A room in PETRUCHIO'S house.

[Enter KATE and GRUMIO]

Grumio No, no, forsooth, I dare not for my life.	1	
Kate The more my wrong, the more his spite appears.		
What, did he marry me to famish me?		
Beggars that come unto my father's door		
Upon entreaty have a present alms.	5	
If not, elsewhere they meet with charity.		
But I, who never knew how to entreat,		
Nor never needed that I should entreat,		
Am starv'd for meat, giddy for lack of sleep,		
With oaths kept waking, and with brawling fed.	10	
And that which spites me more than all these wants,		
He does it under name of perfect love,		
As who should say, if I should sleep or eat		
'Twere deadly sickness, or else present death.		
I prithee, go, and get me some repast;	15	
I care not what, so it be wholesome food.		
Grumio What say you to a neat's foot?		
Kate 'Tis passing good. I prithee let me have it.		
Grumio I fear it is too choleric a meat.		
How say you to a fat tripe finely broil'd?	20	
Kate I like it well. Good Grumio, fetch it me.		
Grumio I cannot tell. I fear 'tis choleric.		
What say you to a piece of beef and mustard?		
Kate A dish that I do love to feed upon.		
Grumio Ay, but the mustard is too hot a little.	25	
Kate Why then, the beef, and let the mustard rest.		
Grumio Nay then, I will not. You shall have the mustard		
Or else you get no beef of Grumio.		

NOTES

2. *my wrong:* the wrong I suffer.

5. *present:* prompt.

9. *meat:* food.

11. *spites:* angers.
    wants: deprivations.

13. *As . . . say:* as if to say.

16. so *it be:* so long as it is.

17. *neat's:* calf's.

18. *passing:* very.

19. *choleric:* anger producing.

20. *fat tripe:* the rumen of the stomach of a sheep, usually cooked with onions.

26. *let . . . rest:* do without the mustard.

Kate   Then both, or one, or anything thou wilt.

Grumio   Why then, the mustard without the beef.   30

Kate   Go, get thee gone, thou false deluding slave,
   [Beats him]
That feed'st me with the very name of meat.
Sorrow on thee, and all the pack of you
That triumph thus upon my misery!
Go, get thee gone, I say.   35
   [Enter PETRUCHIO and HORTENSIO, with meat]

Petruchio   How fares my Kate? What, sweeting, all amort?

Hortensio   Mistress, what cheer?

Kate   Faith, as cold as can be.

Petruchio   Pluck up thy spirits. Look cheerfully upon me.
Here, love; thou seest how diligent I am,   40
To dress thy meat myself, and bring it thee.
   [Sets the dish on a table]
I am sure, sweet Kate, this kindness merits thanks.
What, not a word? Nay, then thou lov'st it not,
And all my pains is sorted to no proof.
Here, take away this dish.   45

Kate   I pray you, let it stand.

Petruchio   The poorest service is repaid with thanks,
And so shall mine, before you touch the meat.

Kate   I thank you, sir.

Hortensio   Signior Petruchio, fie! you are to blame.   50
Come, Mistress Kate, I'll bear you company.

Petruchio   *[Aside]*   Eat it up all, Hortensio, if thou lovest me.
Much good do it unto thy gentle heart!
Kate, eat apace. And now, my honey love,
Will we return unto thy father's house   55
And revel it as bravely as the best,
With silken coats and caps and golden rings,
With ruffs and cuffs and farthingales and things,
With scarfs and fans and double change of bravery,
With amber bracelets, beads, and all this knavery.   60

32.	*the very name:* only the name.
36.	*sweeting:* darling, sweetheart.
	all amort: depressed, sick to death.
37.	*what cheer:* How are you?
41.	*dress thy meat:* prepare your food.
44.	*pains:* trouble, labor.
	is sorted to no proof: comes to nothing.
46.	*stand:* stay.
50.	*blame:* at fault.
54.	*apace:* immediately.
56.	*bravely:* splendidly.
58.	*ruffs:* starched wheel-like collars.
	farthingales: hooped petticoats.
59.	*bravery:* splendid dress.
60.	*knavery:* tricks of dress.

What, hast thou din'd? The tailor stays thy leisure
To deck thy body with his ruffling treasure.
[Enter TAILOR]
Come, tailor, let us see these ornaments.
Lay forth the gown.
[Enter HABERDASHER]
What news with you, sir?   65

Haberdasher Here is the cap your Worship did bespeak.

Petruchio Why, this was moulded on a porringer!
A velvet dish! Fie, fie, 'tis lewd and filthy.
Why, 'tis a cockle or a walnutshell,
A knack, a toy, a trick, a baby's cap.   70
Away with it! Come, let me have a bigger.

Kate I'll have no bigger. This doth fit the time,
And gentlewomen wear such caps as these.

Petruchio When you are gentle, you shall have one too,
And not till then.   75

Hortensio *[Aside]* That will not be in haste.

Kate Why, sir, I trust I may have leave to speak,
And speak I will. I am no child, no babe.
Your betters have endur'd me say my mind,
And if you cannot, best you stop your ears.   80
My tongue will tell the anger of my heart,
Or else my heart, concealing it, will break,
And, rather than it shall, I will be free
Even to the uttermost, as I please, in words.

Petruchio Why, thou say'st true. It is a paltry cap,   85
A custard-coffin, a bauble, a silken pie.
I love thee well in that thou lik'st it not.

Kate Love me, or love me not, I like the cap,
And it I will have, or I will have none.
[Exit HABERDASHER]

Petruchio Thy gown? Why, ay. Come, tailor, let us see't.   90
O mercy God, what masquing stuff is here?
What's this? A sleeve? 'Tis like a demi-cannon.
What, up and down carv'd like an apple tart?
Here's snip and nip and cut and slish and slash,

61.	*stays:* awaits.
	leisure: pleasure.
62.	*ruffling:* ruffled.
SD:	*Haberdasher:* hat maker.
66.	*bespeak:* order.
67.	*porringer:* porridge bowl.
68.	*lewd:* vulgar.
	filthy: disgusting.
69.	*cockle:* cockleshell.
70.	*knack:* knickknack.
	toy/trick: a play thing.
72.	*fit the time:* is now in fashion.
77.	*leave:* permission.
79.	*endur'd me to say:* allowed me to speak.
86.	*custard-coffin:* crust on a custard.
91.	*masquing stuff:* costumes for people who went to costume parties.
92.	*demi-cannon:* large cannon.
93.	*up and down:* entirely.

Like to a censer in a barber's shop.　　　　　　　95
Why, what a devil's name, tailor, call'st thou this?

Hortensio *[Aside]* I see she's like to have neither cap nor
gown.

Tailor You bid me make it orderly and well,
According to the fashion and the time.

Petruchio Marry, and did. But if you be remember'd,　100
I did not bid you mar it to the time.
Go, hop me over every kennel home,
For you shall hop without my custom, sir.
I'll none of it. Hence, make your best of it.

Kate I never saw a better fashion'd gown,　　　　105
More quaint, more pleasing, nor more commendable.
Belike you mean to make a puppet of me.

Petruchio Why, true, he means to make a puppet of thee.

Tailor She says your Worship means to make a puppet of her.

Petruchio O monstrous arrogance! Thou liest, thou thread,　110
Thou thimble,
Thou yard, three-quarters, half-yard, quarter, nail!
Thou flea, thou nit, thou winter-cricket thou!
Brav'd in mine own house with a skein of thread?
Away, thou rag, thou quantity, thou remnant,　　115
Or I shall so be-mete thee with thy yard
As thou shalt think on prating whilst thou liv'st!
I tell thee, I, that thou hast marr'd her gown.

Tailor Your Worship is deceiv'd. The gown is made
Just as my master had direction.　　　　　　　120
Grumio gave order how it should be done.

Grumio I gave him no order. I gave him the stuff.

Tailor But how did you desire it should be made?

Grumio Marry, sir, with needle and thread.

Tailor But did you not request to have it cut?　　　125

Grumio Thou hast faced many things.

Tailor I have.

Grumio Face not me. Thou hast braved many men; brave
not me.

95.　*censer:* perfuming pan with a perforated lid.

96.　*what a devil's name:* in the name of the devil.

97.　*like:* likely.

100.　*Marry, and did:* Indeed, I did.
　　　be remember'd: remember.

102.　*kennel:* gutter.

103.　*hop:* lose.
　　　custom: trade.

106.　*quaint:* dainty, elegant.

107.　*Belike:* perhaps.
　　　puppet: plaything.

112.　*yard:* yardstick.
　　　quarter: quarter yard.
　　　nail: one-sixteenth yard.

113.　*nit:* louse egg.

114.　*Brav'd:* defied.
　　　with: by.

115.　*quantity:* fragment.

116.　*be-mete:* measure, beat, thrash.

117.　*prating:* chattering.

122.　*stuff:* material for the gown.

126.　*faced:* sewed the trim.

128.　*Face:* challenge.
　　　braved: equipped in splendid finery.
　　　brave: defy.

I will neither be fac'd nor brav'd. I say unto thee, I bid thy
  master cut out the gown, but I did not bid him cut it to
    pieces.   130
  Ergo, thou liest.

Tailor Why, here is the note of the fashion to testify.
[he shows the dress order]

Petruchio Read it.

Grumio The note lies in's throat, if he say I said so.

Tailor *[reading]* "Imprimis, a loose-bodied gown."   135

Grumio Master, if ever I said "loose-bodied gown," sew me
  in the
  skirts of it and beat me to death with a bottom of brown
    thread.
  I said, "a gown."

Petruchio Proceed.

Tailor "With a small compassed cape."   140

Grumio I confess the cape.

Tailor "With a trunk sleeve."

Grumio I confess two sleeves.

Tailor "The sleeves curiously cut."

Petruchio Ay, there's the villainy.   145

Grumio Error i' the bill, sir; error i' the bill! I commanded
  the
  sleeves should be cut out and sew'd up again, and that I'll
  prove upon thee, though thy little finger be armed in a
    thimble.

Tailor This is true that I say. An I had thee in place where,
  thou
  shouldst know it.   150

Grumio I am for thee straight. Take thou the bill, give me
  thy
  mete-yard, and spare not me.

Hortensio God-a-mercy, Grumio! Then he shall have no
  odds.

Petruchio Well, sir, in brief, the gown is not for me.

Grumio You are i' the right, sir, 'tis for my mistress.   155

---

131. *Ergo:* Latin for "therefore."

132. *note . . . fashion:* written instructions for the gown.

134. *in's:* in his.

135. *Imprimis:* Latin for "first."

    loose-bodied gown: dresses worn by prostitutes with pun on word "loose."

137. *bottom:* bobbin, spool.

140. *small compassed:* a small semicircle.

142. *trunk sleeve:* wide sleeve.

144. *curiously:* painstakingly.

148. *prove upon thee:* make good in a fight.

149. *An:* if.

    place where: a fitting place.

151. *straight:* immediately.

152. *mete-yard:* measuring stick.

153. *odds:* advantage.

Petruchio Go, take it up unto thy master's use.

Grumio Villain, not for thy life! Take up my mistress' gown for

thy master's use!

Petruchio Why, sir, what's your conceit in that?

Grumio O, sir, the conceit is deeper than you think for.   160
Take up my mistress' gown to his master's use!
O, fie, fie, fie!

Petruchio *[Aside]* Hortensio, say thou wilt see the tailor paid.
[To Tailor] Go, take it hence. Be gone, and say no more.

Hortensio *[Aside to Tailor]* Tailor, I'll pay thee for thy gown tomorrow.   165
Take no unkindness of his hasty words.
Away, I say! Commend me to thy master.
[Exit TAILOR]

Petruchio Well, come, my Kate, we will unto your father's,
Even in these honest mean habiliments.
Our purses shall be proud, our garments poor,   170
For 'tis the mind that makes the body rich,
And as the sun breaks through the darkest clouds,
So honour peereth in the meanest habit.
What, is the jay more precious than the lark
Because his feathers are more beautiful?   175
Or is the adder better than the eel
Because his painted skin contents the eye?
O no, good Kate. Neither art thou the worse
For this poor furniture and mean array.
If thou account'st it shame, lay it on me,   180
And therefore frolic! We will hence forthwith
To feast and sport us at thy father's house.
[to Grumio] Go, call my men, and let us straight to him,
And bring our horses unto Long-lane end.
There will we mount, and thither walk on foot.   185
Let's see, I think 'tis now some seven o'clock,
And well we may come there by dinnertime.

159. *conceit:* idea.
160. *think for:* expect.

166. *no unkindness of:* on offence at.

169. *mean habiliments:* common clothes.

173. *peereth in:* shows through.
habit: clothes.

176. *adder:* snake.

179. *mean array:* plain clothes.
180. *lay:* blame.

181. *sport:* entertain.

186. *some:* about.
187. *dinnertime:* noon.

Kate I dare assure you, sir, 'tis almost two,
  And 'twill be suppertime ere you come there.

Petruchio It shall be seven ere I go to horse.   190
  Look what I speak, or do, or think to do,
  You are still crossing it. Sirs, let't alone.
  I will not go today, and ere I do,
  It shall be what o'clock I say it is.

Hortensio Why, so, this gallant will command the sun!   195
  [Exeunt]

189.   *suppertime:* about 5:30 p.m.

191.   *Look what:* whatever.

192.   *crossing:* opposing.

       let't alone: stop making preparations to leave.

COMMENTARY

Several days have passed and Kate has had very little food or sleep. She begs Grumio for something to eat, explaining to him that beggars are treated more charitably at her father's house than she is in her own. Grumio merely teases her with the prospect of food and when Kate has had enough, she beats him. Obviously, Kate still has a few lessons to learn before she can graduate from Petruchio's "taming school" but despite his treatment of her in the past few days, Petruchio claims "He does it under name of perfect love."

The motivation of Petruchio

The question raised is, of course, that of Petruchio's true motivations. Is his treatment of Kate in the name of love as he says or in his pursuit of total dominance? In her article, "Civilizing Subordination: Domestic Violence and *The Taming of the Shrew*," published in *Shakespeare Quarterly* (vol. 48, 1997), Emily Detmer considers Petruchio's taming techniques to be nothing less than domestic violence, a form of brutality that goes well beyond physical abuse to include intimidation, seclusion, emotional cruelty, economic manipulation, and sexual assault. According to Detmer, Petruchio's methods for controlling Kate are very similar to the Stockholm Syndrome, a condition originally applied to hostage situations in the twentieth century but later studied and applied to domestic abuse. In both hostage situations and in situations involving domestic abuse, the victim's thoughts and actions are controlled through fear and intimidation. The Stockholm Syndrome occurs when a person threatens another's survival and is perceived by the victim as willing and able to carry out the threat. The threatening person isolates the victim from outsiders and makes it seem impossible for the victim to escape. In the midst of the abuse, the abuser will show the other person a certain amount of kindness, confusing the victim who, after time, feels the only person she can rely on is her abuser.

Comparing Petruchio's actions in the light of the Stockholm Syndrome, the reader could certainly be warranted in identifying Petruchio as the typically abusive husband. After the wedding ceremony, he takes Kate unwillingly into the country, miles away from her family and friends, into an unfamiliar situation where she is surrounded by seemingly hostile entities such as Grumio. By beating his servants in her presence, Kate can only assume that he will eventually do the same to her and, by withholding food and sleep, Petruchio not only weakens Kate's defenses but forces her to rely on him for all of her basic necessities, including life itself. Petruchio confuses Kate by being late to the wedding but then "rescuing" her by showing up. He gives her good food and beautiful clothes only to snatch them away for what he explains is her own good. According to Detmer, these acts of supposed kindness by Petruchio are nothing more than opportunities to deprive Kate and reestablish his control of her environment. This somewhat eases the intense emotional distress the abuser has produced, creating the perfect conditions for emotional dependency. Just as Kate will begin experimenting with ways of pleasing Petruchio, at this point, the victim will begin actively looking for ways to satisfy her captor.

Another opinion concerning Petruchio's treatment of Kate is that he is teaching her an invaluable lesson, one that will make her a functioning and accepted member of society. Education is on a certain level, a way of establishing conformity based on the society's ideal model of acceptable behavior. Undoubtedly the Elizabethan attitude towards education was not the encouragement of free thought but rather to be introduced to a standardized curriculum, approved by the general populace with the final outcome meant to be that students became literate and valuable citizens. Kate does not possess the standard social literacy expected of women in Elizabethan society and Petruchio has taken it upon himself to instruct her on her own possibilities.

Both theories, Kate as the victim of domestic abuse or Kate as the recipient of Petruchio's humanistic education, are valid interpretations and have worked on the stage. A very clear example of the domestic abuse version of the play was Charles Marowitz's collage reworking of the play. In this adaptation, Kate was raped, brutalized, and returned to her father's home in chains, a woman driven to madness by the cruelty she had undergone. Other productions, such as George Devine's production of the play at the Royal Shakespeare Theatre in 1953, bring to life a much more humanistic character. As reported in *The Times* (June 10, 1953), Marius Goring, who played Petruchio in Devine's production, portrayed a Petruchio who perceives the good nature of the girl he has undertaken to woo for her money and is resolved to bring it to life by his own methods, which are admittedly eccentric but carried out without a particle of ill-humor.

Kate's viewpoint

It is also possible to look at this scene from the middle ground, and to do this the reader must look at the events not from Petruchio's perspective so much as from Kate's. Whatever Petruchio's motivations, this woman must be frightened and confused beyond words. At the promise of marriage, Kate surely had some preconceived notions of what her life would be like. Perhaps she was thrilled to be getting away from her neglectful father and hypocritical sister, but certainly she never for a moment considered that she would be spending her honeymoon with a crazed man, in a chaotic house, enduring starvation and sleep deprivation. Her confusion is clear in her first speech when she

struggles to find some comfort or explanation from Grumio. When Petruchio enters with food for her he will not let her eat until she learns to say "thank you" and even then he tells Hortensio to eat it all up before Kate can have any. The haberdasher and tailor enter immediately and once again Kate is tempted with beautiful clothes only to have them torn to pieces.

Compared to the first Act of the play, Kate's silence in the remainder of the play has been almost palatable. Except for a brief show of rebelliousness when Petruchio refused to stay for the wedding banquet, Kate has been uncharacteristically quiet. Granted, she has slapped Grumio, but her words, the weapons that have provided her protection up to this moment, have been put aside. When Petruchio refuses to let Kate have the new cap, she finally breaks down crying, "Why, sir, I trust I may have leave to speak,/And speak I will." Kate wants to believe that Petruchio is telling the truth when he tells her that he is doing what he is doing to her out of perfect love. She has tried to change her behavior and please Petruchio but this is the final straw. Petruchio may control her body and her environment but she tries to explain to him that she must own her words: "My tongue will tell the anger of my heart,/Or else my heart, concealing it, will break." No one has ever before paid attention to Kate unless she expressed herself in a verbally violent way. She knows no other way of expressing her anger and frustration and realizes she will die if she cannot speak. She demands that she "will be free/Even to the uttermost, as I please, in words."

Kate has made her stand but Petruchio ignores her. He turns her statement into a comment on the worthlessness of the hat and proceeds to call in the tailor. In the past, Kate's words would have never been ignored. The reaction to her words may have been negative, but there was a reaction. Without a reaction, Kate is rendered powerless, and without her power she has no choice but to surrender.

In this state of powerlessness, Kate must watch as her new gown is torn to bits. This scene was very effectively staged in Jonathan Miller's production at the Royal Shakespeare Theatre in 1987. Kate was hoisted on to what looked like a pedestal and the new gown was placed on her. As Petruchio became more and more angry with the tailor and the design of the dress he began tearing the dress, piece by piece, off of Kate.

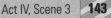

The action made it seem as if Kate were being dismembered and as the men argued over the dress, Kate stood hushed, unnoticed, and devoid of power. By the time the scene was over, Kate was wearing only a white smock, which had been stained and soiled as the men tore the dress from her.

As possible proof of Petruchio's more humanistic nature, in an aside, he assures the tailor that he will be paid and Hortensio entreats him to "Take no unkindness of his hasty words." Apparently this incident has been another lesson taught for Kate's benefit. After everyone has left, Petruchio sits quietly with Kate and explains to her that it is not clothes but "the mind that makes the body rich." Again using animal imagery, comparing the jay to the lark and the adder to the eel, Petruchio wishes Kate to understand that what is important is a person's character. As Shakespeare has made very clear in other parts of this play, a person cannot be judged accurately by his clothing.

Petruchio informs Kate that it is now seven o'clock and that they should be at her father's house by noon. Kate contradicts him, saying it is already two o'clock and that they may get there in time for supper. Although Kate does not scream and yell or throw a tantrum, she has not yet learned the game that Petruchio is trying to teach her. There is almost a sigh of frustration and even resignation in his final speech: "Look what I speak, or do, or think to do,/You are still crossing it. Sirs, let 't alone." Petruchio is not one to give up, however, and he finishes by saying, "I will not go today, and, ere I do,/It shall be what o'clock I say it is."

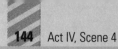

Act IV, Scene 4

The Pedant takes on his role as Lucentio's father Vincentio, and is introduced to Baptista. The Pedant tells Baptista that he agrees to the financial arrangements for the marriage, and the men agree to meet at Tranio's house to continue planning the wedding. Baptista sends Cambio/Lucentio to tell Bianca that the wedding arrangements are being made and Biondello informs Lucentio that now is the perfect time for him to marry Bianca. Lucentio agrees, and Biondello goes off to find a priest.

ACT IV, SCENE 4
Padua. Before BAPTISTA'S house.

[Enter TRANIO,[as Lucentio] and the PEDANT dressed like VINCENTIO]

Tranio Sir, this is the house. Please it you that I call?　　1

Pedant Ay, what else? And but I be deceived,
Signior Baptista may remember me,
Near twenty years ago in Genoa,
Where we were lodgers at the Pegasus.　　5

Tranio 'Tis well. And hold your own in any case
With such austerity as 'longeth to a father.

Pedant I warrant you.
[Enter BIONDELLO]
But, sir, here comes your boy.
'Twere good he were school'd.　　10

Tranio Fear you not him. Sirrah Biondello,
Now do your duty throughly, I advise you.
Imagine 'twere the right Vincentio.

Biondello Tut! Fear not me.

Tranio But hast thou done thy errand to Baptista?　　15

Biondello I told him that your father was at Venice,
And that you look'd for him this day in Padua.

Tranio Thou'rt a tall fellow. Hold thee that to drink
[gives Biondello money]
[Enter Baptista and Lucentio (as Cambio)]
Here comes Baptista. Set your countenance, sir.
Signior Baptista, you are happily met.　　20
[To the PEDANT] Sir, this is the gentleman I told you of.
I pray you stand good father to me now.
Give me Bianca for my patrimony.

NOTES

2.　*what else:* certainly.
　　And but: unless.

5.　*Pegasus:* a tavern named after the winged horse of mythology.

6.　*hold your own:* act your role.

7.　*'longeth:* belongs.

8.　*warrant:* guarantee.

10.　*school'd:* instructed.

12.　*throughly:* thoroughly.

13.　*right:* true.

17.　*look'd for:* expected.

18.　*tall:* excellent.
　　Hold . . . drink: take this money and buy yourself a drink.

20.　*happily:* opportunely.

Pedant Soft, son!
  Sir, by your leave, having come to Padua   25
  To gather in some debts, my son Lucentio
  Made me acquainted with a weighty cause
  Of love between your daughter and himself.
  And, for the good report I hear of you,
  And for the love he beareth to your daughter   30
  And she to him, to stay him not too long,
  I am content, in a good father's care,
  To have him match'd. And, if you please to like
  No worse than I, upon some agreement
  Me shall you find ready and willing   35
  With one consent to have her so bestow'd,
  For curious I cannot be with you,
  Signior Baptista, of whom I hear so well.

Baptista Sir, pardon me in what I have to say.
  Your plainness and your shortness please me well.   40
  Right true it is your son Lucentio here
  Doth love my daughter, and she loveth him,
  Or both dissemble deeply their affections.
  And therefore, if you say no more than this,
  That like a father you will deal with him   45
  And pass my daughter a sufficient dower,
  The match is made, and all is done.
  Your son shall have my daughter with consent.

Tranio I thank you, sir. Where then do you know best
  We be affied and such assurance ta'en   50
  As shall with either part's agreement stand?

Baptista Not in my house, Lucentio, for you know
  Pitchers have ears, and I have many servants.
  Besides, old Gremio is heark'ning still,
  And happily we might be interrupted.   55

Tranio Then at my lodging, an it like you.
  There doth my father lie, and there this night
  We'll pass the business privately and well.
  Send for your daughter by your servant here.
  [*he winks at Lucentio*]
  My boy shall fetch the scrivener presently.   60

24.	*Soft:* hush.
27.	*weighty cause:* serious matter.
31.	*stay:* delay.
36.	*bestow'd:* given in marriage.
37.	*curious:* too demanding.
40.	*shortness:* conciseness.
46.	*pass:* transfer to.
50.	*affied:* formally engaged.
	assurance: guarantee.
51.	*part's:* each party.
53.	*Pitchers have ears:* proverbial: we might be overheard.
54.	*heark'ning still:* listening constantly.
55.	*happily:* by chance.
56.	*an it like you:* if you prefer.
57.	*lie:* stay.
58.	*pass:* transact.
60.	*scrivener:* notary public.

The worst is this: that at so slender warning
You are like to have a thin and slender pittance.

Baptista It likes me well. Cambio, hie you home,
And bid Bianca make her ready straight.
And, if you will, tell what hath happened: 65
Lucentio's father is arriv'd in Padua,
And how she's like to be Lucentio's wife.
[exit Lucentio]

Biondello I pray the gods she may, with all my heart!

Tranio Dally not with the gods, but get thee gone.
[Exit Biondello]
Signior Baptista, shall I lead the way?   70
Welcome! One mess is like to be your cheer.
Come, sir; we will better it in Pisa.

Baptista I follow you.
[Exeunt Tranio, Pedant, and Baptista]
[Enter LUCENTIO and BIONDELLO]

Biondello Cambio!

Lucentio What say'st thou, Biondello?   75

Biondello You saw my master wink and laugh upon you?

Lucentio Biondello, what of that?

Biondello Faith, nothing; but has left me here behind to
expound
the meaning or moral of his signs and tokens.

Lucentio I pray thee, moralize them.   80

Biondello Then thus: Baptista is safe, talking with the
deceiving father of a deceitful son.

Lucentio And what of him?

Biondello His daughter is to be brought by you to the
supper.

Lucentio And then?   85

Biondello The old priest at Saint Luke's church is at your
command at all hours.

Lucentio And what of all this?

---

61. *slender warning:* short notice.

62. *pittance:* refreshment.

63. *likes:* pleases.
    hie: hurry.

64. *straight:* immediately.

67. *like:* likely.

71. *mess:* dish.
    cheer: entertainment, food and drink.

80. *moralize:* explain.

Biondello I cannot tell, except they are busied about a
counterfeit assurance. Take your assurance of her, cum
privilegio　　　　　　　90
ad imprimendum solum. To the church! Take the priest,
clerk, and
some sufficient honest witnesses.
If this be not that you look for, I have more to say,
But bid Bianca farewell forever and a day.

Lucentio Hear'st thou, Biondello?　　　　95

Biondello I cannot tarry. I knew a wench married in an
afternoon
as she went to the garden for parsley to stuff a rabbit, and so
may you, sir. And so adieu, sir. My master hath appointed
me to
go to Saint Luke's to bid the priest be ready to come
against you
come with your appendix.　　　　100
[Exit]

Lucentio I may, and will, if she be so contented.
She will be pleas'd. Then wherefore should I doubt?
Hap what hap may, I'll roundly go about her.
It shall go hard if "Cambio" go without her.　　　104
[Exit]

90.　*counterfeit assurance:* illegal marriage contract.

　cum . . . solum: "with the exclusive right to print." This quote often appeared on books of the time.

92.　*sufficient:* well to do, substantial.

100.　*against you come:* in readiness for your coming.

　appendix: addition; in this case: his wife.

102.　*wherefore:* why.

103.　*Hap what hap may:* whatever may happen.

　roundly: bluntly.

104.　*shall go hard:* will not be for lack of trying.

COMMENTARY

The theme of appearance versus reality again comes into play in this scene as the acts of deception become more and more complicated. The Pedant has been costumed in rich clothes so that he may properly impersonate Lucentio's father, Vincentio, and Tranio, still disguised as Lucentio, escorts the Pedant to Baptista's home so that the two men may agree on Bianca's dowry. While Hortensio and Lucentio have taken on the disguise of teachers, the only real teacher in the play, the Pedant, has taken on the disguise of an aristocrat. The role reversals continue, but soon enough the consequences for the deceptions must be faced.

An important concept

There are certain concepts that arise in much of the literature coming out of the Renaissance and these ideas play important parts in all of Shakespeare's plays, including *The Taming of the Shrew*.

The Great Chain of Being was discussed earlier in a commentary as it applied to Kate and Petruchio. The theory also applies to Lucentio and Bianca but will play itself out in a manner that is opposite to that of Kate and Petruchio. Whereas Petruchio must tame Kate to establish order in his home and thus in his universe, Lucentio erroneously believes that his universe is already

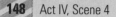

orderly. By ignoring the mutability of the world, Lucentio sets himself up for a fall. In Renaissance England, the common belief was that everything was apt to change and thus the only thing that could truly be considered stable was God. Putting complete faith into something other than God was considered a flaw in human nature, and a flawed existence could only lead to disorder and chaos. Lucentio has placed his hopes and dreams on Bianca, a woman as changing and unstable as any. After their marriage, Lucentio will see the error of his ways as his world-view is shaken by Bianca's transformation from feminine perfection to shrew.

Another important concept explored in Renaissance literature concerns reason versus passion. According to Elizabethan thought, reason, the ability to think clearly and then make decisions based on one's thoughts, is the greatest gift that God gave to man. If man was made in the image of God and God is Reason, then man was meant to be a reasonable creature, separate from the animals that are ruled solely by instincts and passions. Reason should control the passions, but when reason fails and one allows passion to take over, causing one to act irrationally, the reasonable man acts like an unreasonable animal and thus fails in his obligation to God. Therefore one not only commits a sin against God but also lowers himself on the Great Chain of Being. Lucentio has allowed his immense passion for Bianca to cloud his ability to reason. He acts irrationally by lying, disguising himself, and deceiving those around him, and in doing so, abandons reasonable behavior. Reason was often depicted as a masculine trait while passion was considered feminine. As Lucentio has given in to his passions, he loses his masculine authority and as Bianca remains rational, she will assume the role of authority in the relationship as the dynamics of power change and are reversed between the two of

them. Lucentio's punishment for his irrational deeds will be the one thing that has caused him to be irrational: the illusory Bianca.

Even though these issues seem dark and foreboding, they were often portrayed in Renaissance literature in a humorous manner, as is seen in *The Taming of the Shrew*. The story line of Renaissance comedy often derives from the breach of some standard of behavior. If a character conducts himself irrationally, the consequences may seem funny, as when Lucentio and Hortensio find themselves with shrewish wives.

Baptista agrees to the dowry offered by the disguised Pedant, and the two men, accompanied by Tranio, still masquerading as Lucentio, exit to discuss the matter more formally. Baptista believes that Bianca is in love with Tranio/Lucentio, "or both dissemble deeply their affections." Of course, the reader knows that almost everyone in the play is a dissembler, hiding their true natures behind a disguise, making the line humorously ironic. Biondello signals to the real Lucentio, informing him that the priest is available and that he and Bianca should leave to be married at once. Lucentio does not understand right away what Biondello is trying to say, proving once again that often the servants are much smarter and certainly more clever than their masters.

Lacking the humor and deft characterization inherent in the majority of Shakespeare's work, this scene does little more than advance the subplot. Based on these facts, some scholars conjecture that this scene was the work of a collaborator. Considering this was one of Shakespeare's early works, it is also possible that he was just learning the craft at which he would become so proficient.

Act IV, Scene 5

Petruchio and Kate begin their trip back to Padua. On the way, Kate finally understands what she must do to get along with Petruchio. On the journey, Kate, Petruchio, and Hortensio encounter the real Vincentio who is on his way to Padua to see his son Lucentio.

ACT IV, SCENE 5
A public road.

*[Enter PETRUCHIO, KATE, HORTENSIO, and
　SERVANTS]*

Petruchio Come on, i' God's name, once more toward our
　father's.　　　　　　　　　　　　　　　　　　　　　　　1
　Good Lord, how bright and goodly shines the moon!

Kate The moon? The sun! It is not moonlight now.

Petruchio I say it is the moon that shines so bright.

Kate I know it is the sun that shines so bright.　　　　5

Petruchio Now, by my mother's son, and that's myself,
　It shall be moon, or star, or what I list,
　Or e're I journey to your father's house. *[to servants]* Go on,
　and fetch our horses back again.
　Evermore cross'd and cross'd, nothing but cross'd!　10

Hortensio *[to Kate]* Say as he says, or we shall never go.

Kate Forward, I pray, since we have come so far,
　And be it moon, or sun, or what you please.
　And if you please to call it a rush candle,
　Henceforth I vow it shall be so for me.　　　　　　15

Petruchio I say it is the moon.

Kate I know it is the moon.

Petruchio Nay, then you lie. It is the blessed sun.

Kate Then God be bless'd, it is the blessed sun.
　But sun it is not when you say it is not,　　　　　20
　And the moon changes even as your mind.
　What you will have it nam'd, even that it is,
　And so it shall be so for Katherine.

Hortensio Petruchio, go thy ways, the field is won.

Petruchio Well, forward, forward! Thus the bowl
　should run,　　　　　　　　　　　　　　　　　　　25

NOTES

1.　*our father's:* Baptista's.

7.　*list:* please.

8.　*Or e'er I:* before I will ever.

10.　*cross'd:* contradicted.

14.　*rush candle:* cheap candle made by dipping rush
　　in fat.

24.　*go thy ways:* carry on.
　　field: battlefield.

25.　*bowl:* bowling ball.

And not unluckily against the bias.
But, soft! Company is coming here.
[*Enter VINCENTIO*]
[*To Vincentio*] Good-morrow, gentle mistress, where away?
Tell me, sweet Kate, and tell me truly too,
Hast thou beheld a fresher gentlewoman?   30
Such war of white and red within her cheeks!
What stars do spangle heaven with such beauty
As those two eyes become that heavenly face?
Fair lovely maid, once more good day to thee.
Sweet Kate, embrace her for her beauty's sake.   35

Hortensio 'A will make the man mad, to make a woman
   of him.

Kate Young budding virgin, fair and fresh and sweet,
Whither away, or where is thy abode?
Happy the parents of so fair a child.
Happier the man whom favourable stars   40
Allots thee for his lovely bedfellow.

Petruchio Why, how now, Kate? I hope thou art not mad!
This is a man: old, wrinkled, faded, wither'd,
And not a maiden, as thou sayst he is.

Kate Pardon, old father, my mistaking eyes   45
That have been so bedazzled with the sun
That everything I look on seemeth green.
Now I perceive thou art a reverend father.
Pardon, I pray thee, for my mad mistaking.

Petruchio Do, good old grandsire, and withal make known 50
Which way thou travellest. If along with us,
We shall be joyful of thy company.

Vincentio Fair sir, and you my merry mistress,
That with your strange encounter much amaz'd me,
My name is called Vincentio, my dwelling Pisa,   55
And bound I am to Padua, there to visit
A son of mine which long I have not seen.

Petruchio What is his name?

Vincentio Lucentio, gentle sir.

Petruchio Happily met, the happier for thy son.   60

---

26.   *against the bias:* off the natural course.

27.   *soft:* wait a minute, hush.

28.   *where away:* where are you going.

30.   *fresher:* youthful, healthy.

33.   *become:* fit.

36.   *'A:* he.

38.   *Whither away:* where are you going.

40.   *favourable stars:* good fortune.

41.   *Allots:* gives.

47.   *green:* young.

48.   *reverend:* worth of respect.

50.   *withal:* in addition.

54.   *encounter:* greeting.

And now by law as well as reverend age,
I may entitle thee my loving father.
The sister to my wife, this gentlewoman,
Thy son by this hath married. Wonder not,
Nor be not griev'd. She is of good esteem,   65
Her dowry wealthy, and of worthy birth;
Beside, so qualified as may beseem
The spouse of any noble gentleman.
Let me embrace with old Vincentio,
And wander we to see thy honest son,   70
Who will of thy arrival be full joyous.

Vincentio But is this true, or is it else your pleasure,
Like pleasant travellers, to break a jest
Upon the company you overtake?

Hortensio I do assure thee, father, so it is.   75

Petruchio Come, go along and see the truth hereof,
For our first merriment hath made thee jealous.
[Exeunt all but HORTENSIO]

Hortensio Well, Petruchio, this has put me in heart.
Have to my widow, and if she be froward,
Then hast thou taught Hortensio to be untoward.   80
[Exit]

64. *by this:* by now.
65. *esteem:* reputation.
67. *beseem:* befit.
71. *else:* instead.
72. *break a jest:* play a joke.
76. *hereof:* of it.
77. *merriment:* joke.
    jealous: suspicious.
78. *heart:* good spirits.
79. *froward:* headstrong.
80. *untoward:* unruly, stubborn.

COMMENTARY

The climax of the Kate/Petruchio story line occurs in this scene and will continue into the next as the unmasking of all the characters begins. Apparently, Kate has pleased Petruchio enough that they are finally on their way back to her father's house in Padua. In direct contrast to the weather conditions on the trip from Padua to Petruchio's country home, the weather for the trip out of the country is warm and sunny, indicating that a change for the better has taken place in both the characters and their situations.

As they stop to rest, Petruchio comments on how "bright and goodly shines the moon!" Kate, holding on to what she knows to be the truth, crosses him, declaring it to be the sun. Petruchio is angered by her comment and orders the horses turned for home. Hortensio, in an aside to Kate, entreats her to "Say as he says, or we shall never go." At that moment, Kate understands the rules of the game that Petruchio has been trying to teach her. From the stichomythic, rapid-fire repartee of the courting scene, Kate's words have become poetic and warm, exhibiting none of the sarcastic tone she has opted for in the past. Just as her words are transformed, so is she. For all intents and purposes, Kate is now "tamed."

Kate on an ass.
The Raymond Meander and Joe Mitchenson Theatre Collection

he loves her. There is a freedom in that knowledge that allows Kate to see what Petruchio has been trying to teach her all along. She does not have to adhere to the roles that society has enforced upon her. She has the power to take on any role she chooses by channeling her energies into a positive form of play.

Upon Vincentio's entrance, Petruchio gives Kate her final exam by greeting the gentleman as "gentle mistress." Kate takes up the game on her own accord and agrees that Vincentio is a "young budding virgin, fair and fresh and sweet." Seeming to delight in the game for which she has so recently learned the rules, Kate excuses her mistaking of Vincentio by saying that her eyes "have been so bedazzled with the sun/That everything I look on seemeth green." From the dark gloomy moments of the trip to the country, Kate has now awakened. Petruchio is the "sun" that has so bedazzled her eyes and with his nurturing and warmth, the world has become green again with the renewal and rebirth of the spring.

Vincentio introduces himself to the rather puzzling couple, telling them he is going to Padua to visit his son Lucentio. Petruchio informs Vincentio that Lucentio has been recently married to Baptista's daughter Bianca. There is no way Petruchio could know that Bianca and Lucentio have eloped. Their marriage occurred after Kate and Petruchio left for the country and even Hortensio, who left after Kate and Petruchio would not have known about the marriage. This is one of several inconsistencies in the play, a real indicator that this was one of Shakespeare's earlier works.

Dueling viewpoints

Certain feminist scholars would argue that Kate is not so much "tamed" as she is broken, both mentally and physically. In the context of this theory, the reader will see that because of Petruchio's violent and abusive treatment of her, Kate must find a way to stay alive in this universe of masculine power that is both threatening and dangerous. In doing so, she submits to masculine authority, choosing to believe that what a man says is correct even if it is absurd and obviously wrong. To stay alive, she suppresses her own will and her sense of reality to see the world through the eyes of her abuser.

Another theory concerning Kate's submission to Petruchio is that Kate has finally realized that Petruchio's grotesque behavior has been merely a reflection of her own and in that realization, she finds that she has been out-maneuvered by someone whose intensity and intellect equals her own. This man will not bow down to her in fear or walk away from her in disgust because

Notes

Notes

Notes

Notes

THE TAMING OF THE SHREW

ACT V

Petruchio *Marry, peace it bodes, and love, and quiet life,*
An awful rule, and right supremacy,
And, to be short, what not that's sweet and happy.

Act V, Scene 1

Bianca and Lucentio run away to be married. Kate, Petruchio, Hortensio, and Vincentio arrive in Padua at Lucentio's dwelling. The Pedant, still pretending to be Vincentio, is not cordial to the visitors. Biondello pretends not to know Vincentio just as Tranio enters still dressed as Lucentio. Vincentio thinks Lucentio has been killed but Lucentio arrives in time to reassure his father that he is fine. Lucentio and Bianca tell Baptista that they are married and Vincentio agrees to provide the money agreed upon by his imposter, the Pedant. Everyone goes into the house for the wedding banquet, leaving Kate and Petruchio alone on the street. They kiss for the first time, and Petruchio feels his taming is complete and successful.

ACT V, SCENE 1

Padua. Before LUCENTIO'S house.

[Enter BIONDELLO, LUCENTIO, and BIANCA; GREMIO is out before]

Biondello Softly and swiftly, sir, for the priest is ready.　　1

Lucentio I fly, Biondello. But they may chance to need the at home. Therefore leave us.
Exit [with Bianca]

Biondello Nay, faith, I'll see the church a' your back; and then come back to my master's as soon as I can.
[he exits]　　5

Gremio I marvel Cambio comes not all this while.
[Enter PETRUCHIO, KATE, VINCENTIO, GRUMIO, and ATTENDANTS]

Petruchio Sir, here's the door. This is Lucentio's house.
My father's bears more toward the market-place.
Thither must I, and here I leave you, sir.

Vincentio You shall not choose but drink before you go.　　10
I think I shall command your welcome here,
And by all likelihood some cheer is toward.
[Knocks]

Gremio They're busy within. You were best knock louder.
[PEDANT looks out of the window]

Pedant *[as Vincentio]* What's he that knocks as he would beat down the gate?

Vincentio Is Signior Lucentio within, sir?　　15

NOTES

8.　　*bears more toward:* is closer to.

12.　　*cheer is toward:* food and drink can be anticipated.

Pedant He's within, sir, but not to be spoken withal.

Vincentio What if a man bring him a hundred pound or two to make

merry withal?

Pedant Keep your hundred pounds to yourself. He shall need none so

long as I live.   20

Petruchio *[to Vincentio]* Nay, I told you your son was well beloved in Padua. Do

you hear, sir? To leave frivolous circumstances, I pray you tell

Signior Lucentio that his father is come from Pisa and is here

at the door to speak with him.

Pedant Thou liest. His father is come from Padua and here looking   25

out at the window.

Vincentio Art thou his father?

Pedant Ay, sir, so his mother says, if I may believe her.

Petruchio *[to Vincentio]* Why, how now, gentleman! Why, this is flat

knavery, to take upon you another man's name.   30

Pedant Lay hands on the villain. I believe 'a means to cozen

somebody in this city under my countenance.

[Enter BIONDELLO]

Biondello I have seen them in the church together. God send 'em

good shipping! But who is here? Mine old master, Vincentio! Now

we are undone and brought to nothing.   35

Vincentio *[seeing Biondello]* Come hither, crack-hemp.

Biondello I hope I may choose, sir.

Vincentio Come hither, you rogue. What, have you forgot me?

Biondello Forgot you? No, sir! I could not forget you, for I never

saw you before in all my life.   40

Vincentio What, you notorious villain! Didst thou never see thy

master's father, Vincentio?

22.	*frivolous circumstances:* trivial matters.	
29.	*flat:* absolute.	
31.	*cozen:* cheat.	
32.	*under my countenance:* pretending to be me.	
34.	*good shipping:* good journey.	
36.	*crack-hemp:* scoundrel.	
37.	*I may choose:* have some choice in the matter.	
41.	*notorious:* infamous.	

Biondello What, my old worshipful old master? Yes, marry, sir. See

where he looks out of the window.

Vincentio Is't so, indeed?　　　　　　　　　　　　45

[*He beats BIONDELLO*]

Biondello Help, help, help! Here's a madman will murder me.

[*Exit*]

Pedant Help, son! Help, Signior Baptista!

[*Exit from the window*]

Petruchio Prithee, Kate, let's stand aside and see the end of this

controversy.

[*They stand aside*]

[*Enter PEDANT with SERVANTS, BAPTISTA, TRANIO (disguised as Lucentio)*]

Tranio Sir, what are you that offer to beat my servant?　　50

Vincentio What am I, sir? Nay, what are you, sir? O immortal gods!

O fine villain! A silken doublet, a velvet hose, a scarlet cloak,

and a copatain hat! O, I am undone! I am undone! While I play the

good husband at home, my son and my servant spend all at the

university.　　　　　　　　　　　　　　　　55

Tranio How now, what's the matter?

Baptista What, is the man lunatic?

Tranio Sir, you seem a sober ancient gentleman by your habit, but

your words show you a madman. Why, sir, what 'cerns it you if I

wear pearl and gold? I thank my good father,　　60
I am able to

maintain it.

Vincentio Thy father! O villain, he is a sailmaker in Bergamo.

Baptista You mistake, sir, you mistake, sir! Pray, what do you think is his name?

50.	*offer:* venture.
52.	*doublet:* jacket.
53.	*hose:* breeches.
	copatain: high crowned.
	undone: destroyed.
59.	*'cerns:* concerns.
61.	*maintain:* bear the expense of.

Vincentio His name? As if I knew not his name! I have brought him

up ever since he was three years old, and   65
his name is Tranio.

Pedant Away, away, mad ass! His name is Lucentio and he is mine

only son, and heir to the lands of me, Signior Vincentio.

Vincentio Lucentio? O, he hath murdered his master! Lay hold on

him, I charge you, in the Duke's name. O, my son, my son! Tell

me, thou villain, where is my son Lucentio?   70

Tranio Call forth an officer.

[Enter an OFFICER]

Carry this mad knave to the gaol. Father Baptista, I charge you

see that he be forthcoming.

Vincentio Carry me to the gaol!

Gremio Stay, officer. He shall not go to prison.   75

Baptista Talk not, Signior Gremio. I say he shall go to prison.

Gremio Take heed, Signior Baptista, lest you be cony-catched in

this business. I dare swear this is the right Vincentio.

Pedant Swear, if thou darest.   80

Gremio Nay, I dare not swear it.

Tranio Then thou wert best say that I am not Lucentio.

Gremio Yes, I know thee to be Signior Lucentio.

Baptista Away with the dotard! To the gaol with him!

Vincentio Thus strangers may be haled and abus'd. O monstrous   85
villain!

[Enter BIONDELLO, LUCENTIO and BIANCA]

Biondello O, we are spoiled, and yonder he is! Deny him, forswear

him, or else we are all undone.

Lucentio *[kneeling]* Pardon, sweet father.

Vincentio Lives my sweet son?   90

71.   *gaol:* jail.
72.   *forthcoming:* available.

78.   *cony-catched:* cheated, victimized.
79.   *right:* true.

84.   *dotard:* foolish old man.
85.   *haled:* molested.

86.   *spoiled:* ruined.

[BIONDELLO, TRANIO, and PEDANT, exit as fast as may be]

Bianca *[kneeling]* Pardon, dear father.

Baptista How hast thou offended?
　Where is Lucentio?

Lucentio Here's Lucentio,
　Right son to the right Vincentio,　　　　　　　　　　　95
　That have by marriage made thy daughter mine
　While counterfeit supposes blear'd thine eyne.

Gremio Here's packing, with a witness, to deceive us all!

Vincentio Where is that damned villain, Tranio,
　That fac'd and brav'd me in this matter so?　　　　　100

Baptista Why, tell me, is not this my Cambio?

Bianca Cambio is chang'd into Lucentio.

Lucentio Love wrought these miracles. Bianca's love
　Made me exchange my state with Tranio,
　While he did bear my countenance in the town,　　　105
　And happily I have arriv'd at the last
　Unto the wished haven of my bliss.
　What Tranio did, myself enforc'd him to.
　Then pardon him, sweet father, for my sake.

Vincentio I'll slit the villain's nose that would　　　110
　　have sent me to
　the gaol!

Baptista *[to Lucentio]* But do you hear, sir? Have you married my
　daughter without asking my good will?

Vincentio Fear not, Baptista; we will content you. Go to!
　　But I
　will in to be revenged for this villainy.　　　　　　115
　[Exit]

Baptista And I to sound the depth of this knavery.
　[Exit]

Lucentio Look not pale, Bianca. Thy father will not frown.
　[Exeunt LUCENTIO and BIANCA]

Gremio My cake is dough, but I'll in among the rest,

97.　*counterfeit supposes:* false impersonations.
　　eyne: eyes.
98.　*packing:* plotting.
　　with a witness: with a vengeance.
100.　*fac'd and brav'd:* defied.

104.　*state:* status.
105.　*bear my countenance:* take on my identity.

114.　*Go to:* Don't worry.

118.　*My cake is dough:* proverbial: I have failed.

Out of hope of all but my share of the feast.

[Exit]

[Petruchio and Kate advance]

Kate Husband, let's follow to see the end of this ado.   120

Petruchio First kiss me, Kate, and we will.

Kate What, in the midst of the street?

Petruchio What, art thou ashamed of me?

Kate No, sir, God forbid, but ashamed to kiss.

Petruchio Why, then, let's home again. *[to Grumio]* Come,
sirrah, let's away.   125

Kate Nay, I will give thee a kiss. *[she kisses him]* Now pray
thee, love, stay.

Petruchio Is not this well? Come, my sweet Kate.
Better once than never, for never too late.   128

[Exeunt]

120.   *ado:* fuss.

128.   *Better . . . late:* proverbial: "Better late than never."

COMMENTARY

An identifying trait of the majority of Shakespeare's comedies is that by arriving at an understanding of the original problem, the characters achieve reconciliation, and thus, a return to order. Reconciliation and order will be established as the characters understand that their disguises have caused more problems than they have solved. Meanwhile, the unmasking continues as the Lucentio/Bianca subplot reaches its climax and the farcical nature of the play becomes even more apparent in the scene's use of flamboyant deception, disguises, physical violence, and the disturbance of domestic tranquility.

Lucentio, now out of his Cambio disguise, is, with the help of Biondello, on his way to the priest to elope with Bianca. Just as they exit, Petruchio and Kate enter with the real Vincentio. At this point in the play, it is almost as if the roles have been entirely reversed. In the beginning of the play, it was Kate making all of the noise and creating all of the chaos. Now it is Bianca's turn to cause pandemonium.

The character of Bianca, as well as the subplot in general, was derived from a play written in 1566 by George Gascoigne titled *Supposes,* an adaptation of Ariosto's 1509 comedy *Suppositi.* The play dealt with misunderstood circumstances and mistaken identities or "supposes." Bianca's counterpart in Gascoigne is Polynesta, a character that rarely appears on stage even though she is the reason for all of the subterfuge. At the beginning of *Supposes,* Polynesta is pregnant by her lover Erostrato, who, just like Lucentio, has changed places with his servant Dulipo so that he would have easier access to Polynesta, the object of his desire. Just as Tranio aids Lucentio in defeating all the other rivals for Bianca's attention, Duplio assists Erostrato to defeat a rich, elderly suitor similar to Shakespeare's Gremio, for Polynesta. The play *Supposes,* just like *The Taming of the Shrew,* also includes a father who comes to visit his son unexpectedly only to find someone impersonating him and another masquerading as his son. Mistaken identities abound, but in the end, Erostrato and Polynesta are married, and it is revealed that Dulipo is the long lost son of the Gremio character, transforming him immediately from a lowly servant into a true man of status and affluence. Obviously, Shakespeare chose not to include the long-lost child plot twist into his play and based on the Elizabethan sense of right and wrong, elected to make Bianca a virgin as well as a much more developed and integral character.

Back in Padua, Kate and Petruchio have brought Vincentio to Lucentio's home. Vincentio invites Kate and Petruchio in for a drink, but the Pedant, disguised as Vincentio, looks out the window. Vincentio identifies himself as Lucentio's father, but the Pedant, trying to con his way out of this dreadful situation, claims that he is the true Vincentio and the man on the street is a common liar. Petruchio believes the Pedant's story that Vincentio is an imposter and attempts to constrain him. With all of the accusations of impersonation being cast on him, Vincentio, one of the few characters who is who he says he is, could certainly begin to doubt that he is the real Vincentio. Just as Kate believed she was unlovable and unworthy because others told her she was, Vincentio could begin to question his own sanity. So many of the characters are pretending to be someone else that those who are not disguised have as fragile a grasp on reality as those who are disguised.

During this fray, Biondello enters having just come from the wedding of Lucentio and Bianca. Vincentio recognizes Biondello, but Biondello denies having ever seen Vincentio before in his life. To confuse matters even more, Baptista appears with Tranio still disguised as Lucentio. Upon seeing his son's servant in fancy clothes, Vincentio can only assume that Tranio has killed Lucentio and is spending all of his money. An officer is called to the scene and Tranio, trying to find some way out of this predicament, insists that Vincentio is a madman who should be taken to jail and locked up. Just in time to prevent his father from being imprisoned, Lucentio enters with his new bride, Bianca. Upon their arrival, the Pedant, Tranio, and Biondello, knowing the ruse is up, sneak off the stage and make a hasty exit. Lucentio and Bianca explain to their fathers about the "counterfeit supposes" and Vincentio leaves to seek revenge on Tranio.

All of the disguises are removed and the loose ends are tied up rather neatly with Lucentio claiming, "Love wrought these miracles." Love, with its transformative powers is miraculous. Petruchio's love for Kate has astonishingly allowed her to see her potential rather than what society tells her she can be. Love has transformed her from a shrew to a gentle woman of virtue and grace. Even Petruchio has been transformed from the loud, brash, braggart that he was at the beginning of the play into a man who is gentle and eager to please. However, Lucentio's love for Bianca has allowed her to lie, hurt others, and deceive her father. Bianca has not been transformed into anything more than a wife and as Petruchio taught Kate by his actions at their wedding, ritual does not transform. Changes must occur in the heart and soul and Bianca is now merely a married version of her former self. The only change that will be seen in Bianca is that she will take off her disguise as the sweet, accommodating young virgin to reveal the shrew she really was all along.

Baptista storms off the stage leaving Lucentio to assure Bianca that when her father realizes how much money he really has that the marriage will be recognized as beneficial to all. Gremio, the only remaining suitor without a wife, admits his defeat and goes off alone to enjoy Bianca and Lucentio's wedding feast.

Out of the shadows steps the forgotten couple, Kate and Petruchio. They have quietly watched the action unfold and Kate must have enjoyed seeing Bianca, for once, so far removed from her father's favor. Kate suggests to Petruchio that they follow the fray to see how it is all resolved, but Petruchio first asks for a kiss. The two are in the middle of the street and Kate is not receptive to a public display of affection. Petruchio asks, "What, art thou ashamed of me?" This moment can be interpreted in several ways. Petruchio could be asking the question in a threatening way, and the following line, "Why, then, let's home again" would be consistent with the theory that Petruchio is nothing more than an abusive, controlling husband. Kate's kiss would then have to be interpreted as motivated by fear and nothing more. If the order to return home again is delivered in a teasing way, Petruchio might be encouraging the continuation of the play between the two that began in the last scene of Act IV. In this context, Kate's kiss would seal the private contract between the two, a contract that assures the art of play as a basis for their relationship. Kate's final line, "Now pray thee, love, stay" is very telling. For the first time since meeting Petruchio, Kate has used the word love, an indication that her heart is opening to the possibilities that exist with this very unusual man.

Act V, Scene 2

As the wedding banquet continues, the men place wagers on which wife will be the most obedient by coming to the room when called. Both Bianca and the widow refuse to come when called, but Kate, to the surprise of everyone in the room, comes immediately. Kate tells the other women that they owe their husbands their obedience. Petruchio has won the wager and Baptista adds to Kate's dowry because she is such a changed woman. While the guests continue to celebrate, Kate and Petruchio leave the feast for their first real night together as man and wife.

ACT V, SCENE 2

A room in LUCENTIO'S house.

[Enter BAPTISTA, VINCENTIO, GREMIO, the PEDANT, LUCENTIO, and BIANCA, PETRUCHIO, KATE, HORTENSIO and WIDOW; the SERVINGMEN, with TRANIO, BIONDELLO, GRUMIO, bringing in a banquet]

Lucentio At last, though long, our jarring notes agree,   1
   And time it is when raging war is done
   To smile at 'scapes and perils overblown.
   My fair Bianca, bid my father welcome,
   While I with self-same kindness welcome thine.   5
   Brother Petruchio, sister Katherina,
   And thou, Hortensio, with thy loving widow,
   Feast with the best, and welcome to my house.
   My banquet is to close our stomachs up
   After our great good cheer. Pray you, sit down,   10
   For now we sit to chat as well as eat.
   [They sit at table]

Petruchio Nothing but sit and sit, and eat and eat!

Baptista Padua affords this kindness, son Petruchio.

Petruchio Padua affords nothing but what is kind.

Hortensio For both our sakes I would that word   15
   were true.

Petruchio Now, for my life, Hortensio fears his widow!

Widow Then never trust me if I be afeard.

Petruchio You are very sensible, and yet you miss my sense:
   I mean Hortensio is afeard of you.

Widow He that is giddy thinks the world turns round.   20

NOTES

SD.   *banquet:* wine and dessert.

3.   *'scapes:* escapes.
       overblown: past.

10.   *great good cheer:* the wedding feast.

15.   *would:* wish.

17.   *afeard:* suspected, afraid.

Petruchio Roundly replied.

Kate Mistress, how mean you that?

Widow Thus I conceive by him.

Petruchio Conceives by me? How likes Hortensio that?

Hortensio My widow says, thus she conceives her tale. 　25

Petruchio Very well mended. Kiss him for that, good widow.

Kate "He that is giddy thinks the world turns round":
　I pray you tell me what you meant by that.

Widow Your husband, being troubled with a shrew,
　Measures my husband's sorrow by his woe. 　30
　And now you know my meaning.

Kate A very mean meaning.

Widow Right, I mean you.

Kate And I am mean indeed, respecting you.

Petruchio To her, Kate! 　35

Hortensio To her, widow!

Petruchio A hundred marks, my Kate does put her down.

Hortensio That's my office.

Petruchio Spoke like an officer! Ha' to thee, lad.
　[Drinks to Hortensio]

Baptista How likes Gremio these quick-witted folks? 　40

Gremio Believe me, sir, they butt together well.

Bianca Head and butt! An hasty-witted body
　Would say your head and butt were head and horn.

Vincentio Ay, mistress bride, hath that awaken'd you?

Bianca Ay, but not frighted me. Therefore I'll sleep again. 　45

Petruchio Nay, that you shall not. Since you have begun,
　Have at you for a bitter jest or two.

Bianca Am I your bird? I mean to shift my bush,
　And then pursue me as you draw your bow.
　You are welcome all. 　50
　[Exeunt BIANCA, and KATE, and WIDOW]

Petruchio She hath prevented me. Here, Signior Tranio,
　This bird you aim'd at, though you hit her not.

21.　*Roundly:* plainly.

23.　*conceive:* understand.

24.　*Conceives:* becomes pregnant.

30.　*Measures:* estimates.

34.　*mean . . . you:* severe where you are concerned.

37.　*marks:* coins.
　　put her down: defeat her, pun on having intercourse with her referenced in following line.

38.　*office:* job, duty.

39.　*Ha' to:* Here's to.

41.　*butt together:* knock heads.

42.　*body:* person.

43.　*horn:* symbol of a cuckold; phallic.

47.　*Have at you:* I challenge you.

48.　*bird:* prey, target.

Therefore a health to all that shot and miss'd.

Tranio O, sir! Lucentio slipp'd me like his greyhound,
Which runs himself, and catches for his master.   55

Petruchio A good swift simile, but something currish.

Tranio 'Tis well, sir, that you hunted for yourself.
'Tis thought your deer does hold you at a bay.

Baptista O, O, Petruchio! Tranio hits you now.

Lucentio I thank thee for that gird, good Tranio.   60

Hortensio Confess, confess! Hath he not hit you here?

Petruchio A' has a little gall'd me, I confess.
And as the jest did glance away from me,
'Tis ten to one it maim'd you two outright.

Baptista Now, in good sadness, son Petruchio,   65
I think thou hast the veriest shrew of all.

Petruchio Well, I say no. And therefore, for assurance,
Let's each one send unto his wife,
And he whose wife is most obedient
To come at first when he doth send for her   70
Shall win the wager which we will propose.

Hortensio Content. What's the wager?

Lucentio Twenty crowns.

Petruchio Twenty crowns?
I'll venture so much of my hawk or hound,   75
But twenty times so much upon my wife.

Lucentio A hundred, then.

Hortensio Content.

Petruchio A match! 'Tis done.

Hortensio Who shall begin?   80

Lucentio That will I.
Go, Biondello, bid your mistress come to me.

Biondello I go.
 [Exit]

Baptista Son, I'll be your half Bianca comes.

Lucentio I'll have no halves. I'll bear it all myself.   85

53.	*health:* toast.
54.	*slipp'd:* unleashed.
56.	*swift:* quick witted.
	currish: cynical.
58.	*deer . . . bay:* the trapped animal defends itself against its attacker.
60.	*gird:* taunt.
62.	*gall'd:* irritated.
63.	*glance away:* ricocheted off.
65.	*in good sadness:* seriously.
66.	*veriest:* genuine.
67.	*for assurance:* to put to the test.
72.	*Content:* agreed.
75.	*of:* on.
79.	*match:* bet.
84.	*be your half:* take on half your bet.

[Enter BIONDELLO]
How now, what news?

Biondello Sir, my mistress sends you word
That she is busy, and she cannot come.

Petruchio How? "She's busy, and she cannot come!"
Is that an answer?   90

Gremio Ay, and a kind one too.
Pray God, sir, your wife send you not a worse.

Petruchio I hope better.

Hortensio Sirrah Biondello, go and entreat my wife
To come to me forthwith.   95
[Exit Biondello]

Petruchio O, ho, entreat her!
Nay, then, she must needs come.

Hortensio I am afraid, sir,
Do what you can, yours will not be entreated.
[Enter BIONDELLO]
Now, where's my wife?   100

Biondello She says you have some goodly jest in hand.
She will not come. She bids you come to her.

Petruchio Worse and worse. She will not come! O vile,
Intolerable, not to be endur'd!
Sirrah Grumio, go to your mistress,   105
Say I command her come to me.
[Exit Grumio]

Hortensio I know her answer.

Petruchio What?

Hortensio She will not.

Petruchio The fouler fortune mine, and there an end.   110
[Enter KATE]

Baptista Now, by my holidame, here comes Katherina!

Kate What is your will sir, that you send for me?

Petruchio Where is your sister, and Hortensio's wife?

Kate They sit conferring by the parlour fire.

Petruchio Go, fetch them hither. If they deny to come,   115

---

95. *forthwith:* immediately.

110. *there an end:* that's that.

111. *holidame:* Virgin Mary.

114. *conferring:* talking together.

115. *deny:* refuse.

Swinge me them soundly forth unto their husbands.
Away, I say, and bring them hither straight.
[Exit KATE]

Lucentio Here is a wonder, if you talk of a wonder.

Hortensio And so it is. I wonder what it bodes.

Petruchio Marry, peace it bodes, and love, and quiet life,   120
An awful rule, and right supremacy,
And, to be short, what not that's sweet and happy.

Baptista Now fair befall thee, good Petruchio!
The wager thou hast won, and I will add
Unto their losses twenty thousand crowns,   125
Another dowry to another daughter,
For she is chang'd as she had never been.

Petruchio Nay, I will win my wager better yet,
And show more sign of her obedience,
Her new-built virtue and obedience.   130
[Enter KATE, BIANCA, and WIDOW]
See where she comes, and brings your froward wives
As prisoners to her womanly persuasion.
Katherine, that cap of yours becomes you not.
Off with that bauble, throw it underfoot.
[KATE pulls off her cap and throws it down]

Widow Lord, let me never have a cause to sigh   135
Till I be brought to such a silly pass!

Bianca Fie, what a foolish duty call you this?

Lucentio I would your duty were as foolish too.
The wisdom of your duty, fair Bianca,
Hath cost me a hundred crowns since supper-time!   140

Bianca The more fool you for laying on my duty.

Petruchio Katherine, I charge thee tell these headstrong women
What duty they do owe their lords and husbands.

Widow Come, come, you're mocking. We will have no telling.

Petruchio Come on, I say, and first begin with her.   145

Widow She shall not.

Petruchio I say she shall. And first begin with her.

116.	*Swinge me them:* whip them.
118.	*wonder:* miracle.
119.	*bodes:* foretells.
121.	*awful rule:* rule by commanding fear or respect.
	right: proper.
122.	*what not:* everything.
123.	*fair befall thee:* good fortune come to you.
131.	*froward:* uncooperative.
134.	*bauble:* showy trinket of little worth.
135.	*cause:* reason.
136.	*pass:* situation.
137.	*duty:* obedience.
141.	*laying:* wagering.

Kate Fie, fie! Unknit that threatening unkind brow,
And dart not scornful glances from those eyes
To wound thy lord, thy king, thy governor.   150
It blots thy beauty as frosts do bite the meads,
Confounds thy fame as whirlwinds shake fair buds,
And in no sense is meet or amiable.
A woman mov'd is like a fountain troubled,
Muddy, ill-seeming, thick, bereft of beauty,   155
And while it is so, none so dry or thirsty
Will deign to sip or touch one drop of it.
Thy husband is thy lord, thy life, thy keeper,
Thy head, thy sovereign, one that cares for thee,
And for thy maintenance commits his body   160
To painful labour both by sea and land,
To watch the night in storms, the day in cold,
Whilst thou liest warm at home, secure and safe,
And craves no other tribute at thy hands
But love, fair looks, and true obedience-   165
Too little payment for so great a debt.
Such duty as the subject owes the prince,
Even such a woman oweth to her husband;
And when she is froward, peevish, sullen, sour,
And not obedient to his honest will,   170
What is she but a foul contending rebel
And graceless traitor to her loving lord?
I am asham'd that women are so simple
To offer war where they should kneel for peace,
Or seek for rule, supremacy, and sway   175
When they are bound to serve, love, and obey.
Why are our bodies soft and weak and smooth,
Unapt to toil and trouble in the world,
But that our soft conditions and our hearts
Should well agree with our external parts?   180
Come, come, you froward and unable worms!
My mind hath been as big as one of yours,
My heart as great, my reason haply more,
To bandy word for word and frown for frown;
But now I see our lances are but straws,   185
Our strength as weak, our weakness past compare,

151. *blots:* stains, tarnishes.

meads: meadows.

152. *Confounds thy fame:* ruins your reputation.

153. *meet:* fit, proper.

154. *mov'd:* ill tempered.

155. *ill-seeming:* unbecoming.

171. *contending:* antagonistic.

172. *graceless:* ungrateful.

173. *simple:* foolish.

175. *sway:* power.

178. *Unapt:* unsuited.

179. *conditions:* characteristics.

181. *unable:* weak, impotent.

182. *big:* self important.

183. *heart:* courage.

184. *bandy:* exchange.

186. *past compare:* beyond comparison.

That seeming to be most which we indeed least are.
Then vail your stomachs, for it is no boot,
And place your hands below your husband's foot:
In token of which duty, if he please,   190
My hand is ready; may it do him ease.

Petruchio Why, there's a wench! Come on, and kiss me, Kate.
[They kiss]

Lucentio Well, go thy ways, old lad, for thou shalt ha't.

Vincentio 'Tis a good hearing when children are toward.

Lucentio But a harsh hearing when women are froward.   195

Petruchio Come, Kate, we'll to bed.
We three are married, but you two are sped.
[To Lucentio] 'Twas I won the wager, though you hit the
white,
And being a winner, God give you good night!
[Exeunt PETRUCHIO and KATE]

Hortensio Now, go thy ways, thou hast tam'd a curst shrew.200

Lucentio 'Tis a wonder, by your leave, she will be tam'd so.201
[Exeunt]

188.	*vail your stomachs:* conquer your pride.
	no boot: useless.
193.	*ha't:* have it, win.
194.	*toward:* cooperative.
197.	*sped:* done for.
198.	*white:* bull's eye.

COMMENTARY

The "Shrew" play could have easily ended at the conclusion of Act V, Scene 1 with the resolution of the Kate and Petruchio and Bianca and Lucentio story lines. In fact, it is quite unlike Shakespeare to continue a comedy past the marriage of the main characters, but this play does continue with a scene that has caused much debate and even disgusted some readers over the years. Writing about this scene, over 100 years ago, in the November 6, 1897 issue of *Saturday Review,* George Bernard Shaw commented:

" . . . the last scene is altogether disgusting to modern sensibility. No man with any decency of feeling can sit it out in the company of a woman without being extremely ashamed of the lord-of-creation moral implied in the wager and the speech put into the woman's own mouth."

The Taming of the Shrew, as printed in the 1623 Folio, does not include the final scene of the Christopher Sly framework that appears in *The Taming of A Shrew.*

Whether the final scene was lost before printing or never appeared in Shakespeare's play is not clear, but there are apparent parallels between the Induction and the final Act of Shakespeare's play as it stands. For example, just as the Induction includes a great feast for Christopher Sly who has been reconciled with his "wife," this scene takes place at a wedding feast for the three newly married couples and obviously, some sort of reconciliation has occurred between Lucentio and Vincentio and Bianca and Baptista. The conversation is light and occasionally bawdy until the widow, Hortensio's new bride, insults Kate. Kate defends herself and Petruchio and the men, in jest, wager who would win a fight between the two women. Bianca is angered by a comment made by Petruchio and she leaves the room, followed by Kate and the Widow.

The men, left alone at the table, begin discussing their wives and the talk, full of hunting metaphors, is reminiscent of the Lord's entrance in the Induction.

Just as the Lord was quarrelling about his three dogs, the men quarrel about their three wives. With a play on the word "dear," Tranio jibes Petruchio saying, "'Tis thought your deer does hold you at bay" prompting Petruchio to suggest a wager concerning the obedience of their wives. The men will each send for their wife and the man whose wife comes first will win the bet. The original wager of twenty crowns reflects the Lord's proclamation that he would not lose his dog Silver for twenty crowns. In her article "The Ending of *the Shrew*," Margie Burns speculates:

"Indeed, the earlier hunt may echo in the final scene even through the names of the hunting dogs, which chime interestingly with the wives' characters: 'Bellman' suggests Kate's voice and function in the play; 'Silver,' like 'Bianca,' suggests light coloring; and 'Echo,' adequately describes the unnamed widow whose speeches largely just echo Bianca's."

Lucentio is the first to send for his wife, Bianca, who sends Biondello back with the word that "she is busy and cannot come." Hortensio next sends for his wife and she bids him to come to her. To everyone's astonishment, Kate is the only wife to respond to her summons, bringing the other women with her. Baptista is so amazed at Kate's transformation that he ups Kate's dowry by another 20,000 crowns.

In a final gamble, Petruchio commands Kate to "tell these headstrong women/What duty they do owe their Lords and husbands." He has no way of knowing how Kate will respond, the odds being that she will rebel with a tirade against him, marriage, and all men, but instead she delivers a forty-four line monologue defining the woman's role in marriage. Until this moment, Kate has had very little to say, but she is now eloquent and introspective. Depending on the tone with which the speech is delivered, it may take on many meanings. Many actresses deliver the speech with a touch of irony and a metaphorical wink to the audience, saying words she doesn't mean and will not follow. Other actresses have chosen to deliver the speech as a woman too afraid to contradict her husband, and others as a woman disillusioned, knowing she has no way out but to give in. In *Clamorous Voices,* Fiona Shaw, discussing her portrayal of what has often been called Kate's submission speech, explains her interpretation of the speech to Carol Rutter:

"At the end of the play I was determined that Kate and Petruchio were rebels and would remain rebels for ever, so her speech was not predictable . . . This so-called 'submission' speech isn't a submission speech at all: It's a speech about how her spirit has been allowed to soar free. She is not attached to him. He hasn't laid down the rules for her, she has made her own rules, and what he's managed to do is to allow her to have her own vision. It happens that her vision coincides with his. There's a privately shared joke in the speech. And irony. And some blackness. The play is dark; savage sometimes . . . they're going to have a very interesting marriage."

Historically, much of the content of Kate's final speech is taken literally and theoretically from several sources including the *Book of Homilies* used in the Elizabethan Church and *The Instruction of a Christian Woman* written by Juan Luis Vives. "The Sermon of the State of Matrimony" found in the *Book of Homilies* indicates without a doubt that by nature and divine ordinance, women are inferior to men and therefore subject to the rule of their husbands. The wife owes her husband obedience "in the respect of the commandment of God, as St. Paul expresseth it in this form of words: *Let women be subject to their husbands, as to the Lord; for the husband is the head of the woman, as Christ is the head of the church.* Ephesians V. " Of course, the reality between what was commanded and what happened in the home between a husband and his wife was not always carried out as mandated by the Church and *The Taming of the Shrew* explores this theme in a very humorous way.

The Instruction of a Christian Woman was commissioned by and dedicated to Catherine of Aragon, Henry VIII's first wife whom he eventually divorced to marry Anne Boleyn. If Kate's monologue were read without benefit of context or knowledge of Kate's personality, it would be simple to label the speech a guide to the capitulation of women. Rather, the monologue may be interpreted as an almost subversive manifesto, teaching women how to dominate their husbands by appearing to be subservient. In defense of this theory, Juan Luis Vives suggests in his book, one of Shakespeare's sources for this speech, that "A good woman by lowely obeysaunce ruleth her husbande" and goes further to recommend that a woman may "Vanquishe thy cruell husbande rather with obedience." The line is very similar to one delivered by Petruchio's servant Peter in Act IV, Scene 1, when he conjectures that Petruchio's mad behavior towards Kate is an attempt to kill "her in her

A painting of Kate by Claude A. Shepperson, reproduced in Pemrose Annual 1905-6. Mary Evans Picture Library

unspoken message then is to stay calm and refrain from rousing up trouble so that people will not be disinclined to do your bidding.

In an almost direct quote from Vives, Kate declares that "Thy husband is thy lord, thy life, thy keeper, /Thy head, thy sovereign." These very political terms reflect the Elizabethan Chain of Being and the idea that the husband is king of his familial kingdom. However, it is Kate's exaggeration of the line that allows the reader to discern a deeper meaning. In "Refashioning the Shrew," Valerie Wayne suggests:

Just as Petruchio exaggerates his superiority over his servants to tame his wife, so Kate exaggerates her dependence on her husband to prove herself his equal in parodic performance. While her speech evokes the dilemmas of a wife's dependence, Petruchio is also the source of her irony: Like a good humanitarian husband, he has been his wife's teacher; and like an actor, he has taught her to assume a new role. When Kate learns to mimic as well as he, these two easily transcend the role and hierarchies that govern their world.

The Taming of the Shrew compares and contrasts the two paths that ultimately lead to marriage. Bianca and Lucentio, in love with love, take the path that on the surface, seems romantic and desirable. However, in reality, both Bianca and Lucentio are disguised: He as a tutor, she as the ideal woman, and that it is impossible to say that they truly love each other, but rather they are in love with the façades they have allowed each other to see. After the marriage ceremony, when the two drop their disguises, they are both revealed to be shallow and deluded by the roles the other played. Kate and Petruchio travel a different path. They are married quickly but before the marriage is made truly legal by consummation at the very end of the play, Kate and Petruchio tear the masks from each other, and explore, often painfully, the true nature of the other, and in the process they both become better people. The contract made between Kate and Petruchio is more than a legal contract: It is one based on respect, trust, and a true knowledge of the other.

own humor." Just as Petruchio tamed Kate by taking on her shrewish attitude and reflecting it back to her, Kate may be turning the tables on Petruchio, taming him in the same way.

Kate's advice to the other women includes a simile taken directly from Vives. In her speech, Kate says, "A woman moved is like a fountain troubled, /Muddy, ill-seeming, thick, bereft of beauty." In Vives's book, speaking specifically to widows, he advises that if a woman's mind is troubled she cannot pray, "lyke as whan a river or fountayne is troubled a man can drawe no water but full of mudde." In other words, an angry woman stirs up those around her in such a way that no one "Will deign to sip or touch one drop of it." The

Notes

Notes

Notes

Notes

The Taming of the Shrew
CLIFFSCOMPLETE REVIEW

Use this CliffsComplete Review to gauge what you've learned and to build confidence in your understanding of the original text. After you work through the review questions, the problem-solving exercises, and the suggested activities, you're well on your way to understanding and appreciating the works of William Shakespeare.

IDENTIFY THE QUOTATION

Identify the following quotations by answering these questions:

* Who is the speaker of the quote?
* What does it reveal about the speaker's character?
* What does it tell us about other characters within the play?
* Where does it occur within the play?
* What does it show us about the themes of the play?
* What significant imagery do you see in the quote, and how do these images relate to the overall images of the play?

1. I a lord, and have I such a lady?
   Or do I dream? Or have I dreamed till now?

2. Come, madam wife, sit by my side, and let the world slip.
   We shall ne'er be younger.

3. I burn, I pine! I perish, Tranio.

4. I come to wive it wealthily in Padua;
   If wealthily, then happily in Padua.

5. I must dance barefoot on her wedding day
   And, for your love to her, lead apes in hell.

6. Marry, so I mean, sweet Katherine, in thy bed.
   And therefore, setting all this chat aside,
   Thus in plain terms: your father hath consented
   That you shall be my wife, your dowry 'greed on,
   And, will you, nill you, I will marry you.

7. To me she's married, not unto my clothes.

8. He kills her in her own humor.

9. Then God be blest, it [is] the blessed sun.
   But sun it is not, when you say it is not,
   And the moon changes even as your mind.
   What you will have it named, even that it is,
   And so it shall be so for Katherine.

10. Such duty as the subject owes the prince,
    Even such a woman oweth to her husband.

TRUE/FALSE

1. T F The Hostess throws Christopher Sly out of the tavern because he has broken glasses and refused to pay his bill.

2. T F The Lord plans to trick Sly by making him think he is a king.

3. T F Tranio has come to Padua to study at the University.

4. T F Hortensio will disguise himself as an art teacher so that he has closer access to Bianca.

5. T F Petruchio abuses Kate the first time they meet.

6. T F Kate is hurt and angered when Petruchio shows up late to their wedding.

7. T F At Petruchio's home, Kate is not allowed to eat or sleep.

8. T F Petruchio plans to tame Kate as he would a horse.

9. T F Petruchio's servants assist him in his efforts to tame Kate.

10. T F Tranio and Biondello prove that they are much smarter than Lucentio.

11. T F Bianca and Lucentio elope.

12. T F In the duel between the Pedant and Vincentio, the Pedant is slain.

13. T F Because of the change in Kate's attitude, Baptista increases her dowry by 20,000 crowns.

14. T F Baptista disowns Bianca because she has betrayed his trust.

15. T F The widow obeys Hortensio in all things.

MULTIPLE CHOICE

1. Which of the following is not a theme in *The Taming of the Shrew*?

a. The battle of the sexes

b. Appearance vs. reality

c. The struggle between the classes

d. Cruelty to animals

2. Bartholomew, the page disguised as Sly's wife, says she cannot sleep with Sly because:

a. He is actually a boy

b. He has a headache

c. The Doctor has forbidden it so that Sly does not relapse

d. It is time to watch the play

3. The Lord shows Sly some wanton pictures that depict all but one of the following:

a. Icarus

b. Io

c. Venus

d. Adonis

4. Shakespeare uses the work of this poet throughout the play to underscore the theme of transformations:

a. Aristotle

b. Ovid

c. Socrates

d. Plautus

5. The action of the play switches from Warwickshire to:

a. Mantua

b. Pisa

c. Padua

d. Verona

6. Lucentio disguises himself as:

a. A music teacher

b. An artist

c. A Latin tutor

d. A servant

7. Kate has bound Bianca's hands because:

a. Bianca stole Kate's ring

b. Kate is in love with Gremio

c. Bianca slapped Kate for being too shrewish

d. Kate wants to know which suitor Bianca prefers

8. Petruchio claims he will tame Kate by
   a. Beating her
   b. Contradicting everything she says
   c. Locking her away
   d. Kidnapping her

9. Petruchio shows up on his wedding day
   a. Riding an old, run-down horse
   b. In a wagon
   c. On foot
   d. With another woman

10. Vincentio swears to seek revenge on
    a. Lucentio
    b. Tranio
    c. Biondello
    d. Hortensio

11. During the wedding ceremony, Petruchio:
    a. Gives a monetary contribution to the church
    b. Throws wine in Kate's face
    c. Punches the priest
    d. Brawls with Baptista

12. Hortensio complains to Tranio that Bianca:
    a. Is cruel to her sister
    b. Is fickle
    c. Cannot learn to play a musical instrument
    d. Is in love with Biondello

13. In preparation for the trip back Padua, Petruchio:
    a. Arranges for Kate to have new clothes
    b. Instructs his servants to prepare a wedding feast
    c. Goes hunting with his falcon
    d. Goes to the barn to saddle his horse

14. Lucentio took on the disguise of
    a. Litio
    b. Grumio
    c. Cambio
    d. Tranio

15. Couples during the Renaissance were often married
    a. At the altar
    b. In their homes
    c. In the city center
    d. In the doorway of the church

FILL IN THE BLANKS

1. *The Taming of a Shrew* is thought to be a _____ _____ of *The Taming of the Shrew.*

2. *The Taming of the Shrew* is loosely based on the Italian form of comedy known as _____.

3. Shakespeare writes a form of poetry in iambic pentameter known as _____ _____.

4. Lucentio has come to Padua to study _____ at the University.

5. Tranio and _____ are Lucentio's servants.

6. Baptista's youngest daughter is named _____which means _____.

7. A Shrew is both a scolding woman and a _____.

8. Gremio is a _____, a stock character in Italian comedy.

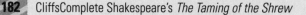

9. The Bianca/Lucentio subplot is taken from George Gascoigne's story, _____.

10. Christopher Sly's professions include _____, _____ and _____.

11. Kate breaks a _____ over Hortensio's head.

12. Biondello must find someone to impersonate _____.

13. A haberdasher is one who makes _____.

14. Kate calls Vincentio a budding, young _____.

15. Petruchio and the other men wager _____ on their wives obedience.

DISCUSSION

1. Based on knowledge acquired in the Induction, what is life like for the aristocracy in Elizabethan England?

2. In your opinion, why does Shakespeare set the play within the play in Italy?

3. What are Petruchio's motivations for marrying Kate? Do they change as the play progresses and, if so, how?

4. Discuss the changes in Bianca's personality from the beginning of the play to the end.

5. In your estimation, why is Kate such a shrew?

6. Clothes play an important part in *The Taming of the Shrew*. Discuss this imagery and its importance to the themes in the play.

7. What parallels do you see between the Induction and the "Shrew" play?

8. How is the image of hunting applied to the women in the play?

9. Is Petruchio tamed at the end of the play? Support your answer with evidence from the text.

10. Why is Kate embarrassed to kiss Petruchio in the street and how does this inform the reader about her character?

IDENTIFYING PLAY ELEMENTS

Find examples of the following elements in the text of *The Taming of the Shrew*.

* Climax
* Diptychs
* Extended Metaphor
* Foreshadowing
* Imagery
* Induction
* Irony
* Metaphor
* Monologue
* Personification
* Prologue
* Soliloquy
* Stichomythia
* Symbolism
* Theme

ACTIVITIES

The following activities can springboard you into further discussions and projects:

1. Make a character mask: Choose a character from the play. Next, cut out a mask in the basic shape of the comedy/tragedy masks. Divide the mask into two parts with a line drawn vertically down the center. Using drawings or pictures cut from a magazine, make a collage on the left side of the mask that represents the character's true nature. On the right side of the mask, make a collage representing the character's disguise or public image.

2. As Lucentio, write a letter to Bianca describing your love for her.

3. In a group, write a scene between Petruchio's servants, discussing Petruchio's taming of Kate.

4. Reading Logs: For each scene, in each act, keep a reading log. The log should consist of a summary of the scene, your personal comments on the scene, questions you may have concerning the scene, vocabulary words you are not familiar with and their definitions, and a line or two from the scene that you found interesting and why.

5. Performance: Pick a scene or monologue from the play. Memorize, rehearse, and perform the scene for your class.

6. Design a set for the play. Explain your choices.

7. Design costumes for four major characters. Explain your choices.

8. Hot Seat: Choose five or six main characters from the play. Divide the class into groups, with each person in the group assigned one of the chosen characters. Students then break from their "home" group and move into a "character" group. For example, all students assigned Kate will move into the Kate group. Each student will then write nonstop for about five minutes an interior dialogue (in first person only) relating the thoughts and feelings of the character. Students then share what they have written within the character group. Next, the students help each other create a minimum of two questions for the perspective of their characters for the characters that are not their own. The Kate group might come up with a question for Baptista such as, "Why did you love Bianca more than me?" Students then return to their original "home" groups. Within the "home group," one student at a time takes the "hot seat." The others ask him questions about his or her behavior in the story and he or she must respond as honestly as possible. After five minutes, change the person on the hot seat.

9. As Petruchio, write a letter to Kate telling her what her final speech from Act V, Scene 2 meant to him.

10. Create a board game based on *The Taming of the Shrew* using the model of an existing game such as Monopoly, Trivial Pursuit, or Life.

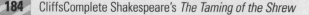

ANSWERS

Identify the quotation

1. Speaker: Sly. Spoken to: Serving men. Location: Ind. 2. Comments: This line highlights the dreamlike quality of the upcoming "Shrew" play: What is real? What is illusion?

2. Speaker: Sly. Spoken to: page (disguised as his wife). Location: Ind. 2. Comments: Sly has accepted his state and is prepared to surrender to the play.

3. Speaker: Lucentio. Spoken to: Tranio. Location: I.1. Comments: This line gives insight into Lucentio's fiery, passionate, and romantic nature.

4. Speaker: Petruchio. Spoken to: Hortensio. Location: I.2. Comments: Petruchio states his motivation for coming to Padua and the reader learns that Petruchio is a blunt, no-nonsense type of character.

5. Speaker: Kate. Spoken to: Baptista. Location: II.1. Comments: Kate is speaking about the proverbs that state an unmarried older sister has to dance barefoot at her younger sister's marriage and lead apes into hell, as she has no children to lead her to heaven. Kate's reaction is one of humiliation and frustration at her status.

6. Speaker: Petruchio. Spoken to: Kate. Location: II.1. Comments: Petruchio gives Kate his command. Her father has sold her to Petruchio and she has no choice but to submit to the will of her father and Petruchio.

7. Speaker: Petruchio. Spoken to: Baptista. Location: III.2. Comments: Clothes are a form of disguise and not an indicator of what lies beneath. Petruchio wants to teach Kate to love the true, undisguised Petruchio.

8. Speaker: Peter. Spoken to: Nathaniel. Location: IV.1. Comments: The servants are commenting on Petruchio's behavior towards Kate. Peter knows that Petruchio is acting like a shrew so that Kate can see her own actions in those of Petruchio.

9. Speaker: Kate. Spoken to: Petruchio. Location: IV.5. Comments: Kate has finally learned and accepted the rules of Petruchio's game.

10. Speaker: Kate. Spoken to: The guests at the wedding banquet. Location: V.2 Comments: Kate is lecturing on the way a wife should respect her husband. She is referring to the Chain of Being where a husband is king in the kingdom of his household.

True/False

1. True 2. False 3. False 4. False 5. False 6. True 7. True 8. False 9. True 10. True 11. True 12. False 13. True 14. False 15. False

Multiple Choice

1. d 2. c 3. a 4. b 5. c 6. c 7. d 8. b 9. a 10. b 11. c 12. b 13. a 14. c 15. d

Fill in the Blanks

1. Memorial reconstruction 2. Commedia dell'arte 3. Blank verse 4. Philosophy 5. Biondello 6. Bianca; white, blank 7. Mouse 8. Pantaloon 9. *Supposes* 10. Cardmaker, bearheard, tinker 11. Lute 12. Vincentio 13. Hats 14. Virgin 15. Twenty crowns

CLIFFSCOMPLETE RESOURCE CENTER

The learning doesn't need to stop here. CliffsComplete Resource Center shows you the best of the best: great links to information in print, on film, and online. And the following aren't all the great resources available to you; visit **www.cliffsnotes.com** for tips on reading literature, writing papers, giving presentations, locating other resources, and testing your knowledge.

BOOKS, ARTICLES, AND MAGAZINES

Bean, John C. "Comic Structure and the Humanizing of Kate in *The Taming of the Shrew.*" *The Woman's Part.* ed. Carolyn Ruth Swift Lenz, Gayle Greene, and Carol Thomas Neely. Urbana: University of Illinois Press. 1980.

An interesting look at the play's use of romance and farce, contending that Kate's final speech is a "humanized vision" of marriage.

Boose, Lynda E. *"The Taming of the Shrew:* Good Husbandry, and Enclosure." *Shakespeare Reread.* ed. Russ McDonald. Ithaca: Cornell University Press. 1994.

The article explores issue of class and status in the play.

Dreher, Diane Elizabeth. *Domination and Defiance: Fathers and Daughters in Shakespeare.* Louisville: The University Press of Kentucky. 1986

Explores the dynamics of the relationships between Baptista and Kate and Bianca.

Gay, Penny. *As She Likes It: Shakespeare's Unruly Women.* London: Routledge Press. 1996.

The book explores Shakespeare's unruly women in performance.

Huston, J. Dennis. "Enter the Hero: The Power of Play in *The Taming of the Shrew.*" *Shakespeare's Comedies of Play.* New York: Columbia University Press. 1981.

Huston argues that Petruchio tames Kate by introducing her to "the human theatre of play."

Kahn, Coppelia. *Man's Estate: Masculine Identity in Shakespeare.* Berkeley. The University of California Press. 1981.

A feminist perspective of marriage and manhood in the play.

Kastan, David Scott, ed. *A Companion to Shakespeare.* Oxford: Blackwell. 1999.

An invaluable resource on Shakespeare and the society that informed his plays.

Marvel, Laura. ed. *Readings on 'The Taming of the Shrew.'* San Diego: Greenhaven Press, Inc. 2000

An anthology of excellent articles on the play dealing with issues of structure, gender, genre, and so on.

Parsons, Keith and Pamela Mason, eds. *Shakespeare in Performance.* London: Salamander Books. 1995.

A beautifully illustrated volume that explores the performance history of each of Shakespeare's plays.

Rutter, Carol. *Clamorous Voices: Shakespeare's Women Today.* Great Britain: The Women's Press Ltd. 1994.

Interviews with women who have successfully played many of Shakespeare's female characters, makes this a fascinating and insightful book.

Saccio, Peter. "Shrewd and Kindly Farce." *Shakespeare Survey* 37 (1984) 33-40.

Explores the farcical aspects of the play.

Wayne, Valerie. "Refashioning the Shrew." *Shakespeare Studies* 17 (1985) 159-87.

Discusses how Shakespeare explored the issues of women and marriage without resorting to the violence usually allotted to shrews in the Elizabethan age.

INTERNET

"The Complete Works of William Shakespeare"
www.the-tech.mit.edu:80/Shakespeare/works.html
HTML versions of the complete works of Shakespeare. (Copyright 1995) Provided by The Tech-MIT. Author: Jeremy Hylton.

"Mr. William Shakespeare and the Internet"
www.daphne.palomar.edu/shakespeare/
This is one of the best Shakespeare sites on the Web, providing information on the plays and poems, Shakespeare's life and times, theatre, and criticism. There are educational materials, links to other related sites, and a guide to searching for Shakespeare on the Internet. Author: Terry A. Gray.

"The Shakespeare Classroom"
www.jetlink.net/~massij/shakes
This site offers teaching materials and study questions for many of Shakespeare's plays. Author: J.M. Massi, Ph.D., Psy.D.

"Shakespeare's Birthplace Trust"
www.shakespeare.org.uk/
Shakespeare's Birthplace Trust is located in Stratford-upon-Avon and oversees the homes associated with Shakespeare, including the house where he was born and Mary Arden's cottage. They also house an excellent library on Shakespeare and offer courses throughout the year. Pictures and descriptions of Shakespeare's homes are offered on this site, along with course information and study materials on the plays.

"Shakespeare Globe USA"
www.shakespeare.uiuc.edu/
A virtual tour of the newly reconstructed Globe Theatre is a highlight of this site. It also offers some very interesting information for teachers and students on Shakespeare's life and plays.

"Internet Shakespeare Editions"
http://web.uvic.ca/shakespeare/Library/SLT/Intro/introsubj.html/
This site offers information on Shakespeare and his life. Included is a wonderful section on the plays including *The Taming of the Shrew.* Author: Michael Best.

FILMS

The Taming of the Shrew. USA/Italy. 122 min. Color. 1967. Directed by: Franco Zeffirelli. With: Elizabeth Taylor and Richard Burton.

A lavish production that concentrates on the Kate and Petruchio plot. Beautiful cinematography enhances this adaptation of the play.

The Taming of the Shrew. USA. 63 min. B&W. 1929. Directed by: Sam Taylor. With: Douglas Fairbanks and Mary Pickford.

This black-and-white film was the first filmed rendition of a Shakespeare play. Fairbanks' use of a whip became standard fare for many subsequent Petruchios.

FILM AND TV ADAPTATIONS

10 Things I Hate About You. USA. 97 min. Color. 1999. Directed by: Gil Junger. With: Julia Stiles and Heath Ledger.

This film adaptation sets the basic structure of Shakespeare's play in a modern American high school.

Kiss Me Kate. USA. 110 min. Color. 1953. Directed by: George Sydney. With: Kathryn Grayson and Howard Keel.

A group of actors work together on a production of *The Taming of the Shrew* in this musical adaptation which has charmed audiences for years.

The Taming of the Shrew
CLIFFSCOMPLETE READING GROUP DISCUSSION GUIDE

Use the following questions and topics to enhance your reading group discussions. The discussion can help get you thinking—and hopefully talking—about Shakespeare in a whole new way!

DISCUSSION QUESTIONS

1. In the light of the twenty-first century, is *The Taming of the Shrew* still relevant to modern audiences and should it continue to be performed?

2. The play has been set in many different eras including the Wild West, the Victorian Age, and the future. Based on the content of the play, is it appropriate to move the play from its Elizabethan roots? Would the play work set in a different time period and if so, which would work the best? Could the play be done in modern dress? How would Kate's character change in each of those different venues?

3. Franco Zeffirelli directed the film version of *The Taming of the Shrew* in the 1960's starring Elizabeth Taylor and Richard Burton. If you were directing a movie version of the play today, whom would you cast in the roles of Petruchio? Kate? Bianca? Lucentio? Baptista? Why?

4. Many times in performance, the Induction is not included as part of the play. Is the play effective without the Induction? Must the Induction be included to maintain the integrity of the play and Shakespeare's vision of it?

5. The silences in Shakespeare's plays are often even more important than what is said. Discuss Kate's silences. What is Kate doing when she is on stage and not speaking? What do her silences say about her character?

6. Discuss Petruchio's taming techniques. Are they abusive or humanistic? Reflect on his treatment of his servants as well as Kate.

7. *The Taming of the Shrew* considers the dynamics of many types of relationships. Discuss the relationships and how authority is exploited or challenged: Master/Servant. Father/Daughter. Husband/Wife. Upper class/Lower class.

8. Society sets certain expectations for each and every citizen. What expectations are placed on Petruchio? Baptista? Kate? Bianca? How do they compare to the expectations that are placed on us today?

9. On the Elizabethan stage, men and boys played all of the parts. What implications arise when one considers that boys played Kate, Bianca, and the Widow? Does this fact add to the themes of role-playing? Appearance versus Reality? Gender issues?

10. Kate's last speech has often been labeled the "Submission Speech." Analyze the speech to determine if she is sincere and truly submissive to her husband. Is she playing Petruchio's own game? Is she being ironic? Is her speech the fulfillment of a male fantasy? How would you direct the actress to play the speech?

Notes

Notes

Notes

Notes

Index